K 600

D1267566

OPINIONS
AND
PERSONALITY

OPINIONS
AND
PERSONALITY

NEW YORK · JOHN WILEY & SONS, INC.

LONDON · CHAPMAN & HALL, LIMITED

M. BREWSTER SMITH

JEROME S. BRUNER

ROBERT W. WHITE

With the collaboration of

David F. Aberle

Stanley G. Estes

Eugenia Hanfmann

Sheldon J. Korchin

COPYRIGHT © 1956
BY
JOHN WILEY & SONS, INC.

All Rights Reserved

*This book or any part thereof must not
be reproduced in any form without
the written permission of the publisher*

Library of Congress Catalog Card Number: 56–6498

PRINTED IN THE UNITED STATES OF AMERICA

PREFACE

In the development of a science, there is a strategy of discovery as well as a strategy of proof. In envy of the precision of method and theory attained by the physical scientists, psychologists and social scientists have in recent years focussed their efforts perhaps too exclusively in the direction of proof. Our purpose in this book, and in the research that underlies it, is of the other sort: not to establish beyond reasonable doubt insights already in our repertory, but to gain new insights into the relations of opinions and personality. We also seek to develop a coherent framework for conceptualizing these relations, and to illustrate this framework sufficiently to encourage more systematic investigation of the research problems to which it gives rise. Our data, drawn as they are from close study of the "opinionings" of ten men, cannot support conclusions about the prevalence of particular phenomena or relationships in a larger population. Our concern, in a word, is with the natural history of holding opinions, and our aspiration is to construct an adequate framework for this task.

The study that gave rise to this book is described in Chapter 4. It is one of a long series of investigations at the Harvard Psychological Clinic in which normal personality has been brought under close scrutiny through case studies carried out by groups of investigators. We gladly register our great indebtedness to Dr. Henry A. Murray for creating this tradition of inquiry in which our plans took form, and for nurturing in earlier years the Clinic as a place congenial to such ventures. To Professor Gordon W. Allport, who has long been concerned with attitudes as an integral and important aspect of personality, we acknowledge another intellectual debt, and we thank him for reading critically an earlier version of the manuscript. Our indebtedness to our collaborators on the Diagnostic Council of the study is properly reflected on the title page. While they cannot be held responsible for our specific formulations, the book rests heavily on consensus reached in discussions by the Diagnostic Council and on case summaries prepared by each member of the research group. A number of other investigators, whose names are recorded in Chapter 4, participated in interviewing and administering test procedures. Our debt to them is obviously great.

The project was one of the first to receive support from the Laboratory of Social Relations. We are most appreciative of the readiness of the Laboratory to invest "risk capital" in support of a project such as ours, and of the personal interest, help, and tolerance of its director, Professor Samuel A. Stouffer. One of us (MBS) held a Demobilization Award of the Social Science Research Council at the time he directed the collection of the data. This aid is gratefully acknowledged.

A word is in order as to how we collaborated on the book. It has gone through many drafts and much reformulation, benefiting along the way from the clarifying impact of our students on whom we tried out successive versions of our ideas. Each of us wrote one of the three central case portraits. It would be meaningless to attempt to disentangle the authorship of the remaining chapters, each of us having had a hand, at one stage or another, in the drafting of nearly all of them. We are grateful for the forbearance of our several families at the numerous critical points in this process. To Dr. M. Ellwood Smith, in particular, we are also indebted for thoughtful and meticulous labors in preparing the index.

To the subjects of our study, busy men who steadfastly made themselves available to our inquisitiveness in the cold evenings of a long Cambridge winter, we owe a special gratitude, and acknowledge our respect and affection. We have exercised care to protect them from embarrassment by using conventional disguises of name, place, and trivial but identifying detail. We hope that those of them who encounter this book will realize that our attempt to formulate in capsule their opinions and personalities, heartless though it may appear, did not detract from our genuine regard for them. A chapter could be written on the attachment each investigator developed for the subjects whose case formulation was his primary responsibility.

A final and very special debt we owe to Mrs. Esther Loud Smith, who as administrative assistant to the project played a role far more significant than the title suggests. Her gracious, discreet, and humane presence was felt throughout our study, in humoring the investigating staff, in scheduling interviews and experimental hours, in maintaining the interest and morale of impatient subjects. In her subsequent role as Secretary to the Psychological Clinic she has seen this manuscript through numerous vicissitudes, while carrying out her mission of making the Clinic a comfortable place in which to work and live. In gratitude we dedicate this book to her.

M. B. S.
J. S. B.
R. W. W.

December, 1955

CONTENTS

CHAPTER 1

INTRODUCTION

Of what use to a man are his opinions? It is with this question that we choose to open our inquiry. A pattern of opinions may be for one man a basis of personal serenity in the face of a changing world, for another a goad to revolutionary activity. Opinions, in short, are part of man's attempt to meet and to master his world. They are an integral part of personality.

If opinions are thus inseparable from the rest of personality, then our task is made clear. Not only must we describe opinions; we must also investigate how they are related to other aspects of the person's life. We ask, in brief, what functions are served by the holding of an opinion. The study of attitudes becomes one phase of the study of complex behavior generally. A "special" psychology of opinion, as Walter Lippmann and William McDougall demonstrated three decades ago, is neither necessary nor to be desired. The theory of opinion in use or of "attitudes in the individual" derives from general principles of personality, of perceiving, remembering, thinking, learning, motivation.

Yet during the first three decades of the century, only two major works appeared with the avowed objective of relating opinions or sentiments to the life processes which constitute personality functioning. One of these, Walter Lippmann's *Public Opinion*,[1] was the work of

[1] New York, The Macmillan Co., 1922.

an inspired amateur who, mindful that men lived in a "personal world" partly of their own fashioning, saw opinions as reflecting the selectivity of man's experience, as means of simplifying the complex social and political world of events to which access was at best indirect. McDougall,[2] on his part, saw the development of opinions or sentiments as the differentiated expression of man's deepest needs, as these were altered in the course of commerce with the environment. For him a sentiment combined a way of striving, a way of knowing the world, and a way of feeling; and insofar as one's needs and sentiments were organized in a pattern of personality, they could never be treated autonomously.

There are perhaps three ways of approaching the study of public opinion. The first and most ancient of these seeks to understand the broad relations between public opinion and political institutions. How does the public, holding what opinions it may, affect the policies of government, its laws, its social and political form? In turn, putting the question more as Aristotle did in the *Politics,* what is the fate of public opinion under various forms of government? That such inquiries seek in the main to form moral judgments on the best relationship between a public and the instruments of government—as in the works of Aristotle, Montesquieu, Locke, or even Machiavelli—underlines the fact that they have often been more normative in spirit than empirical. Such need not, however, be the case. One can indeed understand the relation of government to public opinion prior to evaluating it: and ultimate evaluation may be better for having paused for such dispassionate understanding.

A second approach to the study of opinion, at once less subtle and more empirically demanding than the first, is ecological in spirit. Its emphasis is upon the distribution of opinions in a population and the subgroupings therein. The ecological spirit, in a simple form, is represented by the typical opinion-polling study. What is the division of opinion on an issue? How are opinions on the issue distributed in various segments of the population? And a final question: What accounts for this distribution? More experimentally conceived, such investigations may choose special groups for study in order to test hypotheses: employed and unemployed industrial workers, to study the effect of unemployment on radicalism; veterans and non-veterans, to assess the influence of military service on nationalism; farm workers and farm owners, to analyze the effect of ownership on opinions about government subsidies. Ecological studies of this kind provide a ready

[2] William McDougall, *Social psychology,* London, Methuen, 1908.

if risky springboard into speculation about the psychological origins of group opinion. If the young more than their elders favor socialized medicine, to seize on a speculative example, it is "because" they do not have as firm a sense of vested interest in a career as do their elders, or "because" they are "the depression generation," or "because" they have on the average had more schooling.

The inferences about psychological origins that grow out of ecological studies bring us to the third or psychological approach. The psychologist wants to know what are the various routes by which one comes to favor a given point of view or to oppose it. Specifically, the psychological approach to the study of opinion asks four kinds of questions. The first of these is a _genetic question._ How did an opinion develop? Through what psychological process did it come into being, undergo transformation, or remain unchanged? The second is an _adjustive question._ What function does an opinion serve in the adjustment of the individual? The third is a _relational question._ One asks what other processes are associated with opinions. Does intelligence correlate with differentiation of opinions in a population of subjects? Is there a relationship between degree of parental dominance experienced and the extremeness of opinions on issues involving authority? Out of these relationships there gradually develops more rational theory. Finally, there are _structural questions._ Since we may properly assume that the individual personality is organized or "structured" in a more or less enduring manner, we ask how opinions fit into this organization or structure.

These four questions represent different approaches to the problem of psychological explanation. Possibly they will be reduced some day to a single question. For the time being, however, it is the better part of wisdom to retain all of them, particularly in a field of inquiry as impoverished of theory as the one in which we here find ourselves. In the present study, we shall be concerned with them all. For this is an exploratory investigation whose aims are those of both the naturalist and the theorist.

The plan of the book is to present, first, a general theoretical model in terms of which the opinion processes can be understood psychologically. There follow intensive case analyses of a small group of mature men presented in an effort to trace out the lines of development and maintenance of opinions _in vivo_ as a test of the utility of our conceptual model. The men whose lives and opinions we shall examine, three of them in considerable detail and another seven more schematically, are chosen for study not as typical or representative but for their variety. As we draw together what we learned from these

ten men in a concluding chapter, we shall be concerned with the
implications of our undertaking for the psychology of personality and
for social psychology.

We have said that this investigation was exploratory—and this we
mean with respect to both theory and fact. For we began with woe-
fully few hypotheses for testing and only the most general idea of what
kinds of opinion phenomena we should meet and have to describe.
What we were most sure of was the underdevelopment of the theory
of attitudes in contrast with increasing refinement in their measurement.

For there has developed in psychology a great advance in the theory
and practice of measurement. Notable in this advance has been the
extension of methods of scaling applicable to the ordering of attitudes
and opinions. Thurstone, Stouffer, Likert, Guttman, Lazarsfeld,
Coombs, and many others have contributed to the construction of
scaling models of a highly interesting order. It was our feeling, however, that we needed to know more about the attitude domains themselves. Measurement is an adjunct to theory. Until we have a clearer
conception of the nature of attitudes and the manner in which they
function, we shall not know what aspects of an attitude are worth
measuring. It is a deep question within any branch of psychology to
decide what are the useful units of analysis. Certainly there is no
analogue of the classical centimeters-grams-seconds to guide us.
Before we can apply measurement models effectively to the quantitative description of opinions we must know a lot more about the nature
of opinion. This study, then, since it is concerned with the psychological status of opinions, is a prolegomenon to measurement.

In September 1946, a group of social psychologists, clinical psychologists, and a lone anthropologist met around a table at the Harvard
Psychological Clinic on Plympton Street in Cambridge. The only firm
item on the agenda was that we were going to study the attitudes of
a group of ten mature men with particular reference to the relationship
of attitudes to personality as a whole. We met for three hours that day
and for dozens of other days. At one point, some sociologist colleagues
moved into the back of the room with their recording gadgets to study
our group dynamics. In time even they withdrew, perhaps baffled
by the complexity and confusion of our doings. For successively and
simultaneously we were trying to build a theory, design a study, work
out procedures, analyze cases, refine our methods and our theory, and
generally to remain inquisitive in the face of overwhelmingly numerous
data. This was the Diagnostic Council in 1946 and 1947—writing and

revising theoretical memoranda, designing interview procedures, reaching consensus on case formulations.

In the years since, we have several times recast the rich data generated by this clinical approach. We have drawn on the cases in our teaching, and applied to other problems the frame of analysis that we developed in the study. And after periods in which our materials lay fallow, we came back to them to find them reorganized in our thinking in ways more satisfactory to us. This is not the book we would have written about the study in 1948.

As for the actual scope of the study, practical considerations dictated a narrowing of our interest once it was decided to study the concrete opinions of our subjects and the functions which they served in personality. Obviously we could not study all their opinions. We decided, therefore, to bring the present study into focus upon a limited area of opinion which, though narrow, might provide a pathway into the personalities of our subjects. Our purpose would be served, we felt, if an issue could be found on which opinions were generally well crystallized yet controversial; one generating a certain amount of affect or anxiety; and one, finally, of chronic rather than transitory social and political significance. The topic of Russia and its manifold variations seemed to us, after some reflection, to be a good focus of investigation.

But in two respects attitudes toward Russia and Communism proved somewhat special. In the first place, our subjects had had no opportunity, in the main, for first-hand contact with Russia. There was, moreover, little by way of direct action which our subjects could undertake in support of their attitudes toward Russia. Yet, on the first score, we can exclaim with Walter Lippmann, "How indirectly we know the environment in which nevertheless we live!" Where direct action is concerned, it is perhaps characteristic of modern man in industrial societies that he grows increasingly removed from the instruments of control over his own destiny. What at first seemed special about opinions on Russia may in the end be a source of generality.

This volume is *not*, however, a study of American opinions on Russia in 1947, much less 1955. It is, rather, a study of the psychological processes involved in forming and holding an opinion—any opinion. Insofar as we are able to shed light on American opinions toward Russia, we are gaining an unexpected bounty.

There has been one unforeseen difficulty in writing up this study— a difficulty born of our choice of Russia as a topic. The temper of our times is such that one cannot easily steer a dispassionate course. In assessing the origins of our subjects' attitudes toward Russia, particularly those attitudes which have become identified with "all-out patri-

otism," one sometimes must point to their non-rational bases. Lifted
out of context, such analyses may strike the more zealous guardians
of the American credo as somehow disrespectful or disloyal. We have
been at pains to point out that the motives for holding an opinion
can throw no light whatever on its soundness. More than that we
cannot say. Our object in these pages is never to evaluate. In the
pure sense, we write *ad hominem,* not *ad rem.*

CHAPTER 2

CONVERGING

APPROACHES

IT is characteristic of contemporary psychology that many of its traditional and self-contained compartments are losing some of their distinctiveness by a process of intellectual osmosis. Nowhere is this osmosis more apparent than in the commerce that now exists between the fields of social psychology and the psychology of personality.

Because this study is so much part of a more general movement of convergence in the field of psychology, it is fitting, before setting forth our own theoretical views, to sketch briefly some of the major trends in social psychology and the psychology of personality that have affected research on the nature of the opinion process—our own research included.

Approaches from Social Psychology

The social psychologist has usually approached the empirical study of attitudes with a two-fold objective. One of these has been to describe and/or measure the phenomenon we call an attitude.[1] The second, more interesting psychologically, has been to discover the determinants or correlates of particular attitudes that have proved

[1] The definition of "attitude" will be discussed in the following chapter; it suffices here to note that we consider an attitude to be a predisposition to experience, to be motivated with respect to and to respond to a class of objects in a certain way.

7

amenable to description and measurement. In the next chapter we shall concern ourselves more directly with the dimensions in terms of which an attitude may best be described. Here our concern is with the search for attitude determinants. Our examination will make clearer, we think, the implicit psychological status of this oddly disembodied concept of attitude.

The trait-attitude correlational approach. The first attempts to get at determinants sought to establish simple correlations between attitudes on the one hand and personality traits on the other. Correlational in method, this approach was a direct outgrowth of the academic tradition of attitude measurement. Once the primitive development of attitude scales had made it possible to scale attitudes as more or less pro or con, psychologists began to compute correlations between attitude scores and the other forms of test scores in the psychologist's repertory—intelligence, extroversion, dominance, etc. A large proportion of these studies centered for some reason on radicalism-conservatism, though race prejudice, internationalism, religious attitudes, and others came in for their share of attention.

We need not concern ourselves here with the substantive findings of such studies. The earlier ones have been admirably summarized in Murphy, Murphy, and Newcomb's comprehensive text.[2] It is the conceptual structure of such studies that is of interest. In essence, the approach to personality was analytic and descriptive in nature: what, for convenience, we may call trait psychology. Traits were conceived to be highly generalized dynamic and directive dispositions, hierarchically organized, and subject to modification by experience. Since traits were at core predispositional in nature, the assumption was made that the possession of certain traits would predispose the individual to the adoption of certain general attitudes toward the social world about him.

No better example can be found than radicalism-conservatism. We need not concern ourselves with any searching inquiry of how radicalism scales were constructed, for in the main they were built on rather common-sense principles, items being chosen from current social definitions of what was "radical" and what was "conservative," and items retained in a battery on the basis of highly empirical techniques of item analysis. Once a reliable scale was available, the next question was one of determinants. Let us use a fictitious study as our example, the fictive case being better for reconstructing the logic of the method.

---

[2] G. Murphy, L. B. Murphy, and T. M. Newcomb, *Experimental social psychology*, New York, Harper and Brothers, 1937.

The investigator might reason implicitly as follows: radicalism very likely requires a capacity to disengage oneself from the pressures of a society; unless one can do this, one cannot rebel. It seems reasonable, then, that the introvert would be more likely to exhibit radicalism than the extrovert. Our imaginary investigator then administers the two batteries—an "I–E scale" and a "R–C scale"—to a population of respondents (usually students). He succeeds in obtaining a correlation between introversion-extroversion and radicalism-conservatism high enough to reject reliably the null hypothesis that the two are not related, but not high enough to set his mind at rest about the univocality of a causal relation between them.

Many of these early studies seem somewhat naive today—naive at least in their rather simple conception. For surely there were crucial intervening events between a state of introversion and the adoption of radical political views that had not been encompassed in a simple correlation. If some of the studies later to be described may be characterized as naively psychoanalytic, these studies were innocently *un*psychoanalytic. Little recognition was accorded the hierarchical organization of personality: radicalism, let us say, being treated as though it served the same function in all personalities. There was moreover a curious lack of perceptiveness among those investigators who failed to see, among other things, that opposite extremes of an attitude continuum could be produced by a common cause: that extreme submissiveness and extreme rebelliousness of attitude could both be traced, for instance, to over severe parents. While one need not believe epigrams long in being, one might at least have pondered them, and one of the oldest is *"les extrêmes se touchent."*

Even when trait-attitude investigations sought to employ more powerful and complex statistical techniques for locating relationships, they provided little beyond the sheerly descriptive level. A factor analytic study which could demonstrate that a cluster of questions from a radicalism scale formed a simple structure along with other items from an introversion and dominance scale, could do little more than suggest to the investigator that some hypotheses were needed to transmute this taxonomic yield into a cause-and-effect theory.[3]

We do not mean to indicate that trait-attitude studies were "bad" but rather that they were lacking in comprehensiveness and theoretical guidance. Even so gifted a pair of investigators as Likert and Murphy

[3] The work of Eysenck—notably his *The psychology of politics*, London, Routledge, 1954—is one of the most recent examples of the trait-attitude correlational approach employing the method of factor analysis.

in their painstaking study, *Public Opinion and the Individual*,[4] seemed
able to come up with few findings more solid or reliable than that
radicalism was somewhat associated with dissatisfaction. It is worth
pausing to examine the shortcomings of all such studies in order to
understand better why in later research the emphasis shifted away
from this method.

In the first place, the attitude domains subjected to correlation with
personality traits were *socially* rather than *psychologically* conceived.
However interesting may be the phenomena of radicalism or of pro-
or anti-religiousness, or of reactions to the New Deal, and however
great their political implications, these phenomena were from a psychological point of view in no sense homogeneous. Anti-religious sentiment may in one case stem from conformity to a family norm; in
another instance it may be a reaction *against* the family. To expect
anything approaching a linear correlation between such attitudes and
certain traits of personality was hoping for too much. We shall in a
later section consider studies which chose for investigation attitudes
that were more specifically psychological in meaning: the Adorno,
Frenkel-Brunswik, Levinson, and Sanford study of ethnocentrism,[5] to
take an example.

A second serious fault in the early studies was a lack of proper
concern for situational factors in the determination of attitudes. Few
better cases for documenting this point can be found than Newcomb's
ingenious study [6] of the changes in attitude over time in the Bennington
community—a study showing keen awareness of situation. We need
cite only the fact that the Bennington girls who conformed best to the
community were the ones most likely to show an increase in political
liberalism over their college years. But of course the political tone
of the community, set by a young and vigorous faculty, was politically
liberal. Indeed, there was a period in the mid-Thirties in certain
adolescent groups in the United States when great non-conformist
resources were required of the aspiring young intellectual if he chose
to profess non-revolutionary doctrines! It would be high folly, then,
to search for an "obvious" correlation between a particular political
point of view and the trait of conformity without either holding constant or varying *systematically* the nature of the conformity pressures

[4] G. Murphy and R. Likert, *Public opinion and the individual*, New York,
Harper and Brothers, 1938.

[5] T. W. Adorno, E. Frenkel-Brunswik, D. J. Levinson, and R. N. Sanford, *The
authoritarian personality*, New York, Harper and Brothers, 1950.

[6] T. M. Newcomb, *Personality and social change*, New York, Dryden, 1943.

affecting one's subjects. Yet, few of the earlier studies (and not many of the later ones) were concerned with such precautions.

The most serious shortcoming has already been implied. However great the temptation to empirical vigor in the early stages of development of a field, it is almost inevitable that the vigor will spend itself in a morass of inconclusiveness unless a theory develops to guide it. The theory (or theories) did not emerge out of trait-attitude studies or, to put it differently, the theory implicit in them was narrow and unsatisfactory. Doctoral dissertations moved elsewhere.

The demographic approach to determinants. In the preceding chapter, reference was made to ecological studies of opinion whose objectives are to describe the distribution of opinion in a population and to note major demographic differences in the kinds of opinions held. It was to the immense credit of such studies that they took the investigation of attitudes out of the classroom and into the more representative life of the community or nation at large. It is also true, and almost by the same token, that these studies took the search for opinion determinants out of the realm of purely psychological determinism into a twilight area neither clearly psychological nor sociological. The search for cause in science follows the path of prevailing techniques just as surely as commerce ever followed the flag. The fact of the matter was that when the student of public opinion (one using the sampling poll or survey) came to account for the variance in his results, he could best and most easily account for it by reference to the various demographic subdivisions of his sample. Instead of looking for trait-attitude correlations, the pollster looked for a correlation between opinions and social characteristics.

Since the technique of stratified sampling by quota made it necessary either to sample or control such demographic characteristics as region, size of place, age, sex, socioeconomic status, religion, skin color, marital status, size of family, country of birth, and the like, it was natural enough that the effort to "pin down" certain regularities in opinion should be directed to these variables, knowledge of which was available for all the members of the sample studied. Indeed, it was not long before there developed highly successful techniques of predicting such complex matters as political party preference and even conservatism of sentiments on the basis of one or several of these characteristics.

One of the most serious efforts to use demographic analysis systematically was the classic study of the 1940 election by Lazarsfeld, Berelson, and Gaudet in *The People's Choice*.[7] Repeated interviews with a carefully selected panel of voters in Erie County, Ohio, showed that voting preference could be predicted with a relatively high degree of efficiency by a knowledge of three *social* variables: socioeconomic status, religious preference, and place of residence (whether rural or urban). These authors indeed fashioned a composite index, termed an Index of Political Predisposition, that deserves careful attention— not only for its predictive efficiency and elegance, but also for the reasoning which lies behind its construction. The device is essentially a ranking matrix constructed as tabulated.

Socioeconomic	Protestants		Catholics	
Status	Rural	Urban	Rural	Urban
A, B (well-to-do)	1	2	3	4
C+ (middle)	2	3	4	5
C — (lower middle)	3	4	5	6
D (lower)	4	5	6	7

The greater the rank number of a given cell, the greater the frequency of Democratic voting preference among the members of that cell.[8] What was perhaps as striking as the relation of the Index to voting preference was the fact that the most economical way of predicting vote *shifts* in the campaign or *late decisions* by those who had been undecided was to assume that the campaign had the effect of accentuating the trend represented by the Index rankings.

What "psychologizing" these authors did about the presumed factors underlying their Index was both thoughtful and conservative. They implied, first, that members of a given grouping shared certain experiences and needs which predisposed them in a common direction. While they did not seek to examine in any detail the nature of these common experiences and needs, they posed an interesting research problem in what might be called psycho-anthropology. Perhaps more important, they noted that one of the greatest influences in the determination of political preference was the exercise of *personal influence* by leaders and peers within one's social group—a far more important determinant than, for example, campaign propaganda more narrowly conceived.

[7] P. F. Lazarsfeld, B. Berelson, and H. Gaudet, *The people's choice*, New York, Columbia University Press, 1948 (2nd Edition).

[8] Subsequent research suggests that this close empirical relationship may have been limited to some extent to Erie County, Pennsylvania, in 1940, and to conditions prevailing in an election in which one of the candidates was Franklin D. Roosevelt. *See* M. Janowitz and W. E. Miller, The index of political predisposition in the 1948 election, *Journal of Politics*, 1952, **14**, 710–727.

That the authors were keenly aware of some of the psychological difficulties of their approach is indicated by Lazarsfeld's careful foreword to the second edition of *The People's Choice*. This foreword itself represents an important converging trend in the study of opinion. Before turning to it, however, let us consider wherein the theoretically oriented psychologist finds this type of demographic analysis both challenging and inadequate. First in terms of prediction by such "packaged" variables as socioeconomic status: a large proportion of the respondents in this study (or any cross-sectional study) will fall into the cells ranked or labelled "3" and "4." It is in these groups that prediction is poorest, indeed almost approaching random distribution. Among these groups are the following segments of the population:

> Lower middle-class rural Protestants
> Middle- and lower-middle-class urban Protestants
> Well-to-do and middle-class rural Catholics
> Well-to-do urban Catholics.

It is difficult indeed to assume that either a *common* set of experiences and needs permeates all of these groups or, for that matter, that personal influence is mediated by a common set of psychological factors in all the groups. We may assume, at least, that the motives for political preference not only vary among these groups, but also vary rather widely within any one group.

Nor can one assume that cross-pressures are operating upon members of the various "middle" categories described above. Certainly, these pressures cannot be thought of as sources of psychological conflict. What are such pressures? It is assumed that Catholicism, urbanism, and low socioeconomic status predispose to Democratic preference; their opposites to Republicanism. Placed in opposition to each other— e.g., high economic status combined, say, with Catholicism—they are said to create cross-pressures. Neither psychologically nor sociologically can such a view be supported. Both society and the individual are more than capable of establishing means of negating a conflict of interests: a "Catholics for Willkie" organization handles the matter at the social level; an identification with the business community (cf. Chapter 7) can handle the "cross-pressure" at the psychological level. Certainly Kriesberg's study gives no unequivocal evidence of internal, psychic cross-pressures corresponding to the external ones.[9]

[9] M. Kriesberg, Cross-pressures and attitudes. A study on the influence of conflicting propaganda on opinions regarding American-Soviet relations, *Public Opinion Quarterly*, 1949, **13**, 5–16.

In short, then, the Index of Political Predisposition *locates* possible problems in the social and psychological determination of attitudes. It cannot solve them. And this locating service, we would contend, is the great contribution of demographic analysis generally.

That the matter does not stop there is indicative of the convergence we have noted. For Lazarsfeld, several years after the first appearance of the work, provides in his foreword to the second edition a pattern for the next step toward a more adequate psychological approach.[10] Citing the disappointing yield of external correlations between political preference and demographic variables, he points anew to the superiority of the panel technique. By some such means one can at least locate the specific individuals who change or develop their opinions during a campaign and thereby "pick out a variety of psychological mediators which connect the social situation and the individual decision." [11] Indeed, it is quite clear that the process of picking out these psychological mediators is ultimately dependent upon going beyond demographic analysis to the development of adequate psychological theory and of discriminating methods for psychological research. A recent national study of the 1952 presidential election,[12] in fact, centers on the measurement of just such mediating psychological variables.

But if the demographic approach can be enriched by drawing on intervening psychological variables, it can equally be enriched by the use of sociological ones. Demographic description of a person's income group or religious affiliation is not the same thing as a description of the role and status requirements that such membership entails.[13] It is interesting that Berelson, Lazarsfeld, and McFee in a later study of voting give more emphasis to the proximal effects of group membership—still another example of convergence of approaches.[14]

The search for psychological variables in the opinion process has roots in two trends, and to these we turn next.

The emphasis on "personal significance." The term "personal significance" has, of course, no technical meaning. We refer loosely to a group of attitude and opinion research studies that have inquired about the ways in which the holding or changing of an attitude served

[10] *Op. cit.*

[11] *Op. cit.*, p. xii.

[12] A. Campbell, G. Gurin, and W. E. Miller, *The voter decides,* Chicago, Row, Peterson, and Co., 1954.

[13] T. Parsons and E. A. Shils (eds.), *Toward a general theory of action,* Cambridge, Harvard University Press, 1951.

[14] B. Berelson, P. F. Lazarsfeld, and W. McFee, *Voting,* Chicago, University of Chicago Press, 1954.

some deeper motivational function. The varied guises in which these studies have appeared make their description difficult. A prime source of influence has been the development of the so-called "gratification study" in the field of communications research. Pioneered by a sociologist whose psychological contributions to research on opinion have been nonetheless impressive—Paul Lazarsfeld—these studies have had as their central focus the gratification obtained from various forms of information and entertainment. Lazarsfeld's analysis of the Professor Quiz program,[15] Herzog's brilliant study of the gratification value of the daytime serial-story programs,[16] Merton's subtle analysis of the success of Kate Smith as a marathon bond salesman [17]—these and others of equal merit have done much to focus the attention of research workers on the question which also informs the present book: Of what use to a man are his preferences and opinions? While primarily concerned with the reasons why certain forms of mass communication were gratifying to the consumer, such studies also revealed dramatically the gratifications involved in holding opinions.

Closely related to these investigations are several studies of reactions to specific social situations. An early landmark was Cantril's *Invasion from Mars*, wherein the author examined the predisposing factors to credence in the amazing events portrayed in the famous Orson Welles broadcast of *The War of the Worlds*.[18] In this same category come such other studies as Newcomb's of the Bennington community [19] mentioned earlier in another connection, several investigations of factors underlying the spreading of rumor and information conducted by the Research Center for Group Dynamics at Michigan,[20] quite a few surveys of the gratification factors in electoral choice of which the Bruner and Korchin study of the Curley election is typical,[21] etc.

[15] P. F. Lazarsfeld, *Radio and the printed page*, New York, Duell, Sloan and Pearce, 1940.

[16] Herta Herzog, What do we really know about daytime serial listeners? In P. F. Lazarsfeld and F. Stanton, *Radio research: 1942–1943*, New York, Duell, Sloan and Pearce, 1944.

[17] R. K. Merton (with the assistance of M. Fiske and A. Curtis), *Mass persuasion*, New York, Harper and Brothers, 1946.

[18] H. Cantril (with the assistance of H. Gaudet and H. Herzog), *The invasion from Mars*, Princeton, Princeton University Press, 1940.

[19] *Op. cit.*

[20] L. Festinger, D. Cartwright, K. Barber, J. Fleischl, J. Gottzdanker, A. Keysen, G. Leavitt, A study of a rumor: its origin and spread, *Human Relations*, 1948, **1**, 464–486.

[21] J. S. Bruner and S. J. Korchin, The boss and the vote: case study in city politics, *Public Opinion Quarterly*, 1946, **10**, 1–23.

Typical of the findings of these studies are the following:

Merton, in his study of Kate Smith's war bond sale, emphasizes the pattern of attitudes growing out of the guilt reaction of the civilian in wartime, and the manner in which Smith's personality and appeals played upon these sentiments. He also discusses the opinions stemming from the urbanite's feeling of social alienation—notably his distrust of the "phony" informational environment created by highly competitive advertising.

Cantril in his study outlines the sources of insecurity in the world of 1938 that predisposed people to the utilization of inadequate standards of judgment and the acceptance of catastrophic events beyond their understanding: prolonged depression, the uneasy and incomprehensible state of world affairs, the predominance of a technology that had created means of action beyond popular conception or control.

Bruner and Korchin in their Boston study point to the anonymization of the urban political process and the developing need for a sense of contact with the controlling forces. In this case, the sense of contact was provided by the protective image of Curley, the friend of the poor man, seen as a modern Robin Hood stealing from the rich to aid the poor.

Finally, we may note the development of "open-ended" interview surveys of the kind that have come to be associated with the work of the Survey Research Center at Michigan and several other organizations. The decision to utilize not "yes-no" polling questions but open-ended, general questions in the conduct of opinion studies stemmed from a desire to get a fuller idea of what a given opinion "meant" to the respondent, what its personal significance was. For this departure from standard polling practice there were both practical and theoretical reasons. On the practical side, open-ended surveying had in its early period not only a reportorial task but the task of providing information on which to base Governmental decisions of policy. The policy-maker had to go beyond the *division of opinion* on an issue; he wished to know what people would do and how they could be expected to respond to changes in policy affecting their lives—for example, the farmers' reaction to a new marketing agreement policy. The personal significance of issues was highlighted by the nature of the subject matter to be investigated.

On the theoretical side, several influences are discernible. The spirit of Elton Mayo's approach to the study of industrial society had set into motion such concrete interviewing investigations as the now classic *Management and the Worker*,[22] of Roethlisberger and Dickson. The philosophy behind the interviewing in that study was a permissive one: to let the subject talk, to let him air his views and his grievances

[22] F. J. Roethlisberger and W. J. Dickson, *Management and the worker*, Cambridge, Harvard University Press, 1947.

as he felt, and not to classify his responses into preconceived categories. The early work of Likert in the Department of Agriculture was considerably influenced by this model. Another, later source of influence was Carl Rogers. Interviewers of the Department of Agriculture staff were sent to him for training in non-directive techniques and were, of course, influenced in the direction of considering their task one of allowing the respondent to structure his opinions and needs in terms of his own understanding of the issues involved. The result was that open-ended surveying rapidly became a method both for describing opinions as held by a sample of respondents, and for assessing the personal meaning of these opinions to their holders.

Through all these studies gleamed a refreshing interest in the determinative importance of the "personal significance" of events for the human being affected; yet they were in no sense systematic. In a way, they were a belated answer to the caveat of Thomas and Znaniecki, in *The Polish Peasant:* [23] let the social scientist attend not only to the objective social situation but also to the individual's own definition of that situation. Insofar as they were inspirited by a systematic point of view, it was generally a compound of anthropological emphasis on culture, of dynamic psychology with roots in Freudian theory, and of a non-systematic phenomenological bias. It is of some interest to note that within the field of clinical psychology these theoretical interests were being pursued concurrently and with a more systematic intent.

We turn now to the last of the converging approaches to opinion analysis that grew up in social psychology. In several respects, as we shall see, it differed in content and method, while pursuing the same objective: to understand the psychological processes whereby attitudes come into being.

The cognitive approach. Long before there was even the beginning of research on social attitudes, experimental psychology had occupied itself with such general cognitive concepts as determining tendency, set, task orientation. Until very recent years the bearing of these early studies on the conduct of subsequent investigations of social attitudes was, to be sure, quite indirect—although social psychologists were fond in the interim of hanging this highly respectable family portrait on their wall. Perhaps the major impact of the early tradition, which flourished first at Würzburg, was upon the various definitions of attitude that were current in the Twenties and Thirties, emphasizing directionality and selectivity in readiness to respond to stimulus situations. The fact of the matter was that during these years

[23] W. I. Thomas and F. Znaniecki, *The Polish peasant in Europe and America,* New York, Alfred A. Knopf, 1927.

the temper of American objectivist psychology was so alien to the more "internal" concerns of cognitive theory that the claim of ancestry was little more than a gesture.

But psychology, like the arts, is capable of revaluations and revivals. Insofar as we can locate a birthday for the revival of an interest in the cognitive mechanisms underlying attitude formation, we would perhaps choose the publication date of Sherif's *The Psychology of Social Norms*.[24] If 1936 seems too late, one could with equal justice point to the 1932 publication of Sir Frederick Bartlett's *Remembering*.[25] In any event, the mid-Thirties and the years following saw a steady rise in studies concerned with frames of reference used in judging, with attitude factors in perception and memory, and the like. The studies have been roughly of two kinds. On the one hand, there are ones which, like those by Bartlett, Levine and Murphy,[26] and Postman, Bruner, and McGinnies,[27] have shown the manner in which social attitudes serve as directive factors in memory reproduction or perceptual recognition, thus linking the fields of more traditional general psychology and social psychology. Closely related to these, on the other ·hand, are experiments whose aim has been to elucidate the similarities between attitude and such general cognitive phenomena as judgment,[28] comparison,[29] frames of reference,[30] and hypotheses.[31]

[24] M. Sherif, *The psychology of social norms*, New York, Harper and Brothers, 1936.

[25] F. C. Bartlett, *Remembering*, Cambridge, Cambridge University Press, 1932.

[26] J. Levine and G. Murphy, The learning and forgetting of controversial material, *Journal of abnormal and social Psychology*, 1943, **37**, 507–517.

[27] L. Postman, J. S. Bruner, and E. McGinnies, Personal values as selective factors in perception, *Journal of abnormal and social Psychology*, 1948, **43**, 142–154.

[28] For example, M. E. Tresselt and J. Volkmann, The production of uniform opinion by non-social stimulation, *Journal of abnormal and social Psychology*, 1942, **37**, 234–243; C. I. Hovland and M. Sherif, Judgmental phenomena and scales of attitude measurement: item displacement in Thurstone scales, *Journal of abnormal and social Psychology*, 1952, **47**, 822–832.

[29] J. Volkmann, Scales of judgment and their implications for social psychology. Chapt. 11 in J. H. Rohrer and M. Sherif (eds.), *Social Psychology at the Crossroads*, New York, Harper and Brothers, 1951.

[30] M. Sherif, A study of some social factors in perception, *Archives of Psychology*, 1935, No. 187.

[31] J. S. Bruner, Personality dynamics and the process of perceiving. Chapt. 5 in R. R. Blake and G. V. Ramsey (eds.), *Perception: an approach to personality*, New York, The Ronald Press Co., 1951; and L. Postman, Toward a general theory of cognition. Chapt. 10 in J. H. Rohrer and M. Sherif (eds.), *Social psychology at the crossroads*, New York, Harper and Brothers, 1951.

This is not the place to pass this rather specialized literature under review.[32] Rather, let our object be to note the effect of this body of research on current conceptions of attitude. Perhaps its prime systematic effect has been to rescue the concept "attitude" from its disembodied state by linking it to more general processes of mental functioning. Illustrative of the trend is the theoretical position of one of the early post-war textbooks in the field of social psychology: Krech and Crutchfield's *Theory and Problems of Social Psychology*.[33] Of attitudes, for example, they have this to say: "An attitude can be defined as an enduring organization of motivational, emotional, perceptual, and cognitive processes with respect to some aspect of the individual's world" (p. 152). The laws, then, of attitude formation and maintenance are an extension of the laws of motivation, emotion, perception, and cognition.

From the *theoretical* point of view, the value of such a formulation is evident—granting that this approach to the theory of attitudes is only one of several possible ones.[34] In terms of *practical* consequences for attitude research, an evaluation is more difficult to formulate at this point in history. At very least, the cognitive approach does provide a directive for the things about an attitude that one might profitably investigate. Thus, we do well in our interviewing to investigate the characteristically selective manner in which our respondents experience events related to their attitudes, the anchoring of the scales of judgment they apply to these events, the character of the remembered residue of information the subject brings to his appraisal of an event, and so on.

If the trend toward examining the personal significance of attitudes has brought opinion research to a livelier realization of the importance of motivation, the cognitive approach has on its part underlined the fact that motivation operates on attitude formation in ways far more complex and subtle than simple projection or wish fulfillment.

[32] For three recent reviews of the complex contemporary state of this field, see F. H. Allport, *Theories of perception and the concept of structure*, New York, John Wiley & Sons, 1955; M. D. Vernon, *A further study of visual perception*, Cambridge, Cambridge University Press, 1952; D. M. Johnson, *Psychology of thought and judgment*, New York, Harper and Brothers, 1955.

[33] D. Krech and R. Crutchfield, *Theory and problems of social psychology*, New York, McGraw-Hill Book Co., 1948.

[34] An alternative to the cognitive approach has been the attempt to apply Hullian learning theory to the study of attitude formation and change. Cf. L. W. Doob, *Public opinion and propaganda*, New York, Henry Holt, 1949; and C. I. Hovland, I. L. Janis, and H. H. Kelley, *Communication and persuasion*, New Haven, Yale University Press, 1953.

Approaches from the Psychology of Personality

The approach inspired by psychoanalysis. In the most flamboyant period of the application of psychoanalysis to social phenomena, the convention was to focus this new instrument on those opinions and beliefs which in the light of modern science were "illusions." Typical was Freud's treatment of religion and the religious sentiment in his *Civilization and Its Discontents*.[35] The religious sentiment could be completely explained by reference to unresolved dependency needs, needs for a strong and protective parent to guard us against our lingering feelings of infantile helplessness. "The ordinary man," Freud says, "cannot imagine . . . Providence in any other form but that of a greatly exalted Father, for only such a one could understand the needs of the sons of men, or be softened by their prayers and placated by the signs of their remorse" (p. 23). With rationalization and other elaboration, the religious sentiment and religious doctrine are disguised in a form that makes them acceptable to those more mature aspects of personality not directly gratified by the comforts of religion. The same type of reduction of cognitive and social factors was applied to other value systems, although religion was the favorite topic.[36]

The emphasis of this work was unidirectional in the sense that opinions or values were "explained" in terms of inner motivational dynamics. Much less interest was bestowed upon the possible importance of opinions and values for the inner functioning of the person. Explanation in this period was always from the inside out, never from the outside in. Values and opinions were something cast into consciousness by the upheavals and vicissitudes of the impulsive life. The function of personal ideology as a crucial stabilizing factor in ego development and maintenance was little regarded.

Typical of the emphasis was Harold Lasswell's early work, notably his *Psychopathology and Politics,* a pioneering venture in the application of psychoanalysis to political phenomena by an accepted political scientist.[37] "The significance of political opinions," stated Lasswell (p. 172), "is not to be grasped apart from the private motives which they symbolize." Displacement and rationalization are the major devices whereby "private motives" come to be transformed into political

[35] S. Freud, *Civilization and its discontents,* New York, Jonathan Cape, 1930.

[36] *See,* for example, E. Jones, Essays in folklore and religion, being Volume II of *Essays in applied psychoanalysis,* London, Hogarth Press, 1951, and various other psychoanalytic works in the period from 1920 to 1935.

[37] H. D. Lasswell, *Psychopathology and politics,* Chicago, University of Chicago Press, 1930.

opinions. In Lasswell's words: "The most general formula which expresses the developmental facts about the fully developed political man reads thus: $p \} d \} r = P$, where p equals private motives; d equals displacement onto a public object; r equals rationalization in terms of public interest; P equals the political man; and $\}$ equals transformed into" (pp. 75–76). Or, to cite another quotation: "Political prejudices, preferences, and creeds are often formulated in highly rational form, but they are grown in highly irrational ways" (p. 153). Through the presentation of case histories, Lasswell sought to demonstrate that the main function of political opinion was to externalize or displace some inner motive of long standing upon some external political or social issue. The role of opinions and values in character formation and ego function, their importance as a tool for testing reality, their utility in lending consistency to behavior, their aid in facilitating a sense of group membership—these and other *positive* functions of an opinion were not in this early study subjects of discussion.

Perhaps the turning point in the development of psychoanalytic approaches to the realm of values and ideology was the clearer formulation of ego-functioning that appeared in Freud's *Hemmung, Symptom, und Angst* in 1926.[38] We need not concern ourselves with the technical details of Freud's formulation save to recall that Freud in this book increased the role given the ego in personality dynamics by postulating ego defensive functions aroused by the presence of anxiety. Of prime interest are the developments that stemmed from the reformulation. Two are worth particular attention. One of these was Alexander's paper (1934) on the synthetic functions of the ego;[39] the other, Anna Freud's book, *The Ego and the Mechanisms of Defense*, in 1936.[40] The ego is no longer the powerless rider on the powerful horse. It is the function of the ego to create a compromise between the demands of the impulses of the id, the parental prohibitions and standards of the superego, and the exigencies of external reality. Still more recent developments in psychoanalytic "ego psychology"[41] give

[38] S. Freud, *Hemmung, Symptom und Angst*, Leipzig, Internationaler psychoanalytischer Verlag, 1926. Translated as *The problem of anxiety*, New York, W. W. Norton & Co., 1936.

[39] F. Alexander, Über das Verhältnis von Struktur zu Triebkonflikten, *Internationale Zeitschrift für Psychoanalyse*, 1934, **20**, 33–53.

[40] A. Freud, *The ego and the mechanisms of defense*, London, Hogarth Press, 1937.

[41] Cf. H. Hartmann, Ego psychology and the problem of adaptation, in D. Rappaport (ed.), *Organization and pathology of thought*, New York, Columbia University Press, 1951, pp. 362–396.

further emphasis to constructive functions of the ego, now seen as in important respects autonomous of the id. Psychoanalysis converges here with psychology generally.

With the introduction of this conception, it became possible to talk about the maturity, the strength, or the creativity of the ego's functioning. A philosophy of life, a system of values, or a set of opinions—all aspects of the ego—could no longer be simply conceived as displacements of unruly and anxiety-provoking impulses but must be viewed as an attempt to cope simultaneously with the demands of conscience, impulse, and reality. As the person achieves psychological maturity, moreover, the compulsiveness or demandingness of id and superego are gradually reduced to a point where the individual becomes increasingly capable of orienting himself effectively to reality.

The rise of "neo-Freudian" theory ran parallel, of course, to this development within psychoanalytic theory proper. Formulations such as Horney's,[42] along with the new development in psychoanalysis, brought to a close the first period of psychoanalytic reductionism. Before this turning point, the commerce between social science and psychoanalytic dynamic psychology had been a one-way domination. The psychoanalyst is less inclined than formerly to dismiss as of secondary relevance the social scientist's interest in the social and cultural environment of the individual.

The California study of ethnocentrism by Adorno, Frenkel-Brunswik, Levinson, and Sanford [43] reflects this changed orientation in a study that combined conventional attitude scaling with various techniques for making inferences about the functioning of personality. The reader will recall that the general method of this investigation was to compare subjects found to be at the extreme ends of a distribution of scores on a test of ethnocentrism, one extreme being a high degree of ethnocentrism and intolerance, the other a marked degree of liberalism and tolerance. Could one find any homogeneous character structure at the high and at the low extremes of ethnocentrism? This was the major research question of the project.

Personality studies of their extreme subjects showed the extreme ethnocentric subjects as members of a rather homogeneous "anthropological species," the *authoritarian personality*. A syndrome of nine authoritarian character traits was enumerated, typical of the ethnocentric individual.

[42] K. Horney, *The neurotic personality of our time*, New York, W. W. Norton & Co., 1937.
[43] *Op. cit.*

Conventionalism
Submission to idealized authority figures
Hostility toward those violating social norms
Dislike of subjectivity: "anti-intraception"
Superstitiousness and stereotypy
Preoccupation with strength and toughness
Destructive cynicism toward human nature
Tendency to project unacceptable impulses
Exaggerated concern with sexual "goings on"

There are serious questions to be raised about this research. Authoritarian personalities, as defined by the authors, may and do embrace certain liberal, tolerant ideologies with a rigidity and intolerance matching the bigot's devotion to prejudice. There are authoritarian liberals too. We are, moreover, dealing here with an extreme type, and it is important to remember that neither the extremely tolerant cases nor the great range of middle-of-the-road people are so easily categorized as an "anthropological species." Limited though the results may be, they nonetheless point to an important convergence in the study of opinions. For here, in essence, is a "gratification study"— the gratification inherent in adopting an ideology—but one in which the meaning of gratification is not *ad hoc,* as in the studies earlier cited, but founded upon our current knowledge of psychodynamics.

Though this is not an appropriate place to discuss the matter in detail, it is also of interest to note that these studies made contact with the "cognitive approach" discussed earlier. Several of the California workers have carried their analysis further to deal with generalized intolerance for ambiguity as a cognitive and affective trait, tracing the influence of affective constriction on the authoritarian's mode of cognitive functioning.

A recent critical appraisal of *The Authoritarian Personality,* which also reviews some of this more recent work that it stimulated,[44] calls repeated attention to a complementary set of considerations which, in the view of these critics, the authors of the California studies kept insufficiently in mind. Surely the antisemitism of the Nazi in search of any potential scapegoat with the veriest trace of Jewish blood no matter what his professed religion is a far cry from the medieval antisemite, whose hatred for the Jew could be transformed into tolerance and even respect if the Jew but entered the true church as a confessant. The characterological origins of proneness to antisemitism probably differ drastically in the Californian, the Nazi, and the enthusiastic but

[44] R. Christie and M. Jahoda (eds.), *Studies in the scope and method of the authoritarian personality,* Glencoe, Ill., The Free Press, 1954.

horrified spectator at the *auto-da-fé*. And within contemporary society, different meanings probably attach to virulent prejudice as an expression of cynical embitteredness in the lower social strata and as a middle-class deviation from the polite conventions of the "gentlemen's agreement." The California account of ethnocentrism is incomplete without reference to these cultural and social determinants.

Once having raised the question of social or cultural factors, the same problem that bedevils the student of demographic determinants, we must turn at once to the second major trend in personality theory and research that has affected the study of opinion determinants.

The culture-personality approach. Perhaps the best way of summarizing the effect of culture-personality research on psychodynamic theory is to say that it made the student of personality even more concretely aware of the social vicissitudes. In this sense, "culture-and-personality" as an idea hastened the progress already developing within psychoanalytic theory, noted in some detail in the previous section. One may even argue that it was the work of the psychologically oriented anthropologist which gave the *coup de grâce* to the unblushingly 19th century instinctivism that dominated the beginnings of psychoanalytic theory. Malinowski's book, *The Father in Primitive Psychology*,[45] to choose one of the important landmarks in this development, challenged the assumptions of the Freud of *Totem and Taboo*.[46] If in the period that followed there were published books with such titles as *The Neurotic Personality of Our Time*, their appearance was no accident. A happy circumstance had brought within a single purview the first-hand observation of the free-associating patient and the first-hand observation of primitive peoples.

A detailed review of the developments in this area would not serve our purpose here.[47] Our object is simply to outline briefly the forces which led personality psychologists to an interest in opinion, attitudes, values, and personal ideology. Let us, as we have done before, sample a few of the ferments more in the spirit of illustrating a trend than in chronicling it.

In terms of the most general theoretical influence, the students of culture-and-personality made the dynamic psychologist aware of two

[45] B. Malinowski, *The father in primitive psychology*, New York, W. W. Norton & Co., 1927.

[46] S. Freud, *Totem and taboo*, New York, New Republic, 1927.

[47] *See* A. Inkeles and D. J. Levinson, National character; and C. Kluckhohn, Culture and behavior, In G. Lindzey (ed.), *Handbook of social psychology*, Cambridge, Addison-Wesley, 1954.

points out of which much theoretical tilting was to come. The first of these was that each culture, indeed each subculture, created a special plight to which the individual must adjust. The human plight was in no sense universal save in this fact: that however different the culture might be, it had certain common problems to deal with—death, childbirth, gathering food, etc. But each culture handled these problems differently, developed a special way of life. These ways of life created special needs, special responses, and led to the development of special personality patterns.

The second point, equally "obvious," was this: given a set of problems to face, each culture provided a limited range of responses which the person could adopt if he was to avoid the status of a deviant. These permissible response patterns—involving not only overt but also covert responses—again differed from culture to culture and even from sub-culture to subculture. In short, then, the term "culture" implied both a specialized patterning of the individual stimulus situation, and a special patterning of the response that could be made to it.[48]

With these two basic ideas as points of departure, various anthropologists and students of personality have attempted to erect theories to account for the way in which different culture patterns bring about specialized response-repertories in the individuals of that culture. Explanations exclusively in terms of direct learning seemed not to be sufficient or economical. It was rather generally assumed by writers in this field—Linton,[49] Kardiner,[50] Kluckhohn,[51] and others—that an easier and more adequate method of dealing with the problem was in terms of the patterning of personality. Thus Kardiner says, "There is a limit to the sort of culture content that can be transmitted by direct learning processes"[52] (p. 433). As an "operational tool" he chooses something which he has called "basic personality structure." Its gen-

[48] For a fuller account of "patterning," *see* C. Kluckhohn, Patterning as exemplified in Navaho culture, In *Language, culture and personality* (pp. 109–130), Essays in Honor of Edward Sapir, Menasha, Wis., Sapir Memorial Publication Fund, 1941.

[49] R. Linton, *The cultural background of personality*, New York, Appleton-Century, 1945.

[50] A. Kardiner, *The individual and his society*, New York, Columbia University Press, 1939.

[51] C. Kluckhohn, Culture and behavior, In G. Lindzey (ed.), *Handbook of social psychology*, Cambridge, Addison-Wesley, 1954.

[52] A. Kardiner, The concept of basic personality structure as an operational tool in the social sciences, In D. G. Haring, *Personal character and cultural milieu*, Syracuse, Syracuse University Press, 1948.

eral conception can be sketched in a few sentences. Certain primary institutions exist in every culture, traditional behavior patterns concerning the nurture and discipline of the young child. The effect of these primary institutions is to set up various "projective systems" in the individual, including among other things "basic attitudes toward parents," which achieve their fulfillment in the creation of other, secondary institutions. The historical process whereby secondary institutions are created thus guarantees a cultural environment appropriate to the needs, character, and demands of the individual raised in it. Linton, reflecting the functionalism of American anthropology, points out that the attitudes and values created by primary institutions are those which have maximum relevance to the survival of the culture and may in some cases be antithetical to the eventual well-being (defined, say, as prolongation of life) of the individual.[53] In any event, it is by this process that the basic personality structure of a culture develops.

To be sure, the Kardiner account of the formation of attitudes, personality, and secondary institutions reflects the genetic bias of Freudian theory: i.e., early childhood disciplines create the invariant *anlage* for all that is to follow in the life of the individual. Our interest, however, is not in the content of his theory, but in his approach. And the approach is notable for its recognition of the formative influence of varying cultural patterns. The collaboration of a psychiatrist, Kardiner, and an anthropologist, Linton, in the analysis of Marquesan, Tanala, Comanche, and other cultural materials, led to a fruitful series of other researches, the net effect of which has been to make dynamic psychology keenly aware of the cultural patterning of the personality mechanisms which before were treated as though *sui generis.*

There is a proverb that "the fish will be the last to discover water." Through the cross-cultural reports of the anthropologists, psychiatry and the psychology of personality have discovered their own culture. The result on the domestic scene has been a growth of interest in *subcultural* differences within our own society—and it is at this point that we come to a direct contact between the work of the culture-personality students and the preoccupations of those interested in the demographic variables with which opinions are related. For now we find the sociologist, psychologist, and anthropologist concerned not with social class, say, as a demographic variable, but as a description of certain enculturating forces which shape the needs, experiences, and personalities of class members. "Middle-class" in the writings of Davis

[53] R. Linton, *op. cit.*

and Havighurst [54] or of Hollingshead [55] means not simply a position in the class hierarchy but, rather, is a descriptive label for a set of cultural patterns: patterned situations with which the middle-class member must cope, and responses to these situations permitted by middle-class culture. We do not speak simply of the common needs and experiences of middle-class members, but refer rather to characteristic ambivalence about sex and aggression, to certain compulsive strivings for upward mobility, to certain retentive attitudes toward property, etc. The individual can then be described not by class position alone, but by reference to the extent to which he has introcepted and been formed by class values.

One last point is worth noting. We have said nothing about the relationship between the cognitive approach of certain social psychologists and the culture-personality theorists. To spell out the converging trend here requires more space than we have at our disposal in a book of this sort. Yet convergence there has been, though its importance for the theory of opinion is primarily in the future. Linton,[56] Hallowell,[57] Kluckhohn and Kroeber,[58] and Dennis [59] speak of the importance of the cultural patterning of perception, imagination, and categorical thinking as devices whereby enculturation is vastly facilitated. It is through such patterning of cognition that uniformity of attitudes and beliefs is maintained in spite of the existence, whatever the culture, of events which might bring into question a man's approved and sanctioned beliefs—beliefs as open to "stimulus contradiction" as the Trobriand notion of impregnation by spirits which is supported by a failure of Trobrianders to recognize the facial similarities of fathers and sons.

A Convergent Approach

The contemporary student of the opinion process who is interested in the determinants of opinion has a harder row to hoe than his

[54] A. Davis and R. J. Havighurst, *Father of the man,* Boston, Houghton Mifflin Co., 1947.

[55] H. Hollingshead, *Elmtown's youth,* New York, John Wiley & Sons, 1949.

[56] R. Linton, *op. cit.,* cf. p. 87 f.

[57] A. I. Hallowell, Cultural factors in the structuralization of perception, Chapt. 7 in J. H. Rohrer and M. Sherif, *Social psychology at the crossroads,* New York, Harper and Brothers, 1951.

[58] A. L. Kroeber and C. Kluckhohn, *Culture: a critical review of concepts and definitions,* Papers of the Peabody Museum, 1952, **47,** No. 1.

[59] W. Dennis, Cultural and developmental factors in perception, In R. R. Blake and G. V. Ramsey (eds.), *Perception: an approach to personality,* New York, Ronald, 1951.

predecessor of the 1920's. He cannot operate without a theory of personality. He cannot be unmindful of the importance of cultural forces which pattern the belief systems, values, and personality of his respondents. Nor can he neglect the contemporary, social environment to which the individual is adjusting himself in an effort to gratify both inner demands and reality demands. He must, if his account is to be complete, show a proper mindfulness of the intricate processes of cognition from which emerge the "finished" attitudes and beliefs of his subject.

But this is not the best of all possible worlds, and the scholar cannot be expected in any one inquiry to attempt answers to all the relevant questions. We have been at pains to sketch the various converging trends in the study of the determinants of opinion not as a means of providing a stencil for future inquiry, but rather as a means of making explicit what our own aspirations might be.

In the next chapter we present the point of view about opinions, values, and personality which is at the base of the present study. It is, we believe, a useful framework in terms of which an increasingly rigorous theory must be worked out. Like the various studies cited in the present chapter, our study is another evidence of convergence within psychology toward *a* psychology and away from the classical autonomous "topical" fields.

CHAPTER 3

ON UNDERSTANDING

AN OPINION

Some Assumptions about Personality

We have made much of the axiom that the total behavior of a person—including his opinions—reflects certain underlying regularities of functioning. It is this underlying regularity that lends predictability to behavior. The description of this regularity is the description of personality. Our first duty, then, is to make explicit our own assumptions about the nature of personality.

An individual's opinions are but one of a number of consistent and regular forms of behavior which characterize him. From these consistencies in his behavior we infer the individual's *personality*. Personality, then, is an inferred construct to which we ascribe certain dynamic properties—striving, adaptation, defense, etc. Opinions, like all behavior, both constitute part of the data from which personality is inferred and are in turn a function of personality. We account for consistencies in a person's opinions in the same theoretical terms that we use to account for his consistencies of gesture, emotional expression, or purposive action. And since we have learned to regard the various expressions of personality as highly interdependent, we may expect to find important relationships between a person's opinions and other forms of his behavior.

How shall we describe *personality*, the context in which a person's opinions exist? Perhaps the most widely shared point of view on human behavior is what may roughly be called *functionalism.* The human being, according to this approach, is not governed by a rational calculus, nor is he a blank slate on which experience traces its inexorable mark. Nor yet is man an ingenious machine translating physical stimuli into bodily response. Like all animals, he is an organism, a system of life processes that somehow maintains its identity in active interplay with its environment. An organism is never passive, but survives and grows through constant striving, responding selectively to relevant aspects of its environment, and reaching out to incorporate, modify, fend off, or attain. Final passivity is death; in life there is always striving to maintain the delicate adaptation of the needs of the organism to its environment.

The process of striving and adaptation is a two-sided affair. Not only do organisms modify the environment to fulfill their needs; they in turn are modified by it. Organisms grow and learn. They learn more effective techniques for altering the environment to suit their needs; at the same time they learn to modify the very needs underlying their striving. Although the nature of the life processes and of the environment imposes finite limits on the extent to which the needs of the organism are modifiable, it is still true that the range of flexibility in human beings is enormous.

Behavior occurs as an interaction between striving organism and environment. What of the environment? Clearly it exists *as environment* only in relation to some organism. Its conceivably infinite potential takes on significance only in terms of benefit or harm to that organism. The warden and the churchmouse live in very different environments. Each, through his needs, interests, and aversions defines what for him constitutes the *effective* environment, what Lewin called the "life space." A person does not passively read off his experience; he selects the characters and settings to weave into the plot of his own purposes.

For man, the *social environment* provided by other human beings is particularly significant. Unlike the social environments of other gregarious animals, the potential complexity of the human environment is enormously increased by the fact that man has developed language as a means of communication and as a way of conserving, symbolizing, and manipulating experience. The essential social character of language and its traditionalized categories of thought are of incalculable importance in giving "human nature" its distinctively human character. Indeed, both Freud [1] in his conceptions of superego and ego-ideal and

[1] S. Freud, *New introductory lectures on psychoanalysis,* New York, W. W. Norton & Co., 1933.

George Herbert Mead [2] in his theory of the self have remarked that much of what we label personality represents an invasion of the human organism by his social environment. Personality as we know it is an essentially social product, inconceivable in the completely isolated human being.

With growth, the human organism's strivings become increasingly adapted to the social environment. But the nature of these basic strivings still presents a problem. Psychologists are in dispute in regard to their source in the adult personality. McDougall [3] and Freud [4] have sought the ultimate source of all human strivings in basic biological instincts or propensities. Others, notably G. W. Allport,[5] while granting that the infant organism gets its start toward personality in the satisfaction of simple biological needs, hold that the more complex motives of the adult bear little significant relation to the biological satisfactions around which they perhaps took form. Still others, among them Murray,[6] offer classifications of universally important motives without taking a stand as to their ultimate source. While the source and genesis of adult human motivation must remain subject to controversy until the nature of the learning process is more fully understood, the pervasiveness and multifariousness of striving as a significant fact of personality cannot be gainsaid. As Edward Tolman has put it, "behavior reeks with purpose." [7]

The complicated derivation of human personality allows adaptive striving to go on at very different levels of complexity and effectiveness. When more adequate adaptation is not feasible, man seems capable of reshaping his knowledge and perceptions to find makeshift gratifications and avert the awareness of dangers. Although the healthy individual must somehow come to terms with social reality, the range of latitude within which he can constitute his picture of self and reality remains great. His psychological environment inevitably represents a compromise between inner forces and the outer given.

Such adaptive compromises are made particularly necessary by the fact of conflict, an inevitable corollary of the complexity of human motivation, so clearly stressed by Freud. People want many different

[2] G. H. Mead, *Mind, self, and society*, Chicago, University of Chicago Press, 1934.

[3] W. McDougall, *The energies of men*, New York, Charles Scribner's Sons, 1933.

[4] *Op. cit.*

[5] G. W. Allport, *Personality: a psychological interpretation*, New York, Henry Holt & Co., 1937.

[6] H. A. Murray, *Explorations in personality*, New York, Oxford University Press, 1938.

[7] *Purposive behavior in animals and men*, New York, Appleton-Century, 1932.

things, things often totally incompatible with one another. A rising executive, to pick an instance at random, wants power and success— but he also wants to be loved, even to be taken care of. Some needs may take precedence over others, in a kind of hierarchical organization. But in the not infrequent case of self-contradictory motivation, either one motive must be totally suppressed or compromise gratifications must be hazarded. And the total suppression of a motive may often lead to other compromises in the perception of social reality, com- promises that are required to make the suppression possible. Not only may our executive get ulcers; his sensitivity to relations of dependency may be warped.

Notwithstanding the fact of conflict, each individual personality achieves at least a minimum degree of integration and congruity. A person's various needs and the adaptive devices that he brings to their service form a more or less integrated structure. Lacking a minimum degree of unity, the organism would be incapable of persistent striving. At one level or another the various activities of the organism must strike a balance of mutual compatibility.

Such are the main lines of the view of personality into which we propose to fit a theory of opinion. In brief, the construct of person- ality that we introduce to account for regularities and consistencies in behavior has the following characteristics in our use:

1) It is marked by *striving*. As an organization of behavior tendencies formed in the process of adaptive striving after goals, it includes the tendency to be selectively aware of objects related to certain goals, to pursue these goals, and to employ certain favored techniques in their pursuit. The aims of striving, most generally stated, are *construction* and *defense.* We seek gratification, learn to adapt to the circumstances in which gratification can take place. This is constructive striving. But we also strive to defend ourselves against what is disruptive and anxiety- arousing, to protect against what upsets gratification and adjustment.

2) *Striving characterizes cognitive activity:* perceiving, remembering, thinking, etc. Not only does cognition function in the service of other needs, but it seems to be intrinsically motivated: an "effort after meaning" or, as Tolman [8] has called it, a "placing need" which can be activated by a lack of structure in the individual's life space.

3) Personality is an *organized* whole rather than an unrelated congeries of tendencies. The various aspects of personality are mutually inter- dependent and mutually adapted. Since not all behavior tendencies are of equal potency, we may expect to find a *hierarchical* organization in which some take precedence over others. Thus, a change in a basic need may bring about a change in a series of related, dependent attitudes.

[8] In T. Parsons and E. G. Shils (eds.), *Toward a general theory of action*, Cam- bridge, Harvard University Press, 1951.

A change in one dominant attitude may change various others which are subservient to it.

4) While the interdependency of personality functioning is sufficient to lead to a considerable degree of *unity, conflict* within the personality as well as between personality and environmental forces often occurs. Such conflicts pose problems for the maintenance and growth of the person. Some of the main lines of development of the personality are determined by the strategy adopted for dealing with them.

5) The social and even the physical environment of the individual are not random series of events; rather, they are patterned by the culture of which he is a member. It is also clear that the opportunities for learning to respond to the environment are finitely delimited by the culture. In this respect, the individual, in Dollard's terms, is not only to be considered in his biological and psychological individuality, but also as a "specimen in a cultural series." [9]

6) Finally, a special place in the hierarchical organization of personality must be given to those inferred processes which underlie the experience of self. Whether we use the term Phenomenal Self, Ego, Self Image, or some other, it is quite apparent that a major contribution to consistency of behavior can be referred to the person's reactions to his experience of self.

This is not the place to develop a theory of personality in greater detail. Our intent here has been to outline a minimal conception of personality, one that skirts controversial issues when they are not immediately crucial to a functional theory of opinion, yet sets the direction that our further account must take.

Describing an Opinion

It follows from our description of personality functioning that we must define an attitude in such a way as to take into account its presumed interrelation with other aspects of personality. With this in mind we define an attitude as a predisposition to experience a class of objects in certain ways, with characteristic affect; to be motivated by this class of objects in characteristic ways; and to act with respect to these objects in a characteristic fashion. In brief, an attitude is a predisposition to experience, to be motivated by, and to act toward, a class of objects in a predictable manner.

We shall not be fussy about the word used to denote the phenomenon described in our definition. Attitude, opinion, sentiment—all of these terms refer to the kind of predisposition we have in mind. The permanence of such a predisposition is less a problem of definition than of measurement. Although it is true that most of the attitudes in which the social psychologist and student of personality are inter-

[9] J. Dollard, *Criteria for the life history*, New Haven, Yale University Press, 1935.

ested are relatively long enduring, we would emphasize the continuity between supposedly short-term "sets" and more long-term "attitudes." Finally, the class of objects around which a sentiment is organized— the object that one is predisposed to experience, to be motivated by, and to act toward in a characteristic manner—need not be restricted as in some definitions of attitude to "social objects" or "controversial issues." For an attitude as we have defined it can be related to any class of objects which exist in the person's life space: moral issues, lifted weights in a psychological experiment, Russia, prime numbers, or what not. The specification of objects is again an empirical matter, not a matter for definition.

The reader will sense that our rather broad definition of attitude or sentiment is in the tradition of Shand and McDougall, and conforms in the main to the usage of most contemporary writers such as Murray, Krech and Crutchfield, and Newcomb. In all honesty we must confess that we do not think the time is ripe to be theoretically solemn about the definition of an attitude. Definitions are matters of convenience, and they attain high status only in the advanced stages of a science. In time, greater precision will come. In the meantime we think that little is served by quarreling about definition in the abstract.

Now let us sketch our descriptive apparatus for distinguishing the *object* of an attitude. As we have indicated, it may be anything in the life space of the individual. In less technical terms, it may be anything which exists for the person.

One problem in the use of words can be set aright here. It is important to distinguish the object as it exists for the person and the object as we designate it in common speech. When the object of a sentiment is specified in terms of some social referent, we shall speak of the *topic* of an attitude. A man, let us say, has a highly negative attitude toward "Russia-as-it-exists-for-him." "Russia-as-it-exists-for-him" is the *object* of his sentiment. When, however, we speak of this man's attitude toward "the Soviet Union" or "Russia" or some other socially defined entity, we shall be speaking of the *topic* of his attitude. Perhaps the use of these two terms will keep us from the pitfall of assuming that attitudes have as their objects the socially defined entities of the history books and newspaper columns.

We may distinguish various characteristics of the object of a sentiment: *differentiation, saliency, time perspective, informational support,* and *object value.* We shall consider each of these in turn.

Differentiation. An attitude toward Russia may be focussed upon a highly amorphous subjective impression of that country or upon a highly differentiated one. One person will see Russia as a highly complex phenomenon comprising many *aspects;* Russia as a social experiment, Russia as an aggressor, Russia as a country capable of producing many of the great literary figures of the 19th century, Russia as an approach to Orwell's *1984*, Russia as a veritable basin of natural resources, Russia as anti-Zionist—all of these may be aspects of one man's view of Russia. To another man, Russia is a collectivity of ignorant peasants guided by a small ruthless band of radical agitators and "trouble-makers"—and that is about all. Not only is the object of an attitude differentiated into various aspects; it also varies with respect to its *organization.* "Degrees" of structure are not readily specified, and we shall not attempt to scale such a dimension. One can, however, specify the manner in which a differentiated object of opinion is organized. In the second hypothetical case cited above, the major, organizing aspect of our man's view of Russia might be the sensed absence of personal liberty in that country, and all other parts of the picture might be subordinated to it. We shall see at least one case of this sort in the case histories of the following chapters. In sum, then, the object of an attitude varies in its differentiation; and given any particular order of differentiation, it also varies in the manner of its organization.

Saliency. By this term we indicate the extent to which a particular object or class of objects is central in the everyday concerns of a person. Russia and Communism were matters of the most personal concern and central attention for one of our subjects—almost the most important things in his life. For another, it was of the most marginal interest.[10] We may also speak of the saliency of various differentiated aspects of a man's view of Russia—saying, for example, that Russian anti-religious activity for a given person is more salient than Russian aggressiveness.

Time perspective. Here we mean the temporal frame of reference applied to the object of a sentiment. In our analysis of cases we found this to be an inescapable and vital characteristic of an attitude. Characterizing time perspective systematically is difficult. Yet if we are to predict anything about the way in which the person will guide his actions, it is essential that we do so. Again in terms of Russia, one person will regard Russia as a matter of only momentary, transitory concern: something that erupts into the headlines for a while and then is gone. Another will take, as one of our subjects did, a long-term

[10] A recent survey of the American public concludes as one of its principal findings that the threat of Communism is very low in saliency for most Americans. *See* S. A. Stouffer, *Communism, conformity, and civil liberties,* New York, Doubleday & Co., 1955.

view, the essential theme of which was: "Russia is an unreasonable child; if we remain firm, she will eventually grow up." Still another will adopt a short-term climactic point of view in which Russia is seen as making tremendous inroads into our strength which, unless stopped immediately, will drive us to disaster. Such characterizations of time perspective are, to be sure, highly qualitative and will undoubtedly vary widely as one goes from one kind of attitude to another. Although we do not pretend to have reached an adequate way of handling time perspective, we are convinced that it is a vital aspect of a person's sentiment.

Informational support. Strictly speaking, this term does not characterize the object itself, but rather the knowledge an individual possesses that is relevant to his attitude. It merely identifies the amount of information a person is capable of bringing to bear in appraising the topic of an attitude. In our studies, for example, we have used rather primitive information tests to determine how much the individual "knows" about various phases of Soviet life and society. We recognize, of course, that there is a very close relationship between the amount of differentiation of an attitude and the amount of its informational support. Differentiation refers to an analysis of the person's subjective conception of Russia (which is based upon many things aside from information): while informational *support* refers merely to the amount of the available information that may go into the building of this conception.

Object value. Here we refer to the affective tone of an object. We had considered the term "object *affect*," our choice of "value" being dictated primarily by the importance of value in the sense of positive, negative, and neutral. For the first thing we usually ask about the object of a person's sentiment is whether it appears as disagreeable, pleasant, or neutral. It goes without saying, of course, that when one has said that Russia is a negatively toned symbol for a given person, one has said very little. One must also specify certain other affective qualities: whether, for example, it is seen as threatening or simply as annoying.

So much for the general description of objects about which people have sentiments. One could doubtless multiply categories in terms of which description can be carried out. We have wanted merely to construct a minimum set of variables which might guide us in our exploration. The task of expanding or contracting our modes of description and of rendering them quantitatively scalable remains, of course, for future work.

Orientation. Our next task is to characterize the action tendencies aroused by the object: what we shall call the *orientation* of an attitude. Given a person's subjective view of Russia, we may ask how he orients himself action-wise. In abstract terms, we may speak of three possible action tendencies: *approach, avoidance,* and *hostility.* Concretely, and again in terms of an attitude toward Russia, approach may mean a wish to go to Russia, the act of taking books out of the library to find out more about Russia, joining the Communist Party, buying the *Daily Worker* to find out about its side of the story, or what not. Avoidance again may take varied forms: anything from motivated indifference to an actual active avoidance of anything having to do with Russia. Hostility we know to be a subtle and complex form of behavior. By it we mean any act whose objective is injury, debasement, or any other form of harm to the object: advocating a preventive war, voting for a rabidly anti-Communist candidate, or even fantasying a counter-revolution in Russia.

Policy stand. The translation of one's orientation into a preference for a particular proposal for collective action (such as a given foreign policy), we shall call the *policy stand* of the person. *Policy stand* indicates preference for a socially defined policy and may or may not be identical with the individual's own *orientation.* So a person may say, "I'm in favor of taking Russia's veto power away, but what I'd really like to do is to take the whole damned Politburo and dump them into the middle of the Atlantic Ocean." Most of the work done in public opinion polling is designed to discover the policy stands of cross-sections of the population. And one of the major differences between the regular polls and the open-ended surveys is that the latter try to determine the orientation of their respondents in addition to their stand on policies.

The Expressive Nature of Opinions

A person's behavior is marked by a certain self-consistency or congruency. Expressive movement, speech, intensity of striving, style of thinking, "temperament"—all of these things and many others seem to constitute a congruent pattern which we think of as typical of the individual. How one comes to know this flavor or style in another person is one of the neglected problems in psychology. Yet in spite of the fact that correlational studies designed to uncover consistency between selected facets of behavior have left unresolved the basis of their congruence, there is no gainsaying that this congruence is one of the primary facts of human behavior.

How much of this consistency can be attributed to innate or constitutional endowment and how much can be referred to the distinctive pattern of adjustment achieved by the person in coping with the world is not a particularly fruitful kind of inquiry. Given a person with certain initial endowments of energy and cognitive equipment, there inevitably develops a style of adjustment to the world which is shaped and limited both by constitution and by the intervening opportunities the person has had for learning and adapting.

Opinions, like any other form of complex behavior, are involved in such a pattern of consistency. They reflect the man's style of operating. When we speak of "the expressive nature of opinions" we refer not to any need for expression, but rather to the simple fact that a man's opinions reflect the deeper-lying pattern of his life—who he has become by virtue of facing a particular kind of world with a particular kind of constitution.

In our analysis of concrete opinions, we explain little by saying that a given opinion is "expressive" of the man. Yet there are times when one can do no better than this. A person, let us say, has as one of his most salient cognitive characteristics an inability to deal with abstractions. He must solve all his problems on the level of mulling over the concrete details of events. Perhaps he got that way in the course of adjusting to the conditions of his life. Yet examination of his intellectual functioning shows a definite limit in his intellectual capacities. We find in this individual's opinions the same lack of generality, the same preoccupation with minor detail that is characteristic of his performance in a mental test. To put the matter in dynamic or functional terms—to say, for example, that his opinions serve the function of keeping the informational environment cut down to manipulable size—would be to stretch things considerably. Granted that this preference for detail may serve a function in the *economy* of his personality, it seems to us evident that his detail-oriented opinions are also to be understood as expressive of the over-all *style* of the person.

Another person, let us say, has a history from earliest childhood of meagre energy and a low fatigue threshold. The adult pattern of life of such a person may reflect an adjustment to this deficit, marked among other things by a lack of interest in affairs of the world outside the immediate circuit of routine daily activities. We may find that this man at age forty is markedly indifferent toward the issues of Russia and foreign policy. Again, one can put the matter in dynamic terms: his opinions are a function of needs to conserve energy. But at the simplest level of analysis one must also note that indifference toward world political affairs in this man is expressive of a more pervading indifference toward the world outside his immediate personal orbit.

We do not want to make an issue of the difference between analysis in terms of "need fulfillment" and description in terms of expressive "consistency." For we shall utilize both approaches. Rather, there are certain points in our study where it seems to us that parsimony is on the side of shunning the dynamic explanation in favor of the less glamorous description. The expression of temperamental traits is one such case. A man of generally vivid affect is likely to feel more vividly than others about his opinions. We shall not seek to find dynamic explanations for it, granting nonetheless that in other kinds of personality research one might be primarily concerned with the psychodynamic origins of vivid affect. The same is true of intellectual functioning. We feel no strong urge to explain the gratifications accruing to the unintelligent man by virtue of having poorly informed opinions. Again, in another context, stupidity may be the object of dynamic analysis. Should the vivid man be apathetic toward a major event or the dull person reveal a fastidiously equipped storehouse of reasoned knowledge on a complex issue—then we too shall be more concerned about the dynamics involved.

The Adjustive Functions of Opinion

We come now to our most central question: What purpose is served by holding an opinion? Put more technically, the question becomes, "What adjustive functions of personality are served by the formation and maintenance of an opinion?"

Let us say at the most general level that one's opinions or attitudes serve as mediators between the inner demands of the person and the outer environment—the material, social, and, most immediately, the informational environment of the person. Figures of speech may be misleading, yet we do well to think of a man's attitudes as his major equipment for dealing with reality. This equipment is not a product solely of basic needs and defenses nor is it fashioned directly according to the blueprint of the world in which the person finds himself. Nor is it simply borrowed ready-made from the groups to which he belongs or aspires. Something of all of these but not quite any one of them, it is, essentially, an apparatus for balancing the demands of inner functioning and the demands of the environment. One cannot predict a man's opinions by knowledge of his personality alone or of his environment alone. Both must enter into any predictive formula.

It is a mistake to restrict the concepts of attitude and opinion to those predispositions which have as their object the issues of contemporary social and political life. Such restriction overlooks the fact that these attitudes are embedded in larger systems of opinion which mediate between the most compelling pressures of the environment and the most imperious and pervasive needs. Perhaps someone will ask, "Why all this searching analysis of a man's half-baked attitudes toward Russia?" The answer is this: look far enough into the origins of any opinion, and one will find not just an opinion but a sample of how the holder of that opinion copes with his world.

Rather than risk later misunderstanding we shall pause for a moment to examine the two meanings that can be attached to "having an opinion." Let us say first that one can *hold* an opinion and at the same time reserve option on when and how the opinion should be *expressed.* It is obvious that the two acts serve somewhat different functions. And while we may be inclined to say that the one is freer of constraints than the other—that a man may hold whatever view he likes so long as he is discreet in its expression—it is the better wisdom to attribute an equal lawfulness to each. Only in a most superficial sense is one "free" to hold whatever opinion he will. The illusion of free choice of opinion is scarcely borne out by closer analysis of the many inner and outer requirements that limit what a person will find acceptable. "I can't believe that," he will say; or, "What an irresponsible, almost despicable point of view that is!"

Once we have said that there is a lawful determination both in the opinions one holds and in the occasions and circumstances of their expression, we must then go on to say that the same laws do not hold for each. The two must be held separate, for separate but concurrent examination. It is true, of course, that the opinions permissible to express are, under some circumstances, the very opinions one wishes to hold. Or, quite the reverse, the rebel may find himself repelled by popular points of view whose expression savors to him of conformism. Such instances do not cancel the need for separate analysis.

In our discussion of the adjustive functions of opinion we shall make no special effort to incarcerate "holding" and "expressing" into separate and purified theoretical categories. They each present somewhat different problems for empirical analysis and we shall, where possible, analyze them separately. Our principal theoretical interest, as the reader must long ago have noted, is in the opinions *held* by the individual. It is a crucial but secondary theoretical problem how a man works out the strategy of their expression.[11]

[11] If one should ask, "How do you know the opinion held by a person save by its expression?" we shall reply that we know it only in that way. Knowledge of a "held" opinion is based upon inference from observation of its expression

There are three functions served by holding an opinion, and we shall call them *object appraisal, social adjustment,* and *externalization.* Let us note briefly the characteristics of each and then return to a more extended discussion of their significance.

Object appraisal. We use this expression in the same sense in which psychoanalysts employ "reality testing." The holding of an attitude provides a ready aid in "sizing up" objects and events in the environment from the point of view of one's major interests and going concerns. Insofar as attitudes are predispositions to experience certain classes of objects, to be motivated by them, and to respond to them, it is evident that their existence permits the individual to check more quickly and efficiently the action-relevancy of the events in the environment around him. Presented with an object or event, he may categorize it in some class of objects and events for which a predisposition to action and experience exists. Once thus categorized, it becomes the focus of an already-established repertory of reactions and feelings, and the person is saved the energy-consuming and sometimes painful process of figuring out *de novo* how he shall relate himself to it. If the environmental fact either defies categorization or is categorized in such a way as to bring harmful consequences to the person, new attitudes may be developed or shifts in categorization may occur. In sum, then, attitudes aid us in classifying for action the objects of the environment, and they make appropriate response tendencies available for coping with these objects. This feature is a basis for holding attitudes in general as well as any particular array of attitudes. In it lies the function served by holding attitudes *per se.* Without them, we should be in the constant throes of determining the relevance of events, of fashioning decisions and of deciding upon actions—all *ab initio.* More specifically, object appraisal is the process whereby the person develops attitudes that are a creative solution to the problems posed by the existence of disparate internal demands and external or environmental demands.

Social adjustment. Opinions can play another role: that of facilitating, disrupting, or simply maintaining an individual's relations with other individuals. It is in this realm particularly that one must take care to distinguish the functions served by holding an opinion and by expressing it, for the strategy of expression is of particular importance in maintaining or cementing one's relationship with what may be called "membership groups"—the individuals with whom one is in direct

under a variety of special situations—including those highly permissive diagnostic situations in which there is neither gain nor loss to be earned or incurred by expressing one's views.

contact. Where there is a need to be accepted in the community, one will more readily and more forthrightly express acceptable attitudes while inhibiting or modulating the expression of less approved ones.

The function of social adjustment served by holding an opinion is at once more subtle and more complex. For it is by holding certain views that one identifies with, or, indeed, differentiates oneself from various "reference groups" within the population. By reference groups we mean here those groups in terms of whose standards the individual judges himself and with which he identifies or feels kinship. They may or may not correspond to the membership groups with which he has face-to-face commerce; moreover, certain reference groups may never be physically present to the individual for interaction. Representative of reference groups are such symbols as "intellectuals," "average middle-class Americans," "decent girls," and so on. The act of holding certain opinions, as Merton,[12] Centers,[13] Warner,[14] and various others have pointed out, is an act of affiliation with reference groups. It is a means of saying, "I am like them."

Reference groups, we shall see, may also play a negative role in opinion functioning. There are groups with which one seeks to reject kinship or identification. Thus, one of our subjects sought as hard to dissociate himself from the bourgeoisie as he sought to associate himself with the *avant-garde* left. When rebelliousness and rejection are prominent features in a man's adjustment, we may expect negative reference groups to play a prominent role in his opinion formation.

Two rather unique kinds of social adjustment can also be achieved by holding opinions of a certain kind. First, one may develop opinions as the expression of a need to be autonomous from others. Such declarations of autonomy—and we must distinguish the term from rebellion—are in a curious backhand way still another mode of identifying oneself with various reference groups. Thus one of our subjects showed a strong need for working out his opinions independently, unswayed by prevailing points of view. This procedure was for him a way of expressing his lack of dependence on others; but it was also a way of identifying with that nebulous category known as "independent and liberal thinkers." And second, it is sometimes convenient to

[12] R. K. Merton and A. S. Kitt, Contributions to the theory of reference-group behavior, In R. K. Merton and P. F. Lazarsfeld (eds.), *Continuities in social research*, Glencoe, Ill., Free Press, 1950.

[13] R. Centers, *The psychology of social classes*, Princeton, Princeton University Press, 1949.

[14] W. L. Warner and P. S. Lunt, *The social life of a modern community*, New Haven, Yale University Press, 1941.

indulge hostility toward others by holding opinions that are at odds with prevailing beliefs. If such an adjustment be neurotic in origin, it is nonetheless a form of negativism one occasionally encounters.

The very act of holding an opinion, whatever its nature, may serve the social adjustment of the individual, as Riesman and Glazer have remarked.[15] Given identification with certain groups—let us take the reference group called "intellectuals"—the individual feels that he *must* have opinions on certain issues to maintain his sense of identification.

We must not, however, leave a false impression. The underlying motive gratified by holding and expressing opinions that aid our social adjustment is neither a conformity need nor its reverse, a need to rebel. A wide variety of psychological mechanisms is at work, motivating us to relate our destinies to those of the concrete membership groups around us and to those of the more remote reference groups to which we adhere. Requirements of ego defense, dependency needs, drives for autonomy, hostility, drives for status, and many other dynamisms may be involved.

Externalization. It would be all too easy to equate externalization of inner requirements with the classical conceptions of projection and displacement. These two mechanisms are two *examples* of what we mean by externalization. Externalization occurs when an individual, often responding unconsciously, senses an analogy between a perceived environmental event and some unresolved inner problem. He adopts an attitude toward the event in question which is a transformed version of his way of dealing with his inner difficulty. By doing so, he may succeed in reducing some of the anxiety which his own difficulty has been producing.

Perhaps an illustration, a case not included in our study, will clarify the process. An adolescent develops a violent hatred for Fascism, the Nazis, and for Hitler, particularly during the 1930's. Although he is not accepted because of his age, he is aroused to the point of volunteering for the Abraham Lincoln Brigade during the Spanish Civil War. Upon entry of the United States into the War, he volunteers, is rejected, but flings himself into a lather of civilian war activity from which he derives a deep satisfaction.

Whence the tremendous intensity of this attitude? Leaving aside the realities of the situation, the grave threat with which Fascism *did* in fact confront the world and which our subject sensed, why was there such an extraordinarily intense compulsion to do something about

[15] D. Riesman and N. Glazer, The meaning of opinion, *Public Opinion Quarterly*, 1948, **12**, 633–648.

his feelings? Analysis reveals in this man a strong and unresolved fear of rejection by powerful figures who can be reached neither through their sympathies nor through their intellect: the figure of an inchoate, powerful, cruel, but basically unreachable force. We need not examine the genesis of this deeply repressed fear. It suffices that it existed. The emergence of Hitler and the Nazis served for the adolescent as a concretization or "binding" for this fearsome and rejecting figure. Hitler in a unique way could serve as the apotheosis of that figure which could be reached neither by sympathy nor by reason. Energies previously directed at coping with the inner problem could now be liberated and focussed on an external object. If anxiety could thereby be reduced, so much the better.

We present this case not only to illustrate externalization but also to show how it differs from run-of-the-mill displacement. Certainly the case illustrates displacement, but that is not all: there are also externalization of affect and externalization of action. An external object is treated in terms relevant to an internal problem: where the internal rejecting figure could not be destroyed by direct assault, the externalized object could become a target for highly energized, creatively destructive planning and action. If the externalization proved an adaptive one, that is partly the good fortune of history and partly the result of adequate object appraisal. The fact that there were active membership groups and palpable reference groups with whom our young man could align himself also helped.

The Functioning of an Opinion

Finally we must discuss the various ways in which opinions operate in carrying out their adjustmental functions. We will be forgiven, perhaps, if our exposition reflects the autobiography of our project, for our stumblings may have a certain didactic value.

Early in our program of interviewing and testing it became apparent to us that our subjects expended considerable energy and ingenuity in maintaining the integrity of their attitudes in the face of changing information encountered by them in the newspapers, on the radio, and in conversation. This impression was most vivid when we observed the behavior of our subjects in two of our procedures: the *Stress Interview* and the *Information Apperception Test*. In the first of these, three interviewers confronted the subject with questions ostensibly aimed at "clearing up a few inconsistencies that we had noticed in the course of looking over your interviews." The real object was to test the stability of expressed opinions by presenting counterarguments and by using the other devices of debate. The second, the

Information Apperception Test, consisted of a series of "factual" statements about Russia—some pro, some neutral, and some anti in intent—about which the subject was asked, "What do you make of this?" and then requested to judge in terms of the degree to which they were "typical" of Russia.

At the outset the behavior evoked in these situations appeared to us to be primarily defensive in character, designed to ward off or to incorporate in revised form information not congruent with established opinions. Indeed, we slipped into the habit of speaking of "opinion defense," no doubt in analogy to the psychoanalytic conception of ego defense.

Two circumstances broke us of this habit by revealing the superficiality of such a conception of simple defense. The first of these was the gradual realization that the psychoanalytic theory of ego defense was itself faulty in conception when applied to our concrete case materials. The classical ego defenses, it turned out, were, so to speak, last ditch stands of the ego against vicissitudes that had come to be too great a burden for normal handling. And so too opinion defense. A normal adult does far more than simply defend his opinions against inimical information. He may be on the alert for supporting information to nourish them. He may welcome occasions to express them, to give them exercise. He may even seek opportunities to test their ability to withstand challenge.

The terminology that we finally adopted reflects the change in our thinking. In place of "ego defenses" we adopted the term "adjustive strategies"; for "opinion defense" we substituted the phrase "opinion maintenance and furtherance." Part of the process is, of course, narrowly defensive. But there is also a considerable amount of continuous "monitoring" of attitudes with the object of testing their fit not only to reality but also to inner requirements. When one looks carefully at the verbatim transcript of an interview in which a man is discussing his opinions of some matter that interests him, one notes a series of "testings" of the conformance of expressed opinions both with deeper and more general values and with available information. Insofar as the person is in the habit of thinking aloud, so to speak, the process is the more noticeable. We may assume that the same process goes on continuously in the course of dealing with the environment.

The tentative proposition can be offered that the freer the individual is of disruptive anxieties and tumultuous inner demands, the more flexible is the process of "testing" opinions inwardly and outwardly. In the hypothetically mature person, the program of opinion furtherance and maintenance would almost be akin to the scientist's approach

to nature. But even in the less-than-mature person, there is a constant
push, however slight, toward greater comprehension of the environment and greater congruence of internal convictions.

The effectiveness of this push toward "actualization" (call it what
you will) is a function not only of the maturity of the person and his
freedom from neurotic trends, but also of the information environment
in which he lives. Where the environment is very homogeneous,
where, for example, only one interpretation of Russia is presented in
the press, over the radio, in magazines, and in conversations, the
information environment ceases to present a challenge, and maturation
of opinion is hindered.

The phrase "opinion maintenance and furtherance" is not meant to
exclude examination of the conditions affecting attitude change, for
attitude change is one of the means whereby the person maintains an
effective balance between inner and outer demands. Let us assume
first that temptation to large-scale shifts in attitude provokes resistances
in the average person. One does not upset one's balance with the
informational environment for minor causes. There is probably some
optimal rate of change in one's attitudes for any given shift in environmental information. As events change, some individuals shift attitudes
rather faster than others: these people we call "flexible," those strikingly
slow to shift, "rigid." In either case, long-term alterations in opinion
are far more frequent than short-term alterations of comparable scope.

Opinion and Action

We end this chapter with a brief mention of the relation between
holding an opinion and doing something about it. However remote
the object of an attitude—Russia *is* remote from a citizen's direct action
—there is still much that an individual may do on behalf of his opinions.
Such actions range from a willingness to express his views to a resolve
to devote his life to their realization. Our study was not designed
to get at these actions; had it been our primary focus to do so, we
should undoubtedly have studied opinion on a different topic. A
satisfactory formulation of this important problem, it nevertheless seems
to us, will have at least two ingredients, and our explorations throw
some light on one of these.

One component of a satisfactory account of action in relation to
opinion arises from the kind of motivational analysis to which most
of this book is devoted. The pertinent question is: To what extent are
the functions served by a person's opinions fulfilled by the mere fact
that he holds them, and to what extent does their fulfillment depend
on some further action on his part? Opinion as part of a person's

orderly world view may serve a "placing" function with no agenda for action being implied. If the scanning of object appraisal turns up relevancies to strong personal interests, however, the function of opinion in readying him for action is incomplete unless he follows through. Similarly with social adjustment: our discussion of the distinction between holding and expressing an opinion has already suggested respects in which the functions of overt behavior may be differentiated from those of the disposition itself. When we come to externalization, the question becomes one that the psychoanalyst discusses under the phrase "acting out." Clinical leads are available as to the kinds of people who externalize in deed as well as thought. Hilary Sullivan, whose case we present in detail, is a striking example of a person whose vehement opinions satisfy urgent personal functions with little action beyond the spoken word being required of him.

The second aspect that we see essential in a satisfactory formulation of the problem of action is an analysis of the situations with which the "actor" is confronted. For attitudes are but half of the formula. We have not examined in systematic detail the action-evoking properties of events and situations. The careful reader of our case histories will, we think, be struck as we were by the importance and complexity of the question. Why do some situations call for the adoption of opinion *and* action, while others can be handled by attitudinal means alone?

CHAPTER 4

LEARNING ABOUT
TEN MEN

THE preceding chapters offered a way of describing a person's attitudes and proposed a variety of ways in which they may be functionally related to his personality. This schema was the outcome of trial and revision throughout the course of our intensive study of ten men and their opinions about Russia; indeed it underwent further metamorphoses up to the final preparation of this book. The materials that we gathered on these ten men were invaluable sources of insight on the functioning of opinions in personality. As our own conceptions developed, the concrete richness of the case records, otherwise an obstacle to systematic analysis, proved advantageous. Selective as they inevitably had to be, the transcriptions and summaries of our sessions seemed to capture some of the subjects' living individuality. We could return to them time and again to put fresh questions.

The chapters that follow illustrate the functioning of opinion as it emerged from our study. It is first necessary, however, to describe briefly the project and its setting. In planning an investigation of attitudes and personality, we could draw on the experience of a succession of intensive personality studies at the Harvard Psychological Clinic. The most recent major project, reported in Murray and Morgan's *A Clinical Study of Sentiments*,[1] was closely related to our problem.

[1] Murray, H. A., and Morgan, C. D., A clinical study of sentiments, *Genetic Psychology Monographs*, 1945, **32**, 3–149, 153–311.

These investigators and their associates, in an intensive study of eleven undergraduates, approached attitudes or sentiments from a study of the total opinion structure of the individual. While they limit their report to a description and analysis of the students' attitudes in four general areas (the war, parents, sex, and religion), their work suffered from a certain diffuseness entailed by the lack of a single focus. The fact that their cases were drawn from a highly restricted student population further limits the usefulness of their conclusions. We hoped to profit from their experience by selecting a single attitude focus for intensive investigation, studying a heterogeneous group of adult men, and complementing the clinical study with field research on a broader sample. Some of the findings of the field research have been reported elsewhere; [2] our present concern is limited to the intensive study.

After reviewing various possibilities, we selected opinion toward Russia for our special attention. The choice was made in the light of several criteria:

(a) The area of opinion should be one about which people have more or less crystallized views; (b) it should be a controversial area on which there is a substantial division of opinion; (c) it should be relatively independent of political party and not be a direct reflection of class membership; (d) it should be reasonably charged with anxiety or other forms of affect; (e) it should be on a socio-political level to parallel the problems normally met in opinion polling; (f) it should be a topic of continuing contemporary interest; (g) it should preferably be a topic of some social and political significance in and of itself.[3]

We wanted a topic on which there would be real differences of opinion, and one that would give us a fair chance to observe the more subjective determinants of opinion. Russia was a good choice. As a topical area, it was conceived broadly, so that its ramifications in the individual's opinions could be followed into whatever related areas—such as Communism—might prove relevant. Two features of the topic presented limitations for our purposes: the deficiency of verifiable information about contemporary Russia, and the small opportunity for observable personal action in support of one's opinions. While we recognized and

[2] M. Brewster Smith, The personal setting of public opinion: a study of attitudes toward Russia, *Public Opinion Quarterly*, 1947, **11**, 507–523; reprinted in D. Katz, D. Cartwright, S. Eldersveld, and A. M. Lee (eds.), *Public opinion and propaganda*, New York, Dryden, 1954, pp. 295–305; Personal values as determinants of a political attitude, *Journal of Psychology*, 1949, **28**, 477–486.

[3] Smith, M. B., Bruner, J. S., and White, R. W., A group research project on the dynamics and measurement of opinion, *International Journal of Opinion and Attitude Research*, 1947, **1**, 78–82.

regretted these limitations, they are shared, we felt, by many of the issues usually studied by opinion polls.

The subjects who submitted their personalities and attitudes to intensive study were adult men, all married, and pursuing their livelihood, with one exception, in the Greater Boston community. Obtained through various channels of personal contact, they were in no sense a representative sample of any population. The attempt was made to select men sufficiently intelligent to be verbally productive, but coming from a wide variety of social backgrounds and walks of life. Identified by the pseudonyms we will use henceforth, the subjects were as tabulated.

Pseudonym	Occupation	Age	Education	Wechsler I.Q.	Religion	Income
John Chatwell	Law clerk; law student	27	Coll. grad.	142	P	$3,600
Charles Lanlin	Salesman	41	H.S., Bus. Sch.	120	C	$5,000
Hilary Sullivan	Journalist	46	2 yrs. H.S.	128	Ex-C	$3,200
Ernest Daniel	Factory operative	37	3 yrs. H.S.	128	P	$2,500
Sam Hodder	Factory worker	48	6 yrs. Grade Sch.	113	C	$2,700
Clarence Clark	Accountant	43	H.S., Bus. Sch.	125	C	$3,500
Benjamin Kleinfeld	Shopkeeper	34	1 yr. Coll.	123	J	$3,300
Albert Rock	Contractor	45	Coll. grad.	126	C	$20,000
Grafton Upjohn	Civil Service administrator	48	Coll. grad.	127	P	$5,100
Dana Osgood	Real estate agent	38	Coll. grad.	129	P	$10,000

With the exception of the fact that nearly all of our men were considerably above average in intelligence, and none was in financial difficulty at the time of the study, it would be hard to find a more various group.

Although the subjects were paid, money was a real incentive for participation in only two or three cases. For the rest, payment was mainly an indication of our seriousness and good faith, if it served any purpose at all. As we were later able to ferret them out, a variety of motives contributed to the men's interest and cooperation. Some appreciated an attentive audience; others hoped to gain a better understanding of themselves; still others expected help in their personal problems, sought to associate themselves with an institution of prestige, or accepted their part in the project as a kind of civic responsibility. As the sessions progressed, most of them came to feel very warmly toward the investigators and desired to help them out; the few to whom the weekly sessions became understandably irksome stuck it out to the end as an obligation to which they had committed themselves. A special interest in Russia or world affairs may have added to the interest of one or two of the subjects during the later stages of the project; it had no influence on their initial compliance since they were not told at the outset the special topic of the investigation. Rather, they were told that we were interested in learning about the personality of normal adults and how they formed some of their opinions.

In its general plan, our study followed the pattern of using multiple procedures and investigators, with responsibility for evaluation and interpretation centralized in a Diagnostic Council of senior staff members.[4] Seventeen different investigators, including graduate students and outside consultants, contributed to the administration of the 28 procedures that were selected to throw light on our subjects' attitudes and personalities. Seven senior members of the staff constituted the Diagnostic Council. These were:

David F. Aberle	Social Anthropologist
Jerome S. Bruner	Social Psychologist
Stanley G. Estes	Clinical Psychologist
Eugenia Hanfmann	Clinical Psychologist
Sheldon J. Korchin	Social Psychologist
M. Brewster Smith	Social Psychologist
Robert W. White	Clinical Psychologist

Several provisions ensured that the members of the Diagnostic Council would be in intimate contact with the case materials. Each was responsible for administering at least one and in most cases two or more of the interviews or procedures, and therefore had intensive personal contact with all ten of the subjects. Reports of each session, often transcribed verbatim, were promptly duplicated and placed in the hands of all Diagnostic Council members. Each member therefore had currently available all the materials on each of the cases. Finally, each Council member was primarily responsible for the analysis of one or more of the cases and conducted certain key interviews with his special charges. This plan, which required careful coordination, had the advantages of an optimum balance between centralization and distribution of responsibility.

During the early phases of the project in the fall of 1946, before the subjects were under study, the Council functioned to select and plan the procedures to be employed. When approximately half the sessions had been completed with a given subject, the Council met to arrive at

[4] Cf. H. A. Murray, *Explorations in personality*, New York, Oxford University Press, 1938, and OSS Assessment Staff, *The assessment of men*, New York, Henry Holt & Co., 1948.

a preliminary formulation of the case. In these meetings, the responsible member would present his interpretative summary of the dynamics of the subject's personality and opinions. Having familiarized
themselves with the case materials then available, the other members
would discuss and criticize this formulation, noting points where special information was needed and coming to tentative consensus about
matters where the evidence seemed clear. These preliminary case
discussions guided the member in charge of the case in carrying out a
"Loose Ends Interview" in which matters called in question in the
discussion could be checked, and the gaps in the data filled in. When
the scheduled sessions with the subject were completed, the same
staff member prepared the final case summary, which was then criticized and revised under the scrutiny of the Diagnostic Council as a
whole.

Among the 28 procedures which took the subjects some 15 weekly
2-hour sessions to complete were interviews, standard tests, and test
situations newly devised for the purposes of the study. Each will be
described briefly, starting with those aimed primarily at personality
description and diagnosis, and going on to those mainly aimed at
attitudes toward Russia. Illustrations of the kind of material yielded
by novel procedures may be found in the three long case studies.

The first group of procedures provided the data of personal history.

Enrollment Interview. In this first personal contact with the subject (initial arrangements had been made by telephone), the main
effort was to obtain rapport. A brief data sheet was filled out.

Autobiography. Each subject was asked to write a brief autobiography according to an outline that was provided. With the more
highly educated and conscientious subjects, this proved valuable. The
subjects of low educational level returned documents that were too
sparse to be useful, while the task proved too formidable for two of
the subjects.

Interview on Childhood Memories. Relaxing on a couch in a
darkened room, the subject was requested to recall his earliest memories. The interviewer sought to encourage him but followed no set
guide. Experience suggested that in such an interview near the beginning of the series, better rapport might have been obtained had the
subjects not been required to lie down. The interview was recorded
verbatim.

Interview on Family Background, Ideals, and Discipline. This
interview dealt successively with the following topics: the subject's
ideas about how children should be brought up, the methods he was
using or would use, the methods used upon him by his parents and his

reactions to them, the values for which his parents stood, his parents' participation in the community, the relation of the parents to the grandparents, and the character, social status, values, participation of the grandparents. Full running notes were taken, but the interview was not recorded.

Interview on Educational, Occupational, and Participational History. This supplemented the factual information on education and occupation obtained in the enrollment interview and that on school history, work history, and community life often provided by the autobiography. The subject's personal reaction to experience in these areas was sought. The interviewer kept running notes.

Interview on Health and Sex History. In this interview, late in the series, health and sex problems were discussed as these had affected the subject's adjustment to life. Running notes were kept by the interviewer.

Interview on the Course of a Day. Beginning with when he got up that morning, the subject was asked to tell in detail just what he had done during the day of the interview, up to the time that he came to the Clinic in the evening. The interviewer tried to get his personal reaction to the situations he had met. The interview was transcribed in full.

Loose Ends Interview. Conducted by the staff member responsible for the case, this interview filled in miscellaneous gaps of personal history where preliminary Diagnostic Council discussion indicated that further information was needed. The interview was transcribed in full.

A second group of procedures was the main source of information about the subject's abilities and temperament.

Interview on Temperamental Traits. Traits of emotionality, emotional control, anxiety, mood, and affective organization were sought, emphasis being constantly laid on actual behavior in concrete situations. Note was taken of whether the subject considered each incident unusual for him or typical. Extensive notes were recorded by the interviewer.

Interview on Abilities. The subject was asked to give the basis of his ratings, with examples, after filling out a brief self-rating scale on eleven areas of ability. The abilities rated were: physical, mechanical, business, leadership, social, entertaining, memory, thinking, intuitive, artistic, persistence. Each was briefly defined, and space was provided for the subject to indicate that he was excellent, good, fair, or poor in each ability relative to most men of his age. The ratings and interview were revealing about the subject's insight and evaluation

of his assets and liabilities; as indicators of actual abilities, the ratings
were interpreted with caution.

Rorschach Test. The subject's interpretations of the standard series
of ink-blots provided insight into many of his intellectual and emotional
characteristics.

Wechsler-Bellevue Test of Adult Intelligence. This standard test
yielded a general I.Q. and separate results for verbal and performance
tests, as well as a variety of qualitative information.

Wells-Alpha Intelligence Test. More sensitive than the foregoing
at the higher educational levels, and somewhat different in its content,
this standard test helped to round out the picture of the subject's
intelligence.

Vigotsky Test. This clinical instrument requires the subject to
discover the principle by which an assortment of blocks differing in
size, shape, and color may be sorted into four groups. Besides revealing the nature of the subject's processes of concept formation, it frequently shows his problem-solving behavior in a frustrating situation.

Procedures in the third group sampled the content of the subject's
imaginative and fantasy life, providing clues concerning his personality dynamics.

Free Association Hour. Under the observation of a practicing
psychoanalyst, the subjects were asked to report uncritically whatever
came into their minds, while reclining in a darkened room. The
session was recorded verbatim. While few of the subjects were able
to associate freely, their reactions to the situation and characteristic defenses were as revealing as the content of their associations.

Thematic Apperception Test (TAT). The dramatic stories told
by the subjects around the standard set of pictures presented as a test
of "creative imagination" were analyzed to reveal the subject's characteristic imaginative content and adjustive pattern. The interviewer
recorded the stories in full.

Word Association Test. Under the guise of a test of "ability to
use adjectives to express your own feelings about things," a list of 54
words was presented to the subject, one at a time, with the instruction
that he had 25 seconds to think of all the adjectives he could which in
his opinion applied to the word. Among a matrix of presumably neutral words were some that touched areas usually charged with emotion
and others bearing on Russia and Communism. The test seemed
artificial to the subjects and revealed little if anything that was not
elsewhere available.

Procedures in the next group were directed at the subject's general
pattern of attitudes, interests, and values.

Interview on Personal Values and Religious Sentiments. The subject's personal values and philosophy of life were approached through a discussion of what he believed in, was interested in, and thought important; the most important lessons life had taught him; his early and present ambitions; the kinds of people he admired; his feeling about the way things in general were going in the world; and his religious beliefs. Verbatim transcriptions were made of each interview.

Kuder Preference Blank. The subjects took home to fill out this standard interest inventory, which provides percentile scores on the following interest areas: mechanical, computational, scientific, persuasive, artistic, literary, musical, social service, clerical.

Argument Completion Test. Specially prepared for the study, this test presented the subject with eight situations in which two people were defending opposite points of view. He was instructed to carry on the discussion and to tell how the argument came out and with which side he agreed. An example is the following:

> Y, who is very fond of his son, hears from the school principal that his son is doing badly in matters of discipline. Y goes to see the principal, Mr. X.
> Mr. X says, "The trouble is that the boy has no conception of discipline. The only way to manage him is to maintain firm authority by using punishment."
> Y answers, "You'll never make a good man out of him that way."
> Mr. X says, "I don't agree with you. Let's thrash this thing out."

The remaining procedures provided the main data on the subjects' attitudes toward Russia.

Open-Ended Interview on Russia. The main purpose of this interview was to give the subject a chance to define the situation with respect to Russia as he saw it. At the beginning of the hour the interviewer explained to the subject the special interest we would be taking in his attitudes about Russia. He was then invited at the outset to tell as much as he could about how he felt about Russia and why. Only after non-directive probes had exhausted his flow of talk were topical areas that had not been mentioned broached by the interviewer. With these areas in turn, "pin-down" probes were used only after non-directive probes had yielded a full return. The development of his attitudes toward Russia was given special attention. At the end of the interview the subject was encouraged to bring up anything that he wanted to revert to or that had not been covered. The interview was transcribed verbatim.

Polling Interview. This interview confronted each subject with a standard set of questions, many of them adapted from the national polls. This procedure produced little of value for present purposes.

Information Test. This was a factual quiz of 53 simple multiple-choice items relating to Russia.

Conformity Interview. In this interview the influence of others on the subject's attitudes toward Russia was explored. His principal group identifications and social ties were taken up one by one, and the situations in which he discussed Russia investigated. The latter part of the interview was devoted to his contact with information and opinions about Russia through the various media of communication. The interview was recorded verbatim.

Information Apperception Test (IAT). This was a new technique developed to discover how the subject dealt with items of loaded information that bore on his attitudes. Ten items were presented, one at a time, and the subject was asked in each case what he made of the statement. The instructions were:

> I have here several statements that have been made about Russia in newspapers and magazines. So far as we know, the statements are true. You may have run across some of them yourself in reading or talking about Russia. We are interested in finding out what the statements mean to different people. Mostly they have been used to get across some point of view about Russia; we are trying to find out what they actually do mean to people. After I read each statement to you, I would like you to tell what it means to you personally; what you make of it.

Usually considerable probing was necessary to elicit the subject's full reaction to the item. The statements used were:

1. Stalin said last year that Russia must work to keep the Red Army strong.

2. There is practically no unemployment in Russia. There are jobs for all.

3. The Russian church now holds services in the Soviet Union though most of the worshippers are older people.

4. Factory managers and plant supervisors in Russia receive salaries of around $10,000 a year.

5. The Soviet Union consists of many races and groups with different languages and customs.

6. Russians have been arrested from time to time without knowing what their crime was.

7. In 1939 more books were published in Russia than in any other country—including many translations of such writers as Shakespeare.

8. The children of millions of working mothers in Russia are taken care of during the day in government schools and nurseries.

9. Many Communist leaders in other countries, like Marshal Tito, were trained in Russia.

10. It is now more difficult to get a divorce in Russia than it was ten years ago when divorce was very easy.

The interviewers kept a full running transcript of the subject's responses. This test sometimes required more than one session to complete.

Cartoon Stereotype Test. In this situation, the subject was asked to describe and interpret ten cartoons about Russia, selected from newspapers of the preceding year to include themes both strongly favorable and strongly unfavorable to Russia, as well as some conducive to ambiguity of interpretation. Special attention was given in the analysis to selective description and distortion of meaning. The interviewer took full notes on the subject's responses.

Stress Interview. The purpose of this interview, conducted on the final evening that the subject was seen, was to discover how the subject behaved when his opinions were attacked and inconsistencies in his views pointed out to him. In preparation for the hour, the records of earlier sessions were combed for weak points or contradictions in the subject's statements. Often there were additional places where the staff felt that his attitudes would be clarified if he were made to respond to challenge. The interview was led by a staff member whom the subject had not met up to that time. Two or three members of the Diagnostic Council, including the member primarily responsible for the case, also participated. While the interviews followed no set pattern, the chairman typically led the attack on the subject's position in a formal but not personally aggressive manner. The other interviewers took up the argument as the occasion arose, and now and then spoke in the subject's defense, to see how he would react to such support. The tone of most of the interviews was that of a good-natured argument, but the subject himself set its pitch. To fit each case, the interviewers found themselves arguing now like Communists, now like Trotskyites, and again as stalwart defenders of capitalism and American policy. Markedly different in atmosphere from the non-directive permissiveness that characterized so many of the procedures, the Stress Interview contributed many insights. It was transcribed in full.

Close-Out Interview. In the final interview, conducted by either the project director or the member responsible for the case, the subject was encouraged to talk about his experiences at the Clinic to give us a better picture of the way that he had defined the situation and of the motivating factors underlying his relationship with us. This information was often helpful in the interpretation of his productions. Occasional "loose ends" were also picked up, and the subject (virtually without exception) was left in a cooperative frame of mind.

Of these procedures, ones that were new were pretested extensively before being used on the subjects of the project. The pre-test of the *Open-Ended Interview on Russia* provided an incidental opportunity for the members of the Diagnostic Council to get better acquainted with their own attitudes toward Russia, in the hope that once subjected to analysis they would be less likely to intrude unintentionally in their judgments of the subjects. Each member of the Council submitted to an hour-long intensive interview, and transcripts of the interviews were discussed in terms of the preliminary descriptive scheme with which we began the project. A wide range of attitudes was represented in the Council, from opinions highly favorable to Russia to strongly unfavorable ones that could recognize any merit in Russia only by dint of a studied impartiality.

In drawing up a schedule of procedures, it was recognized that such intensive contact would surely have its influence on the subjects of our study. In general, our guiding principle was therefore to place first the procedures that might be expected to be most influenced by other procedures and to have the least effect on the ones that followed them. A substantial portion of the data on personality was collected before the topic of Russia was introduced. The interview on *Personal Values and Religious Sentiments* came before the more specific *Open-Ended Interview on Russia,* and that in turn preceded the *Information Test* and *Polling Interview,* in order from the less to the more structured. Not until the end of the series were the pressures of the *Stress Interview* introduced. Aside from these considerations, the order followed with each subject was governed by requirements of rapport and exigencies of scheduling. Insofar as possible, procedures were administered in the order listed below, where the persons responsible for each are also named.

Enrollment Interview	Robert W. White
Autobiography (completed at home)	—
Interview on Temperamental Traits	Robert W. White
Argument Completion Test	Albert F. Ax
Rorschach Test	Eugenia Hanfmann
Interview on Childhood Memories (R) [5]	Thelma G. Alper

[5] Fully recorded and transcribed.

Interview on Personal Values and Religious Sentiments (R)	M. Brewster Smith
Wells-Alpha Intelligence Test	Robert A. Harris
Free Association Hour (R)	Walter C. Langer
Interview on Abilities	Bert Kaplan
Interview on Family Background, Ideals, and Discipline	Jerome S. Bruner
Open-Ended Interview on Russia (R)	M. Brewster Smith
Kuder Preference Blank (completed at home)	—
Interview on Educational, Occupational, and Participational History	Stanley G. Estes
Information Test	Sheldon J. Korchin
Loose Ends Interview (R)	(Staff member responsible for the case)
Polling Interview	Sheldon J. Korchin
Interview on the Course of a Day (R)	Jerome S. Bruner
Thematic Apperception Test (given in two parts, on different evenings)	Morris J. Stein (interpretation)
	Barbara Kimball (administration)
Word Association Test	Eugenia Hanfmann
Vigotsky Test	Eugenia Hanfmann
Cartoon Stereotype Test	Henry Weinberg
Wechsler-Bellevue Test of Adult Intelligence	Robert A. Harris
Information Apperception Test	Harold Garfinkel
Interview on Health and Sex History	Robert W. White
Conformity Interview (R)	David F. Aberle
Stress Interview (R)	David M. Schneider, staff member responsible for the case, and two others
Close-Out Interview	M. Brewster Smith or staff member responsible for the case

The upwards of 30 evening hours that we spent with each of our subjects in weekly 2-hour sessions could undoubtedly be reduced without major loss, were we to undertake a similar study. There were several reasons, however, for our decision to include so many procedures. For one thing, we had a strong subsidiary interest in studying the personalities of adult men, a surprisingly unexplored area in psychology. For this purpose we needed more complete data than would have been required to show the grounding of attitudes in personality. Secondly, in exploring unbroken ground in the theory of opinion, we wanted to make sure that possible relationships between personality and attitudes were not lost by default through inadequate personality description. It was better, we felt, to be encumbered by an embarrassment of riches than to find too late that we had failed to

collect necessary information.   Finally, many of our methods were
new.   In spite of pretesting, we could not be certain beforehand that
they would all pay off—as indeed some did not.   With data on both
attitudes toward Russia and personality characteristics collected from
a variety of perspectives, we could be reasonably sure that the essential
facts of each case would be captured.

CHAPTER 5

THE INFORMATION

ENVIRONMENT

FROM the perspective of the Hydrogen Age, the winter and spring of 1947 seem almost serene. Although the Viet Minh was already conducting its guerrilla forays in Indochina, no area was more remote from the concern of most Americans; it was mentioned not once in all of our interviews. Korea was merely one among many far-flung outposts in which the receding tide of war had left American occupation troops. China itself had yet to fall to the Communists. The Berlin airlift, the Cold War as a dominant condition of American life, were still to come. Resting on its unquestioned atomic supremacy, America was demobilized in fact and spirit. Russia did not have the atom bomb, and the dire eventuality that the American monopoly would be broken could still be put aside as a problem for the distant future. Stalin was a fixture in the world scene. The period of perpetual crisis in relations between East and West had only just begun. The years of habituation to impending catastrophe had yet to leave their mark; the crisis of the day seemed sufficient thereto.

The lapse of time across which we must look back on our subjects' discussions is not without advantages. It makes easier an appropriate detachment in our scrutiny of their views on hotly contested matters. It also brings forcefully to mind the importance of brute events in providing the setting against which existing opinion was tested and applied, and in which new opinion took form. Since at this distance it

61

is necessary to recreate explicitly the historical context, we are in less danger of neglecting its impact by taking it for granted. To be sure, the contact between public opinion and public events is not direct. There is the gap that Lippmann so vividly described between events and experience—the private "pictures in our heads." With these pictures we will be concerned shortly when we turn to the ten men with whose opinions this book deals. But first we must pause to look afresh at the web of events that constituted their world and at the informational environment created by the mass media in trying to depict this world.

The Web of Events

Our interviews span the sharp break in American relations with Russia that accompanied the "Truman Doctrine," the beginning of a policy of containment. The intensive interviews on Russia and Communism began in January, before the glimmerings of the Greek crisis appeared on the horizon. They were completed before the promulgation of the "Truman Doctrine," but additional interviews on this development were conducted with all subjects, and we continued to hear our subjects' opinions until our relationship was terminated in May or June. A cursory survey of the headline news of this period may evoke the backdrop of reality against which their opinions had significance.

The beginning of 1947 saw a continuation from the preceding year of the United States–Soviet controversy over the control of atomic energy. January was marked by the resignation of Secretary of State Byrnes and the appointment of General Marshall as his successor. The Foreign Ministers' deputies convened in London to lay the groundwork for a meeting of the Council of Foreign Ministers by discussing the preparation of peace treaties with Germany and Austria. The Polish election was conducted after official United States protests against intimidation of voters by the dominant pro-Soviet group.

February was even more eventful. Early in the month, wide publicity was given to Gerhart Eisler, who was charged by a Congressional committee with carrying Soviet orders to the United States Communist Party. Bernard Baruch, United States delegate to the United Nations Atomic Energy Commission, created a stir by charging that the questions asked by Soviet delegates bespoke secret knowledge about the atomic bomb. An official Soviet protest against Under Secretary of State Acheson's statement that Russian foreign policy was "aggressive and expanding" was rejected by Secretary of State Marshall in a note stating that Acheson had given only a "restrained comment" "in line of duty." Meanwhile, the Foreign Ministers' deputies were making little headway in London, the atomic energy controversy was continuing, and the *New York Times* news summary for February 17 carried the statement that "United States–Soviet relations were reported from Moscow to be at a new low." By the end of the month the Foreign Ministers' deputies had closed their session with no substantial progress. The one optimistic note in the month's news of relations with Russia was the withdrawal of Soviet objections to the American plan for trusteeship over the former Japanese-mandated islands in the Pacific. But even this was heralded as a sinister portent of later Russian claims.

Early in March the first word appeared of possible trouble in Greece. To quote from the *New York Times* summary for March 1:

> President Truman, facing a major policy decision because of Britain's inability to continue financial aid to Greece, was reported to have asked Congressional leaders to consider a $350,000,000 loan to help in stabilizing the military situation there and to keep that country from falling under Soviet influence.

By March 8, the President had postponed a vacation cruise because of the Greek crisis. In these inauspicious circumstances, the Council of Foreign Ministers began on March 10 its session in Moscow to discuss peace terms for Germany and Austria, amid initial disagreements that foreshadowed the inconclusive result of the conference. On March 12 the President addressed Congress in joint session, enunciating the "Truman Doctrine" of aid to Greece and Turkey to combat Communism.

The remainder of the spring was marked primarily by discussion of the Truman Doctrine and by news of the futile meeting of the Foreign Ministers at Moscow, which adjourned on April 24 without substantial agreement. Controversy over the Truman Doctrine came to a somewhat attenuated close with the passage of the aid bill for Greece and Turkey in late April by the Senate (67–23), the House following suit in early May by a margin of 287–108. Also within this period came the presidential executive order instituting loyalty checks on federal employees. On May 22 President Truman signed the aid bill with little fanfare. By the close of the month, newspaper headlines began to tell the story of a Communist coup in Hungary.

The Information Environment

Such were the major events in Russian-American relations during the period of our interviews. But for political reality to become psychologically relevant, it must pass through a double filtration process: first through the selective and distorting screen of the mass communication media and other sources of public information, and then through opacities and magnifications in the individual's outlook on his world. To understand what the men we studied made of Russia, we must first see how things Russian entered their information environment. As is inevitably the case where national or world affairs are concerned, the mass media provided the ultimate supply of information. To gain entry to the mass media, events had to figure as *news;* the principle of the "newsworthy event" doubtless had much to do with the somewhat frantic guise in which Russian matters met the public eye.

Each individual, of course, lives to some degree in an individualized informational environment of his own. His position in society, his habits of reading and listening, his already-established attitudes make some sources of information readily available to him, while virtually excluding him from others that remain accessible to his fellows. One of our intensive interviews was largely devoted to exploring each subject's distinctive channels of information and preformed opinion, particularly in regard to the topic of our study. One may also inquire, however, about the prevalent climate of information within which these social and psychological processes of selection took place. What was being reported and said about Russia in the popular press? Data on this score do not tell us the specific stimuli to which our subjects were exposed. They serve, rather, two other purposes: they describe, however crudely, an atmosphere from which no subject could be wholly isolated, an atmosphere which his opinions were bound in one way or another to take into account. And by depicting the common pool of public information, such data cast into high relief the selectiveness with which each person drew upon it.

Better to assess the informational environment, we had a content analysis made of some of the major popular news sources.[1] Front-page news coverage and content were analyzed for a sample of the morning editions of two Boston papers, representing widely varying viewpoints, the conservative *Herald,* and the Hearst *Record.*[2] The period from February 24 to May 31 was covered.[3] Four mass circulation periodicals were also surveyed for the same period—*Time, Life,* the

---

[1] We are indebted to Mrs. Elizabeth Bellis for carrying out this analysis.

[2] In the case of the *Record* the second and third pages were analyzed, since the cover pages of the tabloid were uniformly devoted to pictures.

[3] The sample for the Boston papers was selected on the following pattern: February 24–March 12, every day; March 13–May 9, every fourth day; May 10–May 31, every day. The boundaries of the three periods were determined in relation to the timing of field surveys reported elsewhere, and have no special significance in the present connection.

Saturday Evening Post, and the *Readers Digest.* The content of each complete magazine issue was analyzed.

In the daily papers, the amount of space given to news concerning Russia or Communism, at a peak through the Greek crisis, dropped sharply thereafter. Average front page lines per day devoted to these topics ran as follows:

	Boston Herald	Boston Record
February 24–March 12	74.5	51.6
March 13–May 8	80.4	50.9
May 10–May 31	36.3	23.6

Of the total number of issues analyzed, 74 per cent of the *Herald's* front pages carried stories with major reference to Russia or Communism, while the corresponding figure for the *Record* was 47 per cent. With the exception of one issue of the *Saturday Evening Post,* every issue of each magazine contained some material on Russia.

It is no surprise to discover that the burden of this attention to Russia was sharply unfavorable. From 65 to 96 per cent of the articles and stories on Russia and Communism in the various media we covered were unfavorable in purport, while virtually none was favorable

TABLE 1

PER CENT OF ARTICLES CONTAINING FAVORABLE, NEUTRAL, AND
UNFAVORABLE COMMENT ON RUSSIA OR COMMUNISM *

Newspaper or Magazine	Favorable	Neutral	Unfavorable	Number of Articles
Boston Herald	6%	29%	65%	68
Boston Record	0	20	80	30
Saturday Evening Post	4	0	96	26
Time	4	8	88	104
Life †	0	24	76	25
Readers Digest	10	10	80	10

* Articles containing entirely "favorable" or "favorable" and "neutral" comment were classified here as "favorable"; articles containing entirely "neutral" comment or both "favorable" and "unfavorable" comment were classed as "neutral"; those containing entirely "unfavorable" or both "unfavorable" and "neutral" comment were classified as "unfavorable." For the themes considered to be "favorable," "unfavorable," and "neutral," see Table 2.

† Includes picture sequences.

(Table 1). The details of this unfavorable picture appear in Table 2, where the content of each article is classified according to the themes it carried. The table may serve to represent the complex message about Russia that was available to all subjects in the spring of 1947.

TABLE 2

NUMBER OF ARTICLES CONTAINING VARIOUS THEMES ABOUT RUSSIA OR
COMMUNISM IN VARIOUS NEWSPAPERS AND MAGAZINES *

	B.H.	B.R.	S.E.P.	Time	Life	R.D.
Unfavorable Themes						
Russia bids for world dominance	3	—	6	7	4	4
Russia seeks to dominate or interfere in weaker countries	5	1	5	6	3	1
Russia is responsible for preventing international accord	9	2	2	18	—	—
The Soviet government is a dictatorship	—	—	5	1	3	3
Russia is a backward, inefficient country	—	—	4	3	1	3
Russia refuses to give out information	—	—	—	8	—	—
Communists in the U.S. are undesirable, subversive, work for Russia	4	3	2	9	3	1
Communists, Russian agents in other countries, work for Russia	—	—	6	21	4	4
Russian professions of good faith are false	—	—	1	1	1	—
Russia criticizes the U.S.	4	1	1	8	1	—
Russia is anti-Christian or interferes with religion	—	1	—	2	2	—
Russian and U.S. ideologies are incompatible	—	—	—	—	—	1
Reported non-U.S. action against Russia	2	1	—	15	—	—
Action against U.S. Communists	3	3	1	5	3	—
Greek-Turkish aid program considered as anti-Soviet	17	7	7	18	8	3
Other U.S. action considered as anti-Soviet	3	5	9	20	8	2
Multilateral, U.N. action against Russia	6	—	1	1	—	—
Miscellaneous unfavorable comment	—	2	—	5	—	—
Neutral or Indeterminate Themes						
Greek-Turkish aid program not considered as anti-Soviet	13	1	—	1	—	—
Reported profession of Russian good faith, desire for peace	2	—	1	2	1	1
Agreement between Russia and U.S. is possible	5	1	—	2	—	—
Russia is in no position to go to war	1	1	2	2	2	3
Action against U.S. Communists is contrary to civil liberties	—	—	2	—	2	—
Miscellaneous neutral	3	4	—	5	5	—
Favorable Themes						
Russia is justly fearful and suspicious of the rest of the world	1	—	1	—	—	—
Miscellaneous favorable	1	—	1	6	—	1
(Number of articles)	(68)	(30)	(26)	(104)	(25)	(10)

* B.H.: *Boston Herald;* B.R.: *Boston Record;* S.E.P.: *Saturday Evening Post;* R.D.: *Readers Digest.*

The actual flavor of the news climate can perhaps best be evoked by representative headlines from the newspapers we surveyed.

Boston Record: "U.S. May 'Take Over' Greece," "Congress to Back Truman Curb of Reds," "Surprise Move by Marshall to Check Molotov on China," "Kick Russia out of UN, Says Byrd," "Bulganin Made Soviet Deputy"—the last, like many items classed as neutral, reporting internal Russian events.

Boston Herald: "U.S. Foreign Policy at Crisis; Greece may Fall into Soviet Orbit if We do not Assume British Obligation There," "Russia Flays 'Vicious' U.S. Atom Rule," "Stalin Film Implies Allies Bled Russia," "Stalin Tells Stassen War Avoidable by Cooperation"—the last being one of the two favorable references.

Among the magazines, *Life* staunchly supported the Truman program to stop "aggressive and expansionist" Russia, while insisting on the need for an even more inclusive program on a global basis. While it emphasized the role of the world Communist movement in forwarding Russia's plans, *Life* opposed outlawing the American Communist Party. Two picture units, nonetheless, dealt with Communism and labor, one pointing out "the shocking extent to which Communism has crept into the labor movement."

Time throughout the period presented Russia as a nation whose bid for world dominance must be stopped. Among the few favorable comments, a number concerned the lightening of the censorship during the Moscow conference, the temporary nature of which *Time* was quick to point out.

The *Saturday Evening Post,* in articles and editorials, lent its support to a program of stopping Russia while revitalizing the European economy. While the bulk of its content was unfavorable to Russia and Communism, it warned against an "anti-Red crusade," and published an article by Edgar Snow entitled "Stalin Must Have Peace."

The *Readers Digest* was markedly unfavorable in content. Titles of the articles illustrate the general tone of *Digest* material: "Down on the Collective Farm," "Help for Our Steadfast Friends, the Greeks," "Red Realm in China," "The Strength of Our New Foreign Policy," "I Didn't Want My Children to Grow Up in Soviet Russia," "The Soviet Spies," and "The Truth About Soviet Russia's 14,000,000 Slaves." The last two articles appeared in the book sections of the *Digest.*

In sum, we see that in spite of the ambiguity and complexity inherent in events themselves, the portrayal of events in the media sampled was most unambiguous and stripped to a striking simplicity. These were the years before either events or news had brought home to the mass audience the subtleties and frustrations of the Western alliance and the pattern of Communist operations. The Marshall Plan, the North Atlantic Treaty, the revival of European economies were yet to shape the European picture. The fall of Nationalist China, the Korean War, the rise to power of Communist China, the neutralism of India, and the Indochina crisis—none of these had claimed the attention of America. The Far East was a province for experts. At home, loyalty programs had only begun to be instituted in large scale, Alger Hiss was unheard of, McCarthy unknown. "The Bomb" was our shield and our monopoly. This was the spring of 1947.

CHAPTER 6

JOHN CHATWELL

T HIS chapter is the first of three case reports drawn from our pool of ten carefully studied men. We have chosen these three for detailed analysis because of their fitness to represent the range of our findings. The three men differ widely in economic status, cultural background, and educational opportunity. Their opinions on general affairs fall roughly into the categories of liberal, conservative, and radical, and their attitudes toward Russia range from bitter opposition to warm espousal. They seemed to us, furthermore, to show distinctly different patterns of relationship between opinions and those processes in personality which we have come to deem significant in opinion formation. In reporting at length on these three cases we hope to convey enough of our method and our thinking so that the grounds for our conclusions shall not be left in obscurity. The remaining seven cases will be presented in much briefer form, mainly to show the personal variations in pattern—the ten distinct individuals—that confronted us at the end of our clinical study.

Before we begin to describe the first case it will be well to guard against misunderstanding on two points. In the first place, the functional analysis of an opinion is not for us a way of deciding upon the soundness of that opinion. When we show that a man's outlook is influenced by conformity pressures, by anxieties and defenses, by obscure personal motives, it is not for the purpose of discrediting his outlook or suggesting that he must be wrong. It would be a grave mistake to assume that because an opinion serves purposes in the economy of personal adjustment it must to that extent be incorrect. Often enough an opinion cannot serve its purpose in this economy unless it is fortified by facts and translated into active participation, unless the person knows he can defend it and is willing to gamble his vote and his action on its correctness. Under these circumstances he is motivated to test reality, learn facts, exchange views with others, and in general perform those very operations whereby soundness of opinion is achieved. Being personally involved does not, of course, free the person from bias, but it does often mean that he has given thought to the matter and retained information about it. One might ask what chance an opinion has of being well grounded in fact when it serves no function in the economy of personal adjustment. When there is really nothing at stake one learns little, remembers less, and very likely forms no opinion at all. In short, the soundness or truth of an opinion must be judged by criteria other than its adaptive service to the person who holds it, and its adaptive service should by no means be conceived as simply a source of error.

The second point on which we wish to forestall misunderstanding has to do with the generality of our findings. In presenting single cases we run the risk of being taken to imply that each case is typical of everyone who happens to subscribe to the same political philosophy. Our method may lead to the hasty impression that we consider John Chatwell a typical liberal, Charles Lanlin typical of conservatives, and Hilary Sullivan representative of sympathizers with Communism. Let it be clear that such is not our intention. As regards the simplistic notion, described in the first chapter, that each brand of political philosophy might be associated with a particular pattern of functions in personality, we can only repeat that we neither expected it to be true nor designed our study to bear upon its truth. In presenting our cases we are merely setting forth some individual examples of the functions of opinions in personality.

Introductory Sketch

John Chatwell was the subject of two detailed studies at the Harvard Psychological Clinic, separated by an interval of nearly six years. He was first known at the Clinic during his undergraduate years when he served as a subject in personality studies then under way. After graduation he saw four years of military service, then returned to his home in Wellfield, a suburb of New York City, and entered a law office while studying for his law degree in evening classes. He had been thus occupied for two years and was just short of 28 years old when we recalled him for the present project. The sessions were held eight hours a day for a three-day weekend in order to complete the schedule in a single visit from New York. Chatwell was motivated to make this visit less by the financial compensation than by a desire to escape briefly from his tiring routine, revisit the scene of his college years, and renew his friendship with the investigator who had chiefly worked with him before. As one who always cherished Josiah Royce's remark that talking is the easiest form of breathing, he did not shrink from the formidable schedule of tests and interviews, and treated the visit as an interesting adventure.

The earlier study caught Chatwell at a poor time, at loose ends with himself as an undergraduate. Coming to Harvard from a prominent career in Wellfield's small Episcopal Academy, he felt lost in the big lecture courses and diffuse social life of a large university. He took little part in organized student activities and felt truly identified with no groups. He was bored by his studies, which he found unchallenging and little related to life. Impatience with laboratory work led him to abandon biochemistry and concentrate in social studies. He reached no firm decisions as to the kind of work he wanted to take up after graduation. With his interest thus feebly engaged, he made a mediocre academic record. His time was pleasantly occupied by reading, conversation, friendships with girls, poker, and various jobs whereby he helped pay his college expenses. But he was assailed at times by boredom and a feeling of futility. In such moods he would talk as follows:

> Where in the world am I? I need complete reorientation; I don't know where I stand. Should I be in college? How shall I fit myself for what I want to do? What do I want to do? I live entirely in the present and do not face the future. I don't seem to have any guts and I don't seem to care.

Upon graduation from college Chatwell volunteered for military service. After an impatient month in basic training, he offered his services as an instructor and was soon competently handling classes of five hundred men in a scientific subject. This success raised his self-esteem and placed him in daily contact with "excellent and congenial officers." Assigned presently to Officer Candidate School, he became an intelligence and communications officer, in which capacity he saw eighteen months of overseas duty.

Some months after entering military service Chatwell married a girl with whom he had fallen in love during his senior year at college.

At the time of the second study he was the father of twin boys with another child on the way. After the war the family lived temporarily in Wellfield, then for the time being in an apartment in New York City near the office and the law school. Chatwell's salary as a law clerk in training was $70 a week, with good prospects for the future in a small but stable and prosperous firm. In contrast to his mood as an undergraduate he was now on high land of optimism and self-confidence. The war was behind him, his marriage was turning out well, and his chosen profession was stimulating his capacities and interests to the utmost. No wonder his own summary struck a note of exuberance:

> I am very, very happy, busy as hell, with independence, a measure of security in a form in which I can accept it, a future with several broad avenues besides the attractive one I'm on, and plenty of problems—interesting problems, and none beyond my abilities.

Physically Chatwell was lightly built, though of a little more than average height. His slender and rather small-boned frame suggested agility and a certain wiry strength.[1] Regular features and an animated expression counted as distinct social assets, and his alertness, good humor, and readiness to talk made him a colorful participant in discussions and a highly productive informant in interviews. At the time of the earlier study he was one of a group of twenty undergraduates whose speech style was analyzed in great detail by F. H. Sanford.[2] His speech was characterized as "colorful, varied, emphatic, direct, active, progressing always in a forward direction." In comparison with the other undergraduates it was unusually well coordinated and closely connected, and his talk tended to cover wide areas, though sometimes at the expense of detail. "His speech is confident, definite, independent," Sanford concluded; "in general he appears to use speech to express his own individuality and to impress the auditor." The intervening years had done little to change these characteristics. Although tired from his current strenuous life, he talked with even more vigor and animation, discussing his life and his views with zest and evident relish. The transcriptions showed that he usually spoke in complete, coherent sentences, was rarely at a loss for words, and even in the *Stress Interview* maintained remarkable clarity and self-possession.

[1] The somatotype, measured during the earlier study according to Sheldon's technique, was 2½–3½–5. Cf. W. H. Sheldon, *The varieties of human physique*, New York & London, Harper and Brothers, 1940.

[2] F. H. Sanford, Speech and personality: a comparative study, *Character & Personality*, 1942, **10**, 169–198.

Chatwell's relationship to the members of the staff was colored by his previous service as a subject and his acquaintance with one of the interviewers, with whom he was on a first-name basis and at whose home he stayed during the visit. This disposed him to a feeling of equality and even of oneness with the group. He was certainly not overawed by the proceedings; in fact, at the end of the *Stress Interview* he congratulated his tormentors on the lawyer-like way they had handled themselves. His rapport with the staff was favorable for many kinds of self-revelation, particularly for discussing political questions, but on the other hand Chatwell was somewhat more concerned to maintain an advantageous self-picture in this group of equals than he had been in the earlier study, when the relationship to the interviewer had evoked needs for help and encouragement.

Chatwell's Values

The system of values and beliefs that Chatwell had built up in the course of his life was undoubtedly influenced by his perception of his own place in the social order. He conceived of himself as well born, well equipped, well educated. On both sides his forebears were successful and respected, the community in which he grew up was an ideal one, the schools he attended were excellent, his own intellectual gifts he knew to be unusual. Economically he was not identified with the highest class, and he felt considerable contempt for the big business man and the very rich person who lacked brains and sensitivity. With respect to what he considered more real values, however, he identified himself with the highest class, the professional class, which alone possessed the inestimable advantage of the trained mind and the power to judge issues without being swamped by personal prejudice. Chatwell felt himself entitled to membership in an aristocracy of brains.

Military experience considerably widened his social horizon. He rubbed shoulders with the common man and came to have much respect for him, particularly because of the common man's competence and ability to take care of himself. Meeting the common man as an American soldier, rather than in civilian life, he was able to perceive the virtues of competence and self-sufficiency without having forced upon him the common man's economic outlook and frustrations. These frustrations were driven home rather by his contacts with Asian civilian populations where he perceived the social system to be organized without any regard for the individual and his rights. The superiority of the American soldier to these enslaved creatures, as he saw them, indicated to Chatwell that the American system, for all its faults, operated effectively to preserve the dignity of the individual. As to his own position, he took it for granted that his training and ability entitled him to officer status and he lost no time and felt no shyness in placing himself in contact with officers.

Chatwell's membership in a relatively secure portion of the professional class exposed him to a set of values derived without much change from 19th century liberalism. From his well-educated parents and from the immediate circle of their friends and neighbors he received a pattern of values in which freedom, enterprise, rationality, and high standards of personal conduct played the leading parts. But Chatwell had done more than receive these values; they had been tried in the crucible of his own experience. He himself had experienced the joy of mastering obstacles and obtaining recognition through an energetic attack on the problems that confronted him. He himself had learned to value freedom and to feel that large organizations and even group decisions tended to hamper his own swift competence. Doubtless the element of his own initiative was more apparent to him than the advantages he enjoyed in the way of class status, education, and relative financial security. Nevertheless his values were not merely borrowed: they were extensively recreated as expressions of his own desires and experience.

When interviewed on *Personal Values and Religious Sentiments* Chatwell spontaneously placed freedom of the individual in the highest position. In another place, the *Conformity Interview,* he was asked on what subjects he felt so strongly that he would not be able to keep still if they were discussed. He replied as follows:

> Why, I have learned to keep quiet about almost anything. Chalk that up to Army service, if you like. But there are many things about which, if there is a general conversation going on—questions of general importance —that I do feel strongly about. Among them are the necessity for active participation by individuals in the processes of government; the assumption of public responsibility, both as voters and as interested citizens, and also to the extent of participating in public life. Actually standing for office, and so on. I feel very strongly about . . . about decentralization of government. One of my fundamental tenets is that, first, there should be as little government as possible, or as little as is absolutely necessary, and that that little shall be performed at the lowest possible level of government, keeping in mind efficiency of operation and so on, but preserving the idea of retaining as much control in the hands of the people concerned as is possible. I feel very strongly about that. Ah . . . I feel also very strongly about restrictions on . . . ah . . . production, artificial restrictions on production, such as tariffs in the international picture, and discriminatory laws within the United States, such as discriminatory taxes on certain commodities like oleomargarine, and things of that sort. Ah . . . generally speaking, I'm opposed to government subsidies of economic

activities, with some exceptions. That's not an absolute statement. Generally speaking I'm opposed to them. I'm extremely interested in the preservation of personal rights. For instance, the idea of expunging the Communist Party is abhorrent to me, even though I completely disagree with their position. And I feel strongly about that.

This set of strongly held values played a prominent part in his views on more specific policy. The protection of individual rights and liberties, the procedural aspects of which he was learning in his legal training, determined his views on many points. When hard pressed in the *Stress Interview* he was able to quote Justice Brandeis to the effect that property rights are personal rights. He believed that the individual's right to make money should be restricted as little as possible by income taxes but that inheritance taxes should be practically confiscatory. He favored little government interference in the price system, and even though he deplored some of the tactics of big business, he believed that relations between management and labor should be left to operate through collective bargaining in a free market. The natural working of economic processes in a free system certainly appealed to him as a model, even though he favored many specific policies that represented interference with nature's design. Enterprise, productivity, personal freedom, were the things he liked, but his discriminating intelligence allowed him to see some of the points at which these values were impractical, as in his recognition that a certain level of security must be achieved as a basis for freedom.

Under the heading of decentralization he held that there should be a minimum of government and that as much as possible should be carried on at the local level where the citizens would be best able to control it. These Jeffersonian sentiments were amplified in a way less archaic than they at first sounded. We found that he favored the TVA project which involves, to be sure, a certain regional decentralization but which has aroused the antipathy of most advocates of less government. He also favored substantial federal grants in aid of education, a course sometimes criticized as opening the way to power over local school committees. In fact he had some difficulty in producing examples of unequivocal decentralization, thinking instead of cases where the public welfare demanded a compromise with this ideal. Conflict was evident between his feeling for radical decentralization and his knowledge of the actual needs of a large interdependent society. Whatever the tone of his general sentiment, his specific policies were not exactly Jeffersonian.

His advocacy of decentralization carried with it, moreover, the idea of citizen control over government, and thus leads us to his insistence

on the duty of active participation. Chatwell accepted it as an obligation of all citizens to keep themselves informed and to seize opportunities to take part in the affairs of community and state. What right,
he asked, had a citizen to criticize the government if he had failed
to vote in the last election?

On the international stage Chatwell believed in active participation
by the United States. He regretted the weakness of the United Nations
Organization and favored transformation of that body into an effective
international government having power to inspect and control armaments and to enforce its decisions on recalcitrant member states. He
did not flinch at the surrender of a portion of United States sovereignty
implied in this program. If the United States were a recalcitrant
member state it should be dealt with as severely as any other state.
His liking for decentralization did not make him an isolationist. The
international scene, realistically perceived, engaged instead his value
of active participation and placed him among the more energetic
advocates of international government. He believed that the world
might best be held in order by the impersonal dictates of law and
justice, his own nation protected but also controlled by a fabric of
legal arrangements.

In the sphere of religion and personal morality Chatwell's views were
much less clearly formulated. Any discussion of religion led straight
into the superordinate value of personal liberty. His own religious
convictions had been rather fully eaten away by the acids of skepticism
and scientific thought. He believed religion had little to offer the
intelligent person, and his concern about it was chiefly that everyone
should be free to believe and worship as he pleased. Like so many
young men of his generation he was guided in his personal life by a
code of fair dealing and kindness about which, however, he would
have thought it offensively priggish to speak. In contrast, he could
be vehement about the ethics of his profession, and told with some
pride how his law firm declined to take work for clients who wanted
to operate in a dishonest fashion.

Chatwell on Russia

In 1947 Russia was not a topic of central concern to Chatwell,
although it was an important one on which he was by no means ill
informed. Under these circumstances we might anticipate that his
attitudes toward Russia would occupy a dependent position as regards
his central value system, representing an application of this system to
problems somewhat removed from the core of his concerns. The topic

was first broached in the *Open-Ended Interview on Russia.* Chatwell at once countered the experimenter's very general question by making a distinction. The transcript reads as follows:

E: So we might start out by my asking you to tell us more or less how you feel about Russia. . . .

S: When you say "Russia," do you mean Russia or the Russians?

E: Well, if you want to make that distinction, that's something you can do.

S: All right. Ah . . . I don't know very many Russians. I've met a few. I know a good many Asiatics of other sorts, and Europeans. And my general feeling about the Russians themselves is that I would have no more quarrel with Ivan than I would with John Smith if Ivan lived next door to me.

E: You think Russians are pretty much like anybody else?

S: Well, I wouldn't say that. I . . . I . . . it depends on what you mean by "anybody else." I'd say they are certainly more like Americans than the Chinese are like Americans, for example. But . . . I certainly have no emotional bias for or against the Russian people, as individuals, I . . . do feel, however, that as nearly as I can determine, and I don't know this, Russia is in effect a police state, and in a police state the individual . . . ah . . . characteristics, or the characteristics of individuals, are not the effective factors in affairs, by and large. My general feeling, even so, and granted that Russia is a police state, I don't have any feeling even toward the Russian government, because it's my own observation that whatever steps Russia has taken, inimical as they may have been to our interests, they have clearly been in the interest of Russia. And I don't think it lies in our mouths to criticize a man who does what he thinks is right for Russia because it isn't the best for us. Ah . . . however, I do think that . . . that they may be wrong about it, and the fact . . . that Russia's national, in the sense of governmental, policies have developed as they have is an unfortunate thing for international relations. Ah . . . Question?

E: I was about to ask you in what ways.

S: Ah . . . principally, I think . . . ah . . . that if the Russians believe in—not Communism, because the Russian organization today isn't Communistic—but if they believe in a nationalized economy, that doesn't necessarily mean that they should be denied the opportunity to experiment in those directions in Russia. And it doesn't necessarily mean that they shouldn't be allowed to influence other people to follow their example, if they think they're right. But I think it does mean that the other people have to be—or should be, morally—given a free choice to accept or reject the economic theories that the Russian government advocates, or that we advocate, as far as that's concerned.

Chatwell went on to discuss the difficulties that must be experienced by Russian leaders in evaluating American opinion. Because of their fear of attack, justified in view of earlier events, they were sacrificing, he felt, magnificent opportunities for economic development within Russia to the need for security through armaments, propaganda, and control over neighboring states. All this, he declared, is understandable, but extremely harmful to international relations. "I hold no brief whatsoever for the infiltration and intimidation of the people in the countries peripheral to Russia," he said, and later, "I have nothing but contempt for the technique of creating confusion." But he was not disposed to blame the atmosphere of hostility and distrust entirely on Russia. The trouble was that each side wanted the other to commit itself first, "which is a not unusual circumstance when the high contracting parties don't trust each other any further than I can throw a piano." The solution would be to show the Russians more fully that our interests were peaceful rather than expansionist, that we would and could achieve a sensible organization of Western Germany in which armament would be minimized and economic development placed foremost.

S: I'd like to see that because I think it will give us an opportunity to establish a capitalistic or semi-capitalistic or semi-democratic society to operate in competition and comparison with the Russian-dominated zone.

E: You think it would stand up well in comparison?

S: Well, I think it could. I don't say that it will. It could. Depends on who runs it . . . and how . . . and what backing they get from the home folks. And how far they let the Russians go in . . . exacting tribute from it.

At this point the interviewer introduced the recently announced Truman Doctrine, asking Chatwell what he thought of the policy it implied in Greece.

S: I think it's a healthy thing. I think that we're in this world and we've got to pay for our responsibilities. I think, for instance, that England was running Greece with our money and we didn't like the way she did it, and she, very astutely, it seems to me, said, "All right, you fly it for a while." Which is what I would have done under the circumstances. And further, I think that Russia is being aggressive and expansionist, as the Under-Secretary of State said, and I don't see any reason why we shouldn't be at least as alert as they are in going to the extent of guaranteeing those people a free choice. I don't think it goes any further than that. I would like to see each group of people have an opportunity to decide what form of government they want . . . with full stomachs. It's unfortunate that the full stomachs have to be supplied by one of the partisans—that's too bad. Under an ideal situation a third party would fill their stomachs and say, "Now decide." But I don't know how you can arrange that.

Shortly afterward the examiner drew the conversation back to more general issues.

E: I wonder if you'd say in what ways you think Russia and America differ most.

S: Well, I would say that the most important difference is the fact that the American is . . . has . . . is subject to direction from such a multitude of sources. He is abstractly free and, as a factual matter, quite confused, whereas, on the other hand, the Russian is led from a single source and very strongly by a ring through his nose . . . ah . . . so that all issues are quite simple to him and his course is clear. And so's his conscience, probably, which is more than you can say for the American.

E: Do you think there are some drawbacks to both . . . ?

S: Yes. . . . Well, I wouldn't say that. Ah. . . . There are drawbacks, of course. I'll say this. I think that the price in confusion that we pay is well worth while.

E: You think we're bound to be confused?

S: Of course. As long as you preserve any individual freedom of action, you're going to have confusion. You have it in a house, for example.

E: You think the Russians pay too high a price?

S: Yes. They pay a price that is unacceptable to me . . . as an individual. And I think to most Americans.

E: So that the lack of freedom in Russia is a thing that stands out, as far as you're concerned?

S: Yes.

These excerpts from the *Open-Ended Interview on Russia* serve to give us a first picture of Chatwell's general position. He had no quarrel with the Russian people, whom he believed to be much like ourselves. He respected the ability of the Russian leadership, which he felt had been effective in building up Russia. He granted Russians the right to practice and preach their economic doctrines, even though he himself did not agree with any such doctrines. He criticized the United States and its allies for not reaching a decent settlement in Western Europe, reassuring Russia of peaceful intentions, and offering the Eastern zone a fair race between the two economic systems. Thus he struggled to reach a fair-minded appraisal, not blackening the rival nor whitewashing our own behavior; he was able to see beyond American interests and judge our policies as he would judge anyone else's. Nevertheless he was against Russia; that is, against the government's policy of infiltration and expansion and what he denounced as the unfair forcing of the Communist system on people who would never

accept it if allowed free choice on a full stomach. This policy he
believed we should actively oppose, filling the stomachs to the extent
that was necessary for freedom of choice. Above all it was the lack
of personal liberty, the police state and the closing of channels whereby
the individual might freely come to his own decisions, that gave intensity to his opposition toward Russia.

With this general picture in front of us we shall now undertake to
formulate in a systematic way Chatwell's opinions in regard to Russia.
Two simultaneous tasks are here involved. First is the exhaustive
analysis of all that he said on the subject, not only in the *Open-Ended
Interview* from which we have been quoting but also in the *Information
Test, Polling Interview, Information Apperception Test, Conformity
Interview, Cartoon Stereotype Test,* and *Stress Interview.* The second
task consists of applying the conceptual scheme we have developed
for systematically describing an opinion. This calls for describing the
differentiated object of his attitude: the aspects of Russia which he
distinguished, and their arrangement in a structured pattern. It calls
for an estimate of *saliency,* the importance of Russia in his everyday
concerns. The scheme then requires an analysis of *time perspective,*
of *informational support,* and of *object value,* the latter referring to the
affective tone surrounding the object. When Chatwell's opinions have
been thus systematically described we shall be in a position to summarize his *orientation* and *policy stand:* his action tendencies as regards
Russia and their translation into particular public policies.

Differentiated object of attitude. In all his discussions of Russia
Chatwell made a major discrimination between the Russian people on
the one hand and the Communist Party and leaders of the Russian
state on the other. We have already noted his first reference to this
distinction and his picture of the average Russian as being very much
like the average American. Commenting further, he said:

> I would say that the Russian and the American both have a similar
> broad aspect about physical things that arises out of living in a country
> that is much less limited physically than some of the other countries of
> the world. And also in being the heirs of a new political philosophy
> which helps to unfetter the outlook from the past. And also in the
> possession of raw materials from which to start.

In respect to economic confidence he believed the Russian outlook to
be more like ours than the British. When vast natural resources are
everywhere in evidence, "you feel that things are possible."

> But if you know that you have no oil, and no this, and no that, and
> no the other thing, it seems to me that it would make it a lot harder to

have the attitude that you can do big things that, to me, is typical of both the Russians and the Americans.

Only with regard to genius for construction and mechanized things did he believe the Russian people to be different and inferior. This quality, which he referred to variously as a "flair," "interest," and "set," he considered to be peculiar to Americans. Russian failure to exhibit such a trait did not in the least injure the favorable and friendly tone of his attitude toward the Russian people. Throughout the sessions this aspect of his opinion was held consistently and with no little strength of conviction.

Chatwell's opinion concerning the Communist Party and its leaders was less single-minded. As we have seen, he respected their attempts to advance the fortunes of the Russian nation, and he thought it highly understandable, in view of previous history, that they should mistrust the intentions of other nations. He respected also the ability of the leaders. "They weren't born yesterday," he remarked to one interviewer; "they gauge what people will stand better than any other country, and they know better what's going on." On the other hand, several of his comments on Russian Communism were given in a quite sharp and critical tone. To the question in the *Polling Interview* which read, "As far as you know, what do you think the Russians are trying to achieve?" he replied:

> The people, 180 million of them, are trying to achieve what everybody else wants in the rest of the world, a decent life; but 2 million are trying to get it at the expense of the other 180 million, trying to feather their own nests and, in doing so, are doing everything to remain in dominance.

When questioned on the part played by Russia in Communist parties outside Russia, he made his usual distinction that it was not Russia but only the Russian Communist Party that was involved.

S: I would say that what it really amounts to, to put it on a cold basis, is that there are 2 million guys in Russia saying, "Look here, boys, we've taken over here and we're having a hell of a fine time. Why don't you do the same?" Well, I think it's soaped up with a lot of idealistic claptrap on top of that, that they're doing everybody a favor by becoming their masters.

E: You think the ideal is somewhat cynical?

S: Well, I think that every Communist I ever knew had a fond dream that he'd be the Gauleiter of the district, comes the revolution. . . . The revolutionists that I've known were, generally speaking, men who were unable to make a go of it in a free society and felt that they'd be better off to be guaranteed a certain cut and, in addition, had a fancy that they as individuals would do considerably better under such a system.

The tartness of these remarks suggests strong feelings of anger, but the barque of judgment was not swamped. A moment later he made a spirited attack on those who would curb the liberty of Communists in America, and soon after, when asked to compare Russian Communism with German Nazism, he found three evidences of the superiority of Russian motives.

S: By and large, I'll give the Communist in Russia credit for being idealistic. And I believe myself that most of the German fascists were quite cynical and were consciously exploiting the people. Ah . . . secondly, the Communists, I believe, appear to think that everybody should work for it, whereas from what I could see of the fascists, it was an attempt to corral the visible evidences of wealth by force.

E: You think there is some difference in sincerity, then.

S: Yes, I think so . . . I think also that there's a difference in point of view; that while Communists believe that the state is more important than the individual, yet they believe, I think, that in the last analysis the state exists for the individual.

Chatwell thus sharply distinguished the Communist Party and its leaders from the great mass of the Russian people. The leaders and the party were responsible for Russian policy, and of this policy he perceived three main aspects: (1) Russia as a developing nation, (2) Russia as a police state, and (3) Russia as an advocate of world Communism.

(1) Chatwell's opinion of Russia as a developing nation was strongly colored by the many similarities he felt to exist between Russia and the United States. The right of the Russians to develop the huge economic resources of their domain without interference by foreign powers seemed no less sacred to him than the right of the United States to work for the same objectives after its own revolution. The Russians themselves, he believed, had become more concerned with this inner development than with any other goal. Naturally they feared that other powers would not let them alone. Any move to arm Germany would be certain to arouse their fears.

S: I don't think that the Russians' real ultimate objectives are objectives that they have to obtain through war. But I think they are in a position, and understandably so, in which it looks as though the obtainment of their objectives by peaceful means is going to be interfered with, not now, not by any present, immediate threat, but in the future . . . I don't see why Russia should put up with that. And neither do the Russians. Now, I happen to disagree with them that the way to prevent that is to obstruct attempts to settle European affairs. . . . But I think that Russia wants to develop peacefully. Of course, she's got a dichotic personality. She wants to develop Russia, and she also wants to spread the truth and the light, as she fondly imagines them to be, throughout the world. And those two objectives may be inconsistent.

E: Which do you think is the dominant one?

S: Well, I think there's been a change in that respect. I think that prior to the war, probably the dominant one was world revolution. And I think that during the war, and since the war, the dominant emotion of the Russians . . . I'll put it this way: I think that Russianism is more important than Communism now. I think they've developed a nationalistic patriotism which is in direct . . . ah . . . contradiction of the international position previously espoused by the Russians, or by their leaders.

Planned economy in Russia, sometimes singled out by other subjects as a major aspect, appeared to Chatwell a mere detail of national development. As a growing nation Russia naturally tried to find the optimal amount of planning needed for economic progress. Chatwell was prepared to say what he thought optimal for the United States, but he considered the Russian problem to be different. Soviet industrial development under the several plans was undoubtedly a good thing; who could tell whether better results would have been obtained by a less regimented program? Inasmuch as Chatwell believed our own economy to be currently overplanned, his willingness to make Russian planning a subordinate and internal issue testified to his sympathetic interest in Russia as a developing nation and his consistent favorable opinion of this aspect of Russian policy.

(2) In sharp contrast was his opinion of Russia as a police state. Chatwell's tolerance was quickly extinguished and his sentiments became intensely negative when he contemplated the infringements of personal liberty practiced by the Communist regime. He was infuriated at the notion of restriction on free speech, at citizens having to take orders from "some nincompoop who happened to be one step higher," at what he had heard about jails well filled with political prisoners. His feelings came to fullest flower in the *Information Apperception Test* when he was asked to comment on the item, "Russians have been arrested from time to time without knowing what their crime was."

That serves to remind me that Russia is a police state and . . . to me . . . it . . . it epitomizes the worst thing about the Russian system. It's particularly important to me because I'm . . . I have an obsession on the subject of personal liberty and because my training is in the field of

Anglo-Saxon law. I think that the evidence for the statement is question-
able, just like all the evidence of internal things in Russia. But since I
feel more strongly about that one, it *seems* to me that the evidence about
that has been more consistent than other evidence. . . .

To me personal liberty is the most important thing in the world. . . .

If I were to change one thing in Russia, that would be the first thing
I'd change.

The attitude of the Soviet state toward religion he completely subordinated to this issue of personal liberty. As a somewhat doubting
Episcopalian, Chatwell had no ax to grind for the religious bodies
suppressed by Communist policy. He refused to take sides in any
fight between authoritarian religion and authoritarian atheism, but he
did take sides warmly with the right of the individual to make his own
religious decisions and to worship or not as he pleased. He was mis-
trustful of the reported easing of restrictions on religion, believing it to
be a calculated political move rather than an evidence of respect for
individual rights. Chatwell's opinion of Russia as a police state was
uniformly negative and uniformly vehement.

(3) Advocacy of world Communism stood out for Chatwell as the
third main aspect of Russian policy. He found the propagation of
Communism not only distasteful in itself but also responsible for some
of Russia's most damaging actions. The right of the Russians to
"spread the truth and the light" he was prepared to defend, but the
spreading must be done in such a way that the prospective converts
were free to accept or reject the proffered doctrine. On this point he
felt the Communists were constantly at fault. He saw them as trying
to sell a doctrine which the majority of people outside Russia, probably
even inside, did not want. In order to ensure a successful sale they
tried to create conditions under which refusal would be impossible.
The tactics included infiltration, intimidation, confusion, opposing all
peaceful settlement, working to bring about the conditions of empty
stomach and fear under which the free use of judgment would be
prevented. Chatwell envisaged the role of the United States in Greece,
for example, as one of counteracting these tactics—filling the empty
stomachs, as he often expressed it—to the end of securing free judgment. In the *Stress Interview* he was heavily pressed on this point.
The interviewers tried to force him to admit that our intervention implied considerably more than filling stomachs; it meant, they argued,
providing arms and supporting a regime favorable to our economic
interests. Under this grilling, Chatwell conceded that more than food
was involved, but he would not favor the Truman policy if he thought
its purpose went beyond providing "the guarantees of a real election,

not only as to the machinery but as to the climate of discussion and so on, and all the other things that go to make it a real election." Emphatically he would be opposed to "using the food, and all the other things that we sent over as weapons, to cram what *we* think is right down the Greeks' necks." But he was sure that we could be trusted to promote free choice for the Greek people without abusing our position to create a tyranny of our own or a beach-head for preventive war.

It was thus Russia's method of advocating world Communism that met with his strenuous disapproval. This was reflected in his views on the treatment of American Communists. In the *Open-Ended Interview* he said:

> If I had a scheme which I thought would benefit the people, I would bend my efforts to convincing them of it and giving them an opportunity to decide. I respect the other man's right to choose, and I would try to present my argument as forcefully as I could. I would not feel that my argument was so weak that I had to resort to subterfuge and sabotage. . . .
>
> I have nothing but contempt for the technique of creating confusion. . . .
>
> However, I have been very much shocked by the tendency recently to try to outlaw the Communist Party as a political party. And that's for two reasons. The first reason: it's abhorrent to me to deny anybody the right to express his political views through recognized channels. I think that that's a right that can't be taken away. And in the second place, just as a practical matter, it seems to me that it will serve only to drive them underground and make them harder to see.

His second point was amplified in the *Polling Interview* in answer to the question, "What do you think should be done about the Communists in this country?"

> Turn the light on them. Give them all the privileges, responsibilities, and immunities of a political party. As for their other activities, we have laws against treason.

Most of what Chatwell thought about Russian policy belonged under the three main aspects we have now discussed. Those aspects of Russia which might be grouped under the heading of the welfare state did not strike him as of much importance. When asked to comment on full employment in Russia, for instance, he refused to consider the fact in relation to policy, treating it rather as an instance of lawful self-regulation in an economy that is not yet capable of producing a surplus of goods. Provision of state nurseries for the children of working mothers he cast in the same light, as indicative of labor shortage and Russian efforts to increase productivity. The high level of book publication in Russia he did count "to the credit of the Russian authorities," but he was suspicious that this benefit might be prostituted to the goals of propaganda. His perception of what was going on *inside* Russia included little except building up the national economy and the vast expense to personal liberty that accompanied it.

Chatwell's tendency to set up both sides of a controversial question and to make due allowance for differences of viewpoint made it hard at times to discover the overall pattern of his view of Russia. He left us in no final doubt, however, as to the facet that most excited him. He spoke of his "obsession" about personal liberty, "the most important thing in the world," and he characterized the police state features of Russia as the thing he would most want to change. The dominant feature of Chatwell's opinions was his opposition to the infringement of personal liberty. This sentiment proved to be the chief organizing force in his perception of the object. It subordinated his attitude on religion, and it even subordinated one of the major guises under which he perceived Russia—as the advocate of world Communism—where his stand was determined by the Communists' intention to force acceptance of their doctrines rather than respecting personal liberty to weigh and reject. Even his espousal of the Russian people and the development of their national economy was colored by his feeling that outsiders should not interfere with their right to self-determination. The chief structuration in his view of Russia was certainly provided by his passion for personal liberty.

Saliency. Chatwell's willingness to talk and his ready production of ideas about Russia should not be taken to mean that the topic occupied a position of high salience among his concerns. He himself, reading this chapter in 1953, characterized his earlier utterances as poorly founded and largely improvised in response to our questioning. Clearly the intervening years had produced a sharp increase in salience and given him a higher standard as regards informed opinion, but we cannot entirely share his disparaging judgment of his earlier views. Prior to our study he had given the topic considerable thought. He showed awareness of the importance of Russia in the world scene and of the probability that a future collision would threaten his way of life, if not his life itself. He did not, however, attach an urgency to the topic that rivaled his concern with major policy issues within the United States. His vote in a presidential election, he told us, would not be determined by the candidates' attitudes toward Russia. His own life and career were freshly in the making. Problems of rights and liberties under American law were of daily high concern, and he was certainly not preoccupied by a topic no closer than the Soviet Union.

Time perspective. At the level of generalities, Chatwell's time perspective was a long one. Within Russia he foresaw a development probably favorable to peace.

> I think that if the Russian government takes the load off the Russian people's backs so that they can produce for themselves, the larger amount of goods and chattels the individual Russian gets, the more conservative he's going to get and the less interested in collectivism he's going to be, and the more important economic freedom is going to be to him. And the more steady and adequate his diet is, the more important personal liberty is going to be to him. On the other hand, if the burden is not only maintained but increased, it may become intolerable and they may throw out their masters and substitute a new bunch.

Either of these developments would reduce the force of Communist propaganda and thus make for greater international understanding. Another long-range trend making for peace was the growing independence of nations from natural resources possessed only by other nations. Scientific invention moves constantly toward the production of synthetic materials, as has already been done, for instance, with rubber. About the years immediately to come it was Chatwell's opinion that "we'll just muddle through." He foresaw long postponement of a German treaty, probably with a horrible instrument resulting at the end, but at least it would be better than the Treaty of Versailles. He believed that neither Russia nor America wanted war in the immediate future, but ultimately, he said, there was a "good likelihood that there may be a collision. It depends on how the collateral policies are handled," policies such as German rehabilitation or intervention in Greece, any one of which might create a crisis. We might say that his immediate and distant time-perspectives were fairly definite and structured, but the middle range, the one in which war would be most likely to occur, appeared to him somewhat misty.

Informational support. Chatwell was the best informed of our ten subjects. He missed only 2 items of the 53 contained in the *Information Test.* He had not read many books about Russia, and those that he had were literary rather than political and economic. His high level of information came rather from his careful reading of the daily papers, especially the *New York Times,* and a number of magazines which he read because of their connection with his professional activities. His selection of sources was not unbiased, inasmuch as he read no paper or magazine that stood explicitly for the interests of labor or for the extreme left. They sufficed, however, to give him a high level of information on Russian current events.

Object value. In Chatwell's case Russia was a well differentiated object which evoked several quite distinct valuations. Toward the Russian people his feelings were kindly and sympathetic. Toward Russia as a great developing nation he was entirely friendly, in fact rather admiring. Russia as a police state, however, evoked his uncompromising disfavor, and her advocacy of world Communism by techniques other than fair persuasion seemed to him a violation of the rights of supposedly free men. It would be crude indeed to add up an affective score to characterize his attitude as a whole. When we considered, however, the structuration of the several aspects of Russia which Chatwell distinguished, we saw that his passion for personal liberty was the strongest organizing force. The final affective outcome was thus predominantly negative. Friendliness and admiration yielded in the long run to his indignation at the infringement of human rights, to anger at those who would destroy this most precious value.

Orientation. Chatwell's orientation toward Russia contained nothing of avoidance. Primarily he favored approach, in a spirit both friendly and strong. We should not be afraid of the Russians, he believed, nor overawed by their vehemence in councils. With skillful diplomacy we could probably guide the course of events so that major conflict could be avoided and current tensions gradually eased and resolved. Should this program fail, Chatwell was not unprepared to orient himself in a hostile direction. Future war undoubtedly seemed remote, but he had taken part in winning a global war only two years before.

Policy stand. Chatwell was fairly decisive as to what should be done. His major proposal was the strengthening of the United Nations to a point of full power over limitation of armaments. He believed we should work for settlement in western Europe by pressing for a German treaty and for other instruments of understanding. He favored intervention in Greece and possibly elsewhere to ensure free elections, but he urged that at the same time we should do everything possible to assure Russia that we had no imperialistic designs. Russian leaders must be educated to understand our willingness to live and let live in freedom.

These were Chatwell's opinions about Russia. At the beginning of this chapter we gave the barest sketch of his life and values. We now turn to a fuller study of his personality and to our central task of elucidating the relationships between personality and opinions.

Chatwell's Life and Enterprises

John Chatwell was born in 1919, the first child of talented and well educated parents. Both parents were descended from colonial families of English origin. Chatwell's father early distinguished himself by completing high school and college in six years while contributing to the support of his family, which was in restricted economic circumstances. He carried his scientific training to the Ph.D. level at a large university and embarked at once upon his career as a research scientist. Quite soon he succeeded in making some valuable inventions, but his economic situation was not thereby greatly improved, for, as his son wrote, "his whole career has been dogged by business men who have profited greatly by his creations, and at the same time have left little for him." Chatwell's mother was the daughter of an Episcopal clergyman. She went to college and did some graduate work, after which she was a teacher of science for several years until her marriage. At various times after marriage she resumed the position of teacher, and this together with the father's fluctuating earnings made it possible to maintain the home in a wealthy suburb and to plan college careers for the children. Wellfield had been Mrs. Chatwell's home for the quarter century during which her father was rector of its large Episcopal church. It was a pleasant community where a good many professional people made their homes.

Chatwell had a brother two years younger than himself, a sister six years younger, and two more sisters who were eleven and thirteen years younger. The brother, Arthur, was close enough in age to play an important part in his childhood. Chatwell remembered that Arthur was stronger and sometimes beat him up, but on the whole they got along well, sharing not only actual adventures but also those of the imagination, "about the vessels and vehicles we intended to build in which we intended to explore the smallest parts of the universe." According to his mother, Chatwell was timid in most physical activities, in contrast to Arthur who would often lead the way up a tall tree, for example, then return to help John up to the same spot. Although the two boys went to different colleges and were separated throughout the war years, a close and affectionate friendship continued between them.

Chatwell grew up in a lively and colorful home, "always interesting," as he put it, "if not entirely peaceful." He described both parents as "highly nervous," along with their many-sided talents, and this led to frequent debates in which the two boys participated. As an undergraduate he wrote:

We all indulge in continual bickering, generally healthy but occasionally bitter, in which case it is generally a matter of a division of the camp, my mother and I on one side, my father and sometimes my brother on the other. I never remember an argument on any really important subject such as our education; it was generally on some never-proven point such as the question of who gained or lost the most in the World War.

This family bickering undoubtedly had its threatening aspects. In our projective tests he frequently went out of his way to represent all family situations as glowingly harmonious. Yet on the whole it was solidarity rather than discord that seemed to him most characteristic of his home. "I feel strongly for all my family," he wrote at 19, and at 27 he said, "I have never had to think whether they were back of me or not; they are proud of me and would pull me out of holes."

From his mother we learned that Chatwell was a "perfect baby," charming, healthy, free from worrisome deviations in his development. When his brother was born, the parents endeavored to make this event acceptable by stressing the role of big brother and eldest child. Various items in the fantasy material suggest that the next few years were a period of emotional hard sledding for Chatwell. There is, we conceive, an optimal pace, perhaps different for each individual and certainly much dependent on circumstances, at which a child can move toward maturity without having to suppress substantial portions of his more immature emotional tendencies. It was apparently Chatwell's fate at times to exceed this pace. On the whole he was able to take the role prepared for him by his parents, but not without residual tensions. In his undergraduate Thematic Apperception Test and even in his memories and dreams there was a certain stress on sickness and injury, the context suggesting not only fear but also that he was attracted by the exemptions that go with illness. Perhaps it was only when sick that he was allowed to drop his role of self-sufficiency and receive the nurturing ministrations that were otherwise reserved for his younger brother. It happened that his mother was interviewed just after Chatwell had been in the college infirmary with a slight illness. Several of her remarks suggested that she was not fully satisfied with his rate of maturing at college. She wondered, for example, whether the recent illness had not contained elements of malingering, and whether the change of field to psychology did not represent an undesirable turn toward self-pampering introspection. We felt that she seemed unusually aware of possible weaknesses in her eldest son, both now and in earlier years, and that this discernment on her part might have constituted a subtle but strong pressure toward maturity. The subjective sequel of this pressure was strikingly expressed in a

theme written for his freshman English course. Using the impulse
to chase after fire engines as an example, he described the process of
suppressing childlike interests.

> One of the first realizations that came during the period when you
> were supposed to be changing from boyhood to manhood was that "kid-
> stuff" didn't become your dignity. At first, you didn't know exactly why,
> but you definitely avoided any show of enthusiasm for what a few short
> months before had been your very life. Then you began to develop an
> amused tolerance for what you now thought was beneath you, having
> realized that you had outgrown a large part of it.
> Simultaneously with this stage arrived an obscure quality that you
> decided must be judgment. You found that the decisions which had
> formerly needed the pointing finger of parent or teacher now seemed so
> simple that they no longer assumed the proportions of decisions at all,
> but were merely minor choices. . . .
> When you reached this point, you looked back and smiled indulgently
> at the childhood troubles that had seemed so mountainous. You were
> sure that you had attained maturity, and you were right, to a certain
> extent. But then you grew a little more, and you began to wonder
> whether you, or anyone else, for that matter, ever will grow up. You
> realized, for example, the utter aloneness of the man who tries to worry
> things out by himself. You realized also the tremendous urge that every
> man feels to lay his load at the feet of someone stronger and wiser than
> he, for at times it seemed as if there were no possible way for you to
> work out your own salvation.

Chatwell's sharp awareness of the pains of growing up did not prevent him from growing up. During his first year at school he earned
the reputation of being a cry-baby because of his behavior when
reprimanded by the teacher. By the third grade, however, he was
living down this reputation. In alliance with a mischievous companion
he frequently incurred the teacher's wrath but learned to maintain a
composed front even when sent before the principal. He described
himself as outgrowing an early condition of excessive obedience to
become "critical, aggressive, belligerent, but often cooperative." His
enjoyment of school increased greatly when he entered the Episcopal
Academy, located in Wellfield, where classes were small, arguments
and debate were encouraged, and attention was given to the needs and
abilities of each individual. Chatwell had nothing but praise for his
education; all his schools seemed to him to be the best he could have
attended. He was particularly happy in the Upper School at the
Academy. Mixed classes and an expanding social life appealed to him;
he became a member of the student council, president of a social club,
and even a player on the football team. In view of his light weight
and slender physique, we were surprised at this last achievement, even

in a small school. We learned from his mother, however, that unlike Arthur, who was often under the whole heap at the end of the scrimmage, John was usually on the outskirts of the game, and that he got so excited that the family doctor finally advised withdrawing him from football. In other spheres he continued his career of participation and prominence, and graduated at the head of his class.

It seems likely that his relation to his brother Arthur contained much jealousy and rivalry. The superiority which Arthur eventually demonstrated in strength and daring could hardly have been pleasant for John. This situation was resolved by an alliance from which the aggressive elements were suppressed, perhaps by displacement upon mutual enemies such as teachers. In a story completion test given in the undergraduate study, Chatwell was proffered two plots in which rivalry between brothers was the most obvious continuation. In both cases he caused the brothers to be strongly allied. One of the plots was even distorted to the point of throwing the blame for a brother's cheating onto the teacher, who failed to detect the deception. "Larry's resentment," he stated explicitly, "is toward his English teacher, not toward his brother. So he tried to figure out some way to discomfort the teacher without hurting his brother." As far as we could tell, the maneuver of alliance worked out successfully in actual life.

Roughness was again encountered in the path toward maturity when Chatwell passed from small school to large university. During his freshman year at college he tried a number of extracurricular activities to which his verbal and social skills seemed well adapted, but he withdrew from each with a feeling that it was run by a clique or in some other way controlled so as to minimize his own chances of success. In retrospect he realized that he had had bad trouble being a small frog in a big puddle. As we have seen, he did not fully resolve this difficulty during his college years, but he was far from being a discontented isolate. Throughout college he read three or four books a week, mostly serious books that had nothing to do with his courses. The knowledge gained from this reading was quickly transformed into table conversation and debates with his acquaintances and instructors. Life really seemed worth while to him when he was using his wits in verbal contest, and he regretted only that when these battles took place in the classroom he had to let the instructor appear to win. His jobs sometimes served as a real source of amusement and gratification. He was one of the most valuable young men on the list at the student employment office because he would try anything and usually carry it off with distinction. He was particularly happy when the job called for argument, persuasion, sales talk, management, and varied human contacts. One job that especially delighted him involved securing participants for a high school radio program; he had to persuade pupils, teachers, principals, superintendents, even school committees, then organize the volunteers and take them to the studio.

During his college years Chatwell's most significant emotional relationships were with his girls. When we first knew him as a sophomore he was in love, and in his written autobiography he used this relationship as his chief example of the really great experiences, the "ecstatic moments" of life. In contrast to the verbal competitiveness of his relation to other young men, his thoughts about his girl revolved around peaceful situations and cooperative endeavor. "She typifies home and rest," he wrote, "and a working partnership in some duty to society that we two can perform better than anyone else." The romance did not long prosper. The girl was "carried off her feet" and swept out of Chatwell's grasp by a more aggressive suitor. From this experience he learned that it did not pay to be too much an "abject slave," especially with the active and somewhat independent girls who interested him more than the "clinging vines." Thereafter he blended somewhat more of the "cave man" into his behavior. When he finally met his present wife, however, and was "sunk without firing a shot," as he expressed it, he again found the peaceful element exerting a strong appeal. He even worried a little as to whether he was not unduly influenced by the feeling of security she gave him. "I like busy days," he said, "but then I like a place where I can take my shoes off." Nevertheless it was clear that he had found someone who represented more than home and rest. "For the first time," he said, "I got an intellectual and emotional and all the kinds of response that I wanted, all at once." He pursued his courtship actively, and at length persuaded this girl to become his wife.

By the time of the present study Chatwell had found that his role as a husband and father was severely restricted by the combined pressure of his work and study. It was in fact largely to give him more hours at home that he moved his family to the city apartment. Married life was a source of satisfaction even when he could not spare it much time and energy. His wife came from a social background roughly equivalent to his own. She shared his values and ultimate goals and was willing to put up with temporary inconvenience on the way to those goals. He described her as a "rare combination of intelligence, tenderness, and physical attractiveness," spoke of the "complete confidence between us," and stated that all bickering was quickly made up so that no lasting resentments clouded the relationship. As for the children, "we both love them and wanted to have them," and they proved one of the "best bargains" he ever encountered: "it has such a good effect on one's ego to know that there is someone in the world who thinks that you are just perfect."

Chatwell's choice of an occupation, postponed during his college years and finally made only after his return from military service, seemed to be proving uncommonly happy. When he was about 14 one of his aunts suggested that he go into patent law. As a sophomore he still gave this as his goal. He clung to the choice with a certain sense of mission because of his father's unfortunate history of losing the profits of his inventions to unscrupulous business men. "As a small boy," he recalled, "I always had some idea of vindicating my father's injuries." Chatwell's boredom in college turned him against the idea of further study, and during those parts of his military career that permitted daydreaming his thoughts dwelled more on a small business as a manufacturing chemist or some similar application of science. He was particularly intrigued by the idea of a small self-sufficient farm which was to include a small manufactory for added interest and income. On his return to the United States he seriously investigated the possibilities, but neither the farm nor the small manufactory seemed likely to yield support for his growing family. Under these circumstances he turned again to patent law. Partly through personal contacts in Wellfield he was presently in a position to choose between two jobs, both of which offered apprenticeship with salary while he went through evening law school. He rejected the job in the patent department of a large manufacturing corporation and chose the one with a small firm of patent attorneys in private practice. The reason he gave for this choice was that after his experience in the Army he valued independence more than security.

His current life was the source of great satisfaction. About his legal training and his work at the office he wrote as follows:

> The school is wonderful. For the first time in my life I find myself looking forward to classes. I believe that I am at or near the head of my class. The case method was made for me. I am in my element when it comes to tearing a case apart and finding out what makes it tick. And, as you know, I am not unaffected by the sound of my own voice, and therefore I get a big kick out of the class discussions.
>
> As though that weren't enough, I am equally enthusiastic about my work. One day it may be a helicopter, the next day paint, the next electronics, the next an abstruse point of law. Here, rolled into one, are the ancient wisdom of the law, calling for scholarship; the fringe of scientific development, to stimulate the imagination; and constant strife and argument to exact care and method from my disorderly soul. I think

you might have had to go far afield to prescribe a better dose for me than this one.

The social aspect was hardly less satisfactory. The men in the office, all older than Chatwell, formed a congenial group and treated him with more consideration than he felt he deserved. The office itself was the scene of stimulating but friendly arguments, also of moments of relaxation and coffee-drinking. To some extent his business and social worlds overlapped, some members of the firm being also residents of Wellfield. After Chatwell moved to the city his social orbit was practically confined to his business and law school associates.

The Personal Setting of Chatwell's Opinions

Our task now is to try to formulate the effective traits and forces in Chatwell's personality, with a view to understanding more fully the formation of his opinions. The plan we adopted for our conferences and case summaries calls for grouping our findings under three main headings. First comes a survey of *capacities and traits.* It is obviously impossible to talk at present about innate, structurally determined, and therefore basic traits. We have in mind rather the kind of datum that is yielded by tests of intelligence and aptitude, and the kind of appraisal that can be made from the individual's history of performance in situations requiring leadership, business skill, friendship, mechanical skill, aesthetic sensitivity, persistence, emotional control, and so forth. We do not assume that existing capacities and traits are innate, unchangeable, or insulated from the sphere of motivation, but we do assume that their neglect would leave our account of the person confusingly incomplete. Next comes a consideration of *basic strivings,* in which we undertake to work out the history of such commonly important tendencies as sex and aggression, dependence and autonomy, nurture, recognition, and achievement. Assuming that urges in these directions are the usual result of development, we try to account, through the subject's particular history and present circumstances, for the individual pattern of strengths and weaknesses that is revealed in the record. The third area, that of *adjustive strategies,* contains our analysis of the tactics and techniques that the subject has built up as more or less habitual ways of overcoming obstacles, coping with dangers, and advancing his fortunes. This plan of exposition will permit us to indicate at several points the important relationships between Chatwell's personality and his opinions.

Capacities and traits. On the *Wechsler-Bellevue Adult Intelligence Test* Chatwell had an I.Q. of 142, the highest of the ten subjects. This

figure places him in the highest one per cent of the general population
and well up in the college population. Evidences of unusual conceptual ability were confirmed in the *Vigotsky Test*, the report on
which stated that he manifested the "highest level of abstract thinking,"
a "quick and effective interplay of thinking and acting," and an "elegant
precision of performance that was a pleasure to watch." The two
Rorschach Tests, given nearly eight years apart, were remarkably similar in overall result though different in detail. Both showed zest and
energy in the production of many excellent responses. In both there
was emphasis on details and a versatile and flexible way of handling
them, while whole responses were largely neglected. In view of other
results the lack of whole response could hardly be construed as signify-
ing poor capacity for abstract thinking. It seemed to stem rather from
a desire to control the material, to choose less obvious parts on which
he could exercise his ingenuity. Certain limitations could be detected
in his originality, which expressed itself in selecting and cutting out
rather than in combining or giving the material an unusual content.
He might be described as breezing through the test with little dwelling
on responses, little absorption in the material. If there was any difference between the two records it lay to the credit of the second,
which could be characterized as less careless and better disciplined
than the undergraduate performance.

As a senior in college Chatwell took the Graduate Record Examination, a test essentially of acquired and retained knowledge. He stood
well above the average college senior not only in his field of concentra-
tion but in all seven of the fields of knowledge covered by the test.
In at least two of these fields his score was well in the range of students
accepted for graduate work. The credit for this showing must go not
so much to his courses, which he took lightly, but to his extensive
outside reading and his habit of translating each topic of interest into
a discussion and argument with his acquaintances. He demonstrated
great facility in picking up and retaining information on all kinds of
subjects. His delight in argument had been shown at least as early
as his geometry class in upper school, where the instructor called him
a nuisance for arguing so much. That it sometimes became an end in
itself was apparent from the following conversation:

E: Incidentally, it would interest me to know if you ever take the unpopular side of an argument just to raise hell.

S: Oh, I'm quite sure I do. I don't know if I've ever consciously done
that, but I've found myself in it many, many times without any
apparent reason, which amounts to the same thing.

E: Have you ever taken a position that you actually disagreed with, just to argue?

S: Not consciously, but I think I've certainly done it many times unconsciously. I *like* to argue.

In both *Rorschach* performances there was felt to be a certain lack of emotional warmth and depth. Intellectual ingenuity took precedence over emotional expression. From the *Rorschach Test* alone it might be inferred that Chatwell's unusual capacity for intellectual control, and his pleasure in utilizing that capacity, made for a stable adjustment but constricted somewhat the operation of deeper feeling and fantasy. His performance in the *Thematic Apperception Test* gave further evidence of the dominance of intellectual control. There was little dwelling on the emotional possibilities of the plots; rather, he tossed off clever, well-organized, sometimes flippant stories which as often as not were left incomplete or brought to a facile ending through coincidence or gratuitous circumstance. One must be guarded, however, in making inferences from these findings, especially in view of the fact that Chatwell was not wholly naive about the purpose of projective tests. His description elsewhere of the experience of being in love provides telling evidence that the realms of feeling were not always constricted.

Our direct investigation of affective traits yielded evidence for a considerable capacity to control disruptive emotion. Anger for Chatwell was "a cold dead calm," not without autonomic manifestations. He liked to be calm when anyone else was angry; indeed, a recent angry and tactless outbreak at one of his teachers in law school had convinced him that he was alarmingly overtired and in need of the change which the visit to Cambridge provided. Anxiety was a familiar experience to him in connection with important situations, such as a football game during his school days, or currently an important interview, one example being our own *Stress Interview*. Under such circumstances he experienced gastric tightness, a dry mouth, and great restlessness, and he was apt to smoke very fast. He declared himself able to deal with these anxieties rationally and talk himself out of them.

We can now indicate an important connection between Chatwell's capacities and his opinions. His mind was quick, flexible, versatile; he retained large quantities of information, and his thinking was facile not only concretely but at the highest levels of abstraction. His opinions about Russia drew two characteristics from his equipment: he was extremely well-informed even though Russia was not one of his main concerns, and he differentiated several aspects of Russia, attaching a different object value to each. The facility with which his mind could operate encouraged both argument and reflection, and these in turn contributed to an articulate organization of his opinions. Chatwell was able to hold sophisticated and differentiated opinions about Russia and this at once distinguishes him from several of our subjects for whom a like mental task would have been probably impossible, certainly distasteful. His ability to attach different values was assisted by the generalized predominance of intellectual control over feeling. He was able, for instance, to approve fully of the Russian leaders in their nation-building activities while disagreeing violently with their policies toward neighbor nations. Both here and elsewhere in his life his affects tended to follow the dictates of his reason.

Turning now to traits of a less intellectual character, we have noted already that Chatwell was physically light but energetic. He declared himself not an athlete, but he had taught swimming at camps and was a good walker and climber. He was always competent with tools, having started early to build radios in his father's workshop. He was an active enjoyer of music and literature, could improvise at the piano, and had tried his hand at writing short stories and essays. In a series of very diverse jobs held during his college years, and in varied military assignments, he showed the versatility and verve that might be inferred from our account of his mental traits. He was well accustomed to approaching new tasks with confidence, throwing himself into them, and achieving success.

This aspect of his career engendered feelings of well-being, self-confidence, and optimism which also left their mark upon his opinions. He felt no qualms about American intentions in Greece, which some of our subjects found distinctly disquieting, and he had high hopes for negotiation and debate. Yet he was not unaware of his personal limitations. Reducing sharply in the present study the extravagant self-rating he had earlier given himself on leadership, he said:

> I've come to realize that in certain kinds of men it's better than in intellectual men. The ability to act promptly. It's not so easy for a person who is analytic to act easily.

Similarly the confidence that characterized his orientation and policy stand with respect to Russia was tempered by considerations of American frailty. He expected that we would do no better than "muddle through" the coming years.

Basic strivings. The strivings that received the strongest impetus from Chatwell's parents were those associated with growing up and being mature. The pressure was in the direction of self-sufficiency and independent accomplishment, with emphasis also on investigation and discussion. The values of gregariousness were less stressed; in fact, there was some shielding from early contacts with children of lower social status. Definitely discouraged were the dependent tendencies: the needs for loving care, comfort in distress, guidance, help in overcoming anxieties. These remained as residual tensions in a personality organized along lines of independent achievement.

The predominant pattern of strivings received further significant shaping as Chatwell tried out his capacities and skills and learned the channels that would lead him to satisfaction. One of the channels he entered was football, but his light weight and fear of injury prevented this from being a real source of gratification. Another channel was argument, and here the gratification was so high that the love of argument became one of the strongest driving forces in his personality. The assertiveness that could not succeed in athletic channels found in discussion and debate an admirable route toward its goals. In a sophomore story-completion Chatwell symbolized this phase of his own development. Given the plot that a football player was not equalling his famous father on the gridiron, Chatwell had the boy realize that he would never be a good player, but then come to feel that the whole sport was organized wrong; so he "suddenly threw himself wholeheartedly into modifying the system, and found that he had just the qualifications for doing this successfully." Politics, persuasion, and human management increasingly appealed to him. In such a role Chatwell won his school success; for the lack of it he was at loose ends in college; resuming it again, he achieved success and rapid advancement in military service.

It is important to see precisely what was involved in this central pattern of strivings. A prominent element was *recognition*, the need to receive the esteem and praise of others, particularly well satisfied in his teaching positions in the service and in his work in the patent law office. His demands in this respect were very high. We have already noted that he explained his delight in his children by mentioning their admiration for him. He tended to lose interest in a line of activity that brought only slow or moderate appreciation, but his ability to work hard for recognition resulted in his obtaining from time to time an amount that equalled what he wanted. Another element we might call *competitive aggressiveness*, a need to surpass rivals and to disparage with no little sarcasm their errors and irrationalities. His private arguments, his work at the law school, and his preparation of cases yielded particular gratification for this part of his striving.

The atmosphere of his home seemed to have been always favorable to the expression of verbal aggression, the outlets being sufficient to keep him from building up resentful tension and hatred. He claimed to be able to "tell a person to go to hell" under almost any circumstances. Still another element was a need to *understand,* an inquiring curiosity which doubtless owed something to the constant example and stimulation of his father's restlessly searching intellect and his mother's scientific interests. Even though Chatwell confessed to occasional argument for the sake of argument, he was not one of those who wants to win regardless of the merit of his cause. On the contrary, he attached great importance to having all the facts, and this doubtless helps to explain his unusual retentiveness. He included this element of his central pattern of motives when asked to describe "what sort of people you admire most or would like most to be like":

> I admire proficiency and competency. I like to read a good opinion or hear a good argument or see a man do a good job of teaching, or do anything well. . . .
> I like to see a man stick his neck out. And I like to see a man who has figured the angles, too. I always enjoy seeing a man who has really thought a problem out and hasn't overlooked anything. I generally feel a little contemptuous of a fellow who makes a pronouncement or adopts a course of action or something of that sort, where there is some fairly obvious factor in the situation that he has either overlooked or discounted that destroys the validity of the position or course he has adopted.

We are probably not wrong in ascribing to Chatwell's need for understanding an even broader significance. Useful in argument, it was further vital as a generalized means of mastering the unknown by rationality.

Chatwell's success-crowned central pattern of motives thus included a number of important satisfactions: he gained recognition, he exercised competitive aggressiveness, and he satisfied curiosity and the search for understanding. Let us consider now some of the things that were *not* satisfied, that were somewhat crowded out by his very success along the central line. One of these, oddly enough, was a feeling of *productivity* in the rather special sense of the creation or extraction of some valuable commodity. In spite of his happiness in legal work, he complained about its possibly parasitic character.

> We're parasites, to a certain extent, and from that point of view there's a little dissatisfaction in the back of my mind, and some day I think I might like to do a little manufacturing or farming or just something that's productive, you see, that's purely productive. . . .
> I recognize that the role of the lawyer is necessary in a complex society,

and I enjoy the work.   But there still is the fact that you can't eat what
the lawyer makes . . . right away.   You have to change it into something else first. . . .
   I think that it probably grows out of the fact that I've had this idea
of economic independence and self-sufficiency and that I haven't by any
means dropped that idea.

Another insufficiently satisfied desire was *independence,* a wish to
be self-sufficient and free to act as he pleased without hindrance from
the needs and interference of others.   It is surprising, in view of the
large amount of personal freedom found in his actual life, that there
should still have been residual tension on this score.   Obviously he
did not take to the restraints of military service, which greatly increased
his liking for an individualistic way of life, but his daily round as law
school student and law clerk seemed admirably suited to satisfy even
a rather uncompromising advocate of personal freedom.   Nevertheless
Chatwell chafed a little under such restraints as existed, and liked
to imagine a more perfect state of independence.

The incompletely satisfied urges toward productivity and independence found interesting expression in his fantasy of a small self-sufficient
farm.   This fantasy was of long standing.   Even as a sophomore, long
before military service appeared on his horizon, he told us about the
small independent economic unit which he hoped might later become
his home and occupation.   Its self-sufficiency was emphasized by the
detail that it would have a brook with a fall of water sufficient to
operate a generating plant for the whole farm.   As we have seen, this
fantasy developed during his military service, to the point that after
discharge he investigated the possibilities for turning it into a reality.
He continued to be fascinated by the idea of small decentralized units.
In the *Stress Interview* he said:

   Take the question of power—light and heat.   I think that our endeavors,
   our scientific and practical endeavors, would be far better channeled into
   the production of a small unit that could supply those things to the
   home, for example, that the individual could own and thus emancipate
   himself from the utility company. . . .
   I would be much happier in the type of democracy or republic that,
   from an economic point of view, Jefferson contemplated, a nation of small
   freeholders.   That's my idea of the way to live.
   I believe that the interdependence that we all have is the thing that
   makes us fear-ridden, hag-ridden. . . . And so that's why I say I would
   prefer us, even at a lower level of physical existence, but with the
   security that comes from knowing that that same level at least will be
   available to us, no matter what happens to somebody else.   That our
   level of living is not dependent on the group decisions of everybody else,
   the way it is now.

It is significant that he gave these most extreme statements of his interest in self-sufficiency when he was under pressure in the *Stress Interview*. Certainly his guard was down when he expressed such opinions to interviewers momentarily bent on shattering his defense of the American as opposed to the Russian system. But this lapse from his usual argumentative skill testifies all the more strongly to the emotional importance these ideas possessed for him.

While we cannot fully reconstruct the history of Chatwell's interest in productivity and independence, it is possible to point out certain features of his earlier life that probably strengthened these tendencies. Mention was previously made of the early impetus he received toward adopting the role of eldest, grown-up child. We notice now that he characterizes dependence as a source of anxiety and conflict, a thing that makes us "fear-ridden, hag-ridden." This suggests that in childhood Chatwell rejected dependence not only out of pride and a wish to sustain the role expected of him, but also because of frustrations, anxieties, and angers which dependence entailed for him. He became definitely soured on dependence and correspondingly fortified in the roles of self-sufficiency and independence that remained available. We notice further that his interest in productivity seemed to carry with it a certain fear of being useless and therefore inferior. The origin of his uneasy feeling that lawyers might be parasites lay possibly in the opinions and experiences of his father, the productive inventor whose profits were stolen by middlemen. Another influence might have been his comparative lack of success in football, and a feeling that in turning to verbal lines of excellence he still did not measure up to the more "real" achievements of his brother and the other boys. In his undergraduate days he often felt the uselessness of his clever argumentativeness; in contrast, after the war he particularly mentioned the satisfaction of going into the jungle and with his own mind and hands transforming a piece of it into a habitable military installation. It was perhaps the college experience that most strongly turned him against verbal symbolic manipulation and that left him with a residue of discontent when later the most available profession was one that operated mainly through verbal channels.

These basic strivings were reflected in several ways in Chatwell's opinions. His central pattern of successful strivings particularly colored his orientation and policy stand toward Russia. He advocated an active course of argument, persuasion, negotiation, and human management. Alike in his everyday life and in his international policy he showed no fear of competition. Argument should be from a position of strength, but Chatwell was well versed through personal experience in building positions of argumentative strength, and he had no difficulty in assigning such a position to the United States.

His concern with productivity and independence put its stamp on his opinions in a somewhat different fashion. The passion for independence colored his theory of taxation, which called for heavy inheritance taxes but the smallest possible tax burdens on individual earnings. It influenced his views on decentralization, where a Jeffersonian ideal which resembled his fantasy of the private self-sufficient farm pushed him at times toward rather extreme general statements. Yet the pressure of this somewhat importunate need was not so great as to threaten reality testing. Plans for the private farm had been made to confront realities and had been discarded; similarly, Chatwell's views on specific domestic policies, such as TVA and federal aid to education, did not conform to the Jeffersonian ideal. His sharp rejection of dependence, symbolized by his views on inheritance taxes in the United States, helps us to understand both his lack of interest in Russia as a welfare state and his quick subordinating of religious problems to those of individual freedom. His feelings about productivity in his personal life find their parallel in his insistence upon citizen participation in government as contrasted with irresponsible criticism. And he was the only one of our subjects who perceived as a major aspect of Russia her opportunity and her task to develop a great productive economy.

Adjustive strategies. An appraisal of Chatwell's current adjustive techniques must begin with recognition of his *initiative* and *enterprise*. While an undergraduate he was willing to take on any kind of job suggested by the student employment office. His military career was similarly marked by initiative in volunteering for assignments and calling himself to the attention of officers. On discharge he seriously investigated quite a few job possibilities and was not backward in suggesting that he might be valuable. Both in law school and in the office he was energetic and forth-putting, leaving few stones unturned when interested in a case.

Chatwell's initiative was by no means an empty gesture. Once having taken the necessary first steps he went on to carry off the task with considerable success. The clue to this adjustive process lay in his versatile and flexible *rational mastery* of the task at hand, coupled often with a skill in *self-dramatization.* Having volunteered as an instructor in basic training, for example, he hurled himself into the task, drew on his well-stored memory and also boned up on the subject he was teaching, devised teaching aids and tests, and quickly became the capable person he had asserted himself to be when he volunteered for the job. In general it was through his mental and verbal gifts that he mastered the situations he got into. His use of these gifts was little if at all impaired by feelings of inferiority or of anxiety.

The technique of *rational mastery*, with its emphasis on reality testing, served admirably for most of the situations of life. We had occasion, however, to observe Chatwell attempting to use this technique in a wholly inappropriate situation, namely, the hour of *Free Association*. The transcript shows that he discussed the price structure for fifteen minutes and the structure and physiology of the hand for considerably longer. By worrying these topics to death he maintained constant control over the course of thought and thus minimized the chances that his associations would be guided by irrational forces. This striking illustration of an adjustive strategy run wild showed how deeply he depended upon the vigilant scouting activity of his intellect as a means of forestalling dangers. So far as we could observe, the threat in free association was not the particular content that might emerge; on other occasions he discussed freely some topics that he evaded here. What seemed to threaten him most was the instruction to lay aside control over his thought processes and thus cancel the operation of his most cherished adjustive technique.

A man who displays initiative and enterprise, who is gifted and experienced in rational mastery, and who rises to challenging situations with colorful self-dramatization, can take a good many things in his stride. At 28 Chatwell had achieved an efficient adjustive technique, a "style of life" which had proved successful under a variety of circumstances. It was a great asset in understanding him that we had known him at an earlier period, when he was still feeling his way and having a certain difficulty in getting his bearings. His behavior as an undergraduate revealed much more clearly the struggle to overcome weaknesses in himself and the avoidance of certain activities that might put him to a dangerous test. Some of the situations that provoked anxiety he met with energetic *counteraction*. He forced himself to learn high diving, just as earlier he had forced himself to play football and still earlier to control his cry-baby tendencies, by disregarding his anxiety or talking himself out of it. Having had an accident while learning to drive a car, he forced himself to continue driving until he could do so without fear. He was uneasy at first about girls and love-making, but this fear too he counteracted by actively seeking female company and by becoming more of a "cave man" after rejection. Sometimes mastering anxiety proved to be the main motive behind an activity, so that his interest lapsed as soon as he attained a feeling of ease. His high level of self-confidence was far less soundly established than we judged it to be in the second study. Furthermore, as an undergraduate he was more inclined to utilize *avoidance* when a situation presented difficulties or could not be mastered quickly. We have already mentioned his withdrawal from freshman activities when he found that the role of big frog was unavailable. The summer before he went to college he made quite a mess of a sales job, and also sponged on friends by living at their home all summer when his parents supposed him to be supporting himself and living at the YMCA. There was also evidence for considerable use of *repression*, especially in earlier stages of his history. His denial that family bickering upset him and his exclusion of quarrelsome or conflictful plots from projective material involving families, suggested that repression had served him in some of the emotional trials of childhood.

The success of Chatwell's strategies of initiative and enterprise disposed him, we can easily believe, to look with special favor on an economic system that demanded and rewarded these virtues. He admired the ideal of a free competitive economy, for example free bargaining between labor and management, even though his views on specific issues added up to a substantial departure from this ideal. His interest in rational mastery had its parallel in his vision of a strengthened United Nations, wherein the member states, bound by a legal framework that would ensure fair play, would argue their causes and negotiate their claims. Chatwell was bitterly opposed to confusion. He deplored Russian tactics in neighbor states because they deliberately created confusion and prevented rational decisions. His strongest insistence, in international affairs as well as in free association, was that things should be kept at the level of rationality, where he was willing to face any challenge.

Opinion Maintenance and Furtherance

Chatwell's opinions were not easily swayed by the bombardment of information and argument to which his gregariousness and wide reading exposed him. To most sources of information he felt equal if not superior. Asked if he used newspaper material in arguments, he said:

> I never use editorials to back myself up in an argument. I always consider that my opinion is at least as good as the editor's. I sometimes refer to some fact which has been reported.

After discussing a number of columnists he swept them all off the board with the following statement:

> Every once in a while one of them writes something about something that I happen to know something about, and that really fixes me because

I find that their ignorance on those subjects is so appalling, and their pronouncements are so majestic, that I have to discount what they say on any subject.

He had no patience with what he called the "rabidly reactionary" columnists and editorial writers, and generally skipped their "trash." Ordinarily he did not read papers or magazines representing leftist views or even standing for the interests of labor, but his contempt for anything "rabid" applied equally to material from these sources. His mind was by no means closed to differences of opinion, however, when these were presented at his preferred level of intellectual detachment. His insistence on rationality was shown in the comment he made about Pegler:

> Once in a while he states a sentiment that I subscribe to, but it's generally in such unreasonable terms that, even if I agree with it, it makes me rather disgusted.

Only one newspaper commanded his complete respect. This one appealed to him for its high intellectual calibre, and also for its nonpartisan effort to present all the news that is fit to print and all sides of a controversial issue.

Chatwell's opinions were never shaken by information that he could consider biased or by arguments that did not meet his standard of rationality. The greatest source of threat lay in well reasoned arguments from a little to the right of his own position. His vulnerability in this direction came partly from the fact that his immediate associates were somewhat to his right, partly from some of his own sentiments, such as his passion for decentralization, which were not incongruent with more rightist policies. Chatwell was indeed under a certain pressure, identified as he was becoming with the law firm, to swing in a rightist direction. In the past he had never been one to alter his views in the interests of conformity. Quite the contrary, his critical and competitive attitude, and his lack of identification with groups, made the formation of his opinions a highly individual enterprise. He had only gradually learned to keep still when there was no hope of persuading others. This technique of silence was already beginning to serve him at the office. The atmosphere there was definitely favorable to discussion, but Chatwell knew well enough that the senior partner objected violently to every feature of Russia and to most features of our domestic policy since 1933. In the office his views on Russia seemed distinctly pink and his acceptance of the TVA experiment a dangerous concession to the principle of the welfare state. Under these circumstances he found himself airing his opinions on

Russia less often, his views on the price system and free market more often. He denied, however, that his own opinions had changed.

In general, then, Chatwell's usual defense of his opinions was conducted partly by judicious avoidance of arguments in certain quarters but mainly by a highly critical attitude toward material presented and toward the prestige of its sources. In spite of this, he read a great deal, exposing himself to whatever information came through the channels he considered worthy. The investigators naturally tried to circumvent his usual techniques for opinion maintenance on the subject of Russia by thrusting new information before him, assailing him with cartoons, and challenging the consistency of his statements. He was not easily flustered, becoming really angry only when he felt that he was being misrepresented and stereotyped as a "corporation lawyer." New information he treated in his usual way, questioning its credentials and criticizing its implications if these conflicted with his own ideas. Cartoons he rejected, whichever side they took, with a searching analysis of their oversimplification and misrepresentation. Criticism he met by a lively attempt to clarify his position and improve its consistency. Occasionally he was cornered and driven to flat assertions that he believed such-and-such to be so and that he might be wrong, but the investigators had to be content with rather small success in their attempts to break through his prepared positions and force him into more improvised methods of defense.

An example of his handling of information was the following response, given to the item, "The Russian Church now holds services in the Soviet Union though most of the worshippers are older people":

S: There is a moral question there, but it is not a new idea to me. The moral code is introduced by the word "now." It implies a restriction of activities previous to that time which I, as a matter of principle, oppose. As a practical matter, I view the statement in context. The fact that it now holds services does not mean that there is religious freedom. The picture is clouded because I realize there isn't religious freedom. I disapprove of that, though it isn't directly stated in the thing.

E: Does the item make you think better or worse of Russia?

S: No, not worse. It actually states an improvement in the situation of which I have been cognizant for some time. I had my reaction to these statements some time back. They are now a part of my set. In all fairness, the fact that there was an increase, assuming it was true, and if I was convinced of its truth, I'd say it was a good thing. Of course, the further problem is the motive of the government. I wonder why Stalin is administering drugs at this time. It may be that the doctor thinks the patient needs drugs.

He challenged the truth of the statement, challenged its motive and meaning if true, told the examiner it was old stuff anyway, and thus parried any possible implication that his views on tyranny in Russia needed moderation. Equally devastating was his analysis of a cartoon which showed a monkey (satellite state), its leash leading to an organ-grinder (Stalin) whose hands were full of money, begging from a citizen (American public) who held a newspaper proclaiming domestic shortages:

> Well, this is one that's got a fundamental economic misconception built into it; that is, giving dollars to foreign countries leads to a decrease in the number of dollars in the United States. The real fact is that the increased purchasing power of the foreign nations means more goods are going out of the country and resulting in shortages. The second thing is that it shows Stalin and the monkey with lots of dollars in their pockets, which isn't true. But if it shows the confusion of the American citizen about sending dollars out of the country and shortages in this country, it's true, because no doubt the average American citizen is confused about it.

In such wise Chatwell maintained his opinions against challenges. His methods of defense were not so rigid as to preclude gradual change. His eagerness for new information and his zest for argument combined to keep his opinions flexible and related to contemporary events. Rational argument was his chief technique for furthering his views. Inclination, practice, and legal training combined to make him a formidable champion of what he believed.

It is of interest to speculate concerning the way his opinions about Russia might change if events took certain possible courses. For example, if the Russian attempt to extend the boundaries of Communism took a sharply militant and threatening form we would predict that his antagonism would rapidly increase and that he would favor vigorous defense. A Russian change in this direction would engage two important values, independence and rational (legal) procedure, both of which would heighten his opposition. At the same time we would expect him to advocate operation through the legally established channels of the United Nations, and we would anticipate that he would be among the last to accept wartime restrictions on individual liberties in his own country. Increased stress would probably touch off his value of active participation so that he would willingly accept a share in the defensive enterprise and even press his services. His conception of the national purpose would not include the destruction of Russia and Communism but rather their firm incorporation in a greatly strengthened international state.

In the event of a prolonged "cold war," irritating but not acutely threatening, a good many influences would operate to keep Chatwell in about his present position. No matter how prolonged the irritation, it would be very difficult to interest him in a preventive war, which he would perceive as an infringement upon Russia's right to be left alone and as a lapse on our part from standards of rational and legal procedure. Furthermore, inasmuch as "rabid reactionaries" tend to infuriate him, he would remain constantly critical of proposals from their quarter, searching relentlessly for irrationality in their appeals. Exposed as he is more directly to the "rabid right" than to the "rabid left," it is even likely that a trend toward Fascism in America would offend him more than any behavior by the Russians that was less than acutely threatening. Antagonism toward reactionaries would not, however, cause him to take sides more strongly with the Russians. This could happen only if Russia abandoned plans for expansion and the spreading of Communism in favor of the task of developing herself as a self-sufficient and productive nation.

A Functional Summing-Up

It is now time to gather up our study of Chatwell and his opinions into the categories proposed in Chapter 3 for making a functional analysis. We distinguished there between the *expressive* nature of opinions and their *adjustive* nature, dividing the latter in turn into *object appraisal, social adjustment,* and *externalization.*

Under the first heading, the *expressive nature of opinions,* we refer not to the expression of needs or purposes but to the way the opinions reflect the more general conditions of temperament, capacity, and acquired personality structure. Chatwell's opinions were in this sense an expression of his mental abilities and of other relevant traits, quite apart from their content and their relation to the satisfaction of his strivings. The outstanding fact is his intellectual competence, which constantly encouraged both argument and reflection. He was well informed, he differentiated several aspects of Russia, he attached different object value to these aspects, and he managed a coherent organization of his opinion as a whole. In all of this he was assisted by a strong intellectual control over feeling. His opinions further reflect the self-confidence engendered by a successful and versatile career, somewhat tempered, however, by a growing appreciation of his own and other people's limitations.

Turning now to the *adjustive nature of opinions,* we first consider Chatwell's opinions about Russia as subserving his needs for *object appraisal.* In the most general sense, a person appraises reality in order to anticipate and prepare for the benefits and harms it holds in store for him. Chatwell's orientation reflected the usual motives of wanting to make a living and achieve security, but his demands did not stop at that point. He needed to find a reality that permitted and called for the free exercise of talent and initiative, that offered choice and change, that would give him the feeling of being able to work enjoyably while accomplishing things of value and distinction. He hoped, in short, that reality would be congenial to the kind of person his early life and situation had allowed him to become. Threats lay in everything that might block him, entangle him, subordinate him, prevent the free egress of his energies. Large portions of reality seemed dedicated to propositions that offered little scope to a person making his demands. Even if he had not had the example of his inquiring parents and the encouragement of his college training, he would have been strongly motivated to understand the not altogether inviting world of his adulthood.

This was perhaps the most general reason for his having a strong urge toward object appraisal. His solution of the problem was embodied in a system of values in which personal liberty and freedom of enterprise were cherished to the utmost that was compatible with security. While by no means overlooking the welfare functions of the modern state, he did not believe that state action should go to the point of hampering individual urges toward invention and productiveness. The abuses of a competitive system he felt could be controlled by properly established legal arrangements all the way from the local to the international scene. These opinions represented a cognitive structure into which his aspirations could be fitted. They led to a discriminated pattern of attitudes toward Russia: he espoused her right to develop her productive economy in her own way, free from outside interference, but he deplored the police state, the suppression of individual initiative, and the forceful, illegal methods of dealing with neighbor countries.

This general urge toward object appraisal was from an early period supported by a more specific motive, that of control through rational mastery. The more sharply cognitive element in this process, the stress on perceiving reality and making it rational, probably had roots in his family's tendency to argue freely on a variety of questions, arguments which were just upsetting enough to challenge his best intellectual efforts. As his skill in debate increased, he began to utilize it with teachers and contemporaries. To acquit himself well in discussion he must be posted as to the facts; he must have "figured all the angles." The effect of constantly exposing his views to social correction was to stimulate in him a zeal for useful information and a desire to make his apprehension of reality inclusive and consistent. On two counts Chatwell did not want to be fooled. He did not want to make a false estimate of the world's congeniality to his purposes lest his whole plan of life come to naught. He did not want to make a false appraisal of existing facts lest he make himself ridiculous in debate.

The service of Chatwell's opinions in *social adjustment* was probably less important than their function in object appraisal. The most common way in which opinions promote social adjustment is through conformity, when the individual adopts or develops opinions harmonious with those of an important membership or reference group. While Chatwell shared the traditional values of Western liberal culture as transmitted through his parents and their community, conformity of opinions to membership groups played scarcely any further part in his highly individual way of life. Even in the office where he worked he conceded little more than a tactful silence on certain red-rag issues without much change in inner conviction. At all times, however, starting in his school days, he used his opinions as a means of establishing his competitive dominance among his peers. Through argument and debate he established a place in the eyes of his teachers as well as in the eyes of his contemporaries. Verbal competitive aggression was probably his prepotent motive in relation to peers of the same sex. His opinions were therefore part of his equipment for obtaining the kind of social adjustment he most craved. For this purpose it was all the better if they did not agree with those of others; the only requirement was that he have opinions and that they be defensible. He used the same technique in working over the offerings of authorities and thus establishing his place in relation to them.

Chatwell's opinions seem to have been distorted to only a minor degree by the *externalization* of inner problems. His perception of the world followed in general the demands of his major expressed strivings rather than of unresolved inner tensions. His faith in legal arrangements and legal procedure, at all levels including the international, was probably strengthened by his favorite adjustive strategy in personal life, rational mastery, and thus perhaps qualifies as an externalization of the problem of maintaining control over disruptive impulses. Apart from this possibility, the two tendencies that showed the clearest evidence of residual tension were independence and productivity. Both combined to produce a fantasy of a small autonomous farm-and-manufacturing unit the operator of which could be maximally free and productive. Probably Chatwell's interest in political and economic decentralization received substantial support from the needs expressed in this fantasy, as did his picture of the Russian people and the Russian enterprise of developing a great independent productive state. Probably his lack of interest in Russia as a welfare state can be traced in part to suppression of dependent needs in his own life. But on the whole there was no reason to assign to repressed needs or to defenses a major part in the shaping of his opinions.

In conclusion, our functional analysis convinces us that in Chatwell's case opinions about Russia received their strongest impetus from his needs for object appraisal. Urges in the direction of social adjustment were important but less influential, and the externalization of inner problems exerted a still less marked effect. In saying this we do not imply that his views were therefore more right or more valid than those of other subjects. An urge toward object appraisal does not guarantee faultless reality testing. The attempt to find the world hospitable to one's interests and skills may indeed end in a considerable falsification of things as they are. Our purpose was not to assess the correctness of Chatwell's opinions but rather to work out the relationships between them and his personality as a whole.

CHAPTER 7

CHARLES LANLIN

O NE cannot, either in a psychological or statistical sense, portray a representative man. Yet Charles Lanlin was a representative man in a way that was true neither of Chatwell nor Sullivan. His identifications were with the values and aspirations of the middle class and in considerable measure his inner security depended upon the approval and recognition of those who, in his view, shared the dominant values of the culture. Lanlin was particularly interesting to us for the illustration he provided of the manner in which conformity needs influence the formation and maintenance not only of political beliefs but also of essential personality mechanisms.

In the preceding chapter we sought to make clear that the analysis of a man's motives for holding a point of view could throw no light upon the validity of that point of view. At the risk of repetitiousness, we must remark that if one believes in the values of competitive business enterprise partly out of a need to conform to a dominant group in the community, one's belief is not thereby credited or discredited.

Lanlin's opinions on Russia and Communism were not intense and were by no means bulwarks in the structure of his personality. The main stream of his energies was directed toward matters much closer to his home and to his work. It is only insofar as Russia and Communism impinged upon these more personal spheres that our subject

113

felt intensely on these issues. As a result, Russia was viewed almost exclusively from the outside; the "threat of Russia" dominated his image of the Soviet Union and Communism while the rationale behind the threat remained shadowy to him. In this sense he is again, perhaps, more typical of the American public at large than our preceding case.

A last point of interest is worth highlighting. Where Sullivan, discussed in the next chapter, adhered to a position bitterly excoriated by the larger community, Lanlin rode the crest of a wave of popular abhorrence toward Russia. So well phalanxed was he by like-minded men and so well supported by the media of communication with which he had contact, that he scarcely needed to justify his position on Russia either to himself or to his fellows. He provides, then, a striking contrast to the other two men whose opinions we examine in detail.

Introductory Sketch

Charles Lanlin, a salesman of heating, cooking, and household appliances, was at the age of 42 the father of four children. He had served for nineteen years as a clerical worker in the appliance company which he had recently come to represent as a salesman at the time of our study. These years of clerical service had been a period of occupational dissatisfaction during which he felt he was "not being constructive." The last eight years of his clerical work were relieved by participation in union activity which did much to assuage his feelings of discontent. Prior to his service with his present employer he had worked briefly in a bank, which he disliked as "too gloomy," and before that in a manufacturing concern where he quit his job when he realized his unpopular position as a member of the Time Study Department.

Lanlin was a genial person whose progress through high school and on into a business trade-school was marked neither by difficulties nor by conspicuous success. Born into a Catholic family, he had maintained his faith and, while not a deeply religious man, was a faithful confessant. His salary, supplemented by income from property left him upon his father's death in 1935, yielded a total income of $5000. Lanlin had to watch his expenditures with some care in order to maintain his wife and four children in a modest house in a middle-class, outlying suburb of Boston. At the time of our study, he was in good health, although he still maintained a diet on which he had been placed eight years before when there had been some suspicion of gastric ulcer. Save for this uncertain incident, his health had never been a problem to him.

Lanlin was engaged as a subject in our investigation through a friend then active in the local labor circles in which our subject moved as a union official. He showed no reluctance to take part in the experiment when its purposes were explained and seemed throughout the course of the study to enjoy the opportunity provided for conversation.

Charles Lanlin gave the appearance of a well-fed, well-cared-for man in his forties. Somewhat heavy in physique and medium in stature, his general build was that of an athlete run to fat. One felt he was conscious of it and that he dressed to minimize the beginnings of a paunch. His complexion, moderately florid, fitted well the growing stoutness of his physique. Such words as "well padded," "sleek," and "bland" described him, although his face and body still had enough of youthful angularity to save him from looking conspicuously soft.

His approach to the world was a smiling one. He laughed and chuckled easily; he was the kind of person who enjoyed a joke—especially when he told it. His aim was to be cordial and pleasant in his contacts with others. Even in repose, his features had a vaguely smiling, if bland, cast. His gesturing too was rather vague and loosely knit. Somehow one had the impression that his face was not quite finished.

Our subject dressed for appearance, consciously so. The image on which he modelled himself was that of a prosperous junior executive. He confided to one interviewer that public speakers always wear double-breasted suits: "it gives you a smooth front." Smooth fabrics of light though modest shades were his favorites; he was almost exclusively given to bow ties. In the months we observed him, he never appeared to be in need of either a pressing, a shine, a haircut, or a change of linen. Yet he was not overdressed.

A highly talkative man, Lanlin's speech nonetheless fell short of simple and conjunctive discourse. His conversations ran to tangents: something reminded him of something else which in turn reminded him of something else, the "something" of the first instance frequently suffering desertion the while. At times, indeed, his tangential chatter made it difficult to keep him to the subject of the interview. If his speech lacked conjunctivity, it lacked neither warmth, humor, nor occasional picturesqueness. He was capable of such colorful concreteness as likening his hemorrhoid operation to an apple coring—a conception punctuated by gestures. Culturally, the level of Lanlin's speech was conventional lower middle-class, grammatical errors being not infrequent, particularly where the verb "to do" was concerned.

Save for one interview, he showed little uneasiness during the various procedures: the exception being one in which he reclined on a couch and gave his responses to questions about childhood memories to a woman interrogator. In several of the early interviews he was somewhat uneasy for several minutes, but once conversation got underway he was quite accessible.

Although Lanlin evidently respected the aims of the project and the importance of what he vaguely understood as "science," he never regarded his task as one of helping the experimenters carry out a difficult piece of research. Nor, on the other hand, did he seem to be needful of help himself. Subjective exploration was not something that interested him greatly. His major motive in continuing to serve as a subject seemed to be a desire for new and prestigeful conversational partners.

Lanlin's Values

Lanlin's attitudes toward Russia and Communism fitted into a broader system of values and attitudes which must be understood before we can fully appreciate why he reacted as he did to the Soviet system.

Lanlin was apolitical in the manner of not a few American businessmen. In appraising world and national affairs, his criterion was not that of politics—the art of composing competing claims for power. Rather, he applied to the political process the yardstick of efficiency and good management—basically the frame of reference of business. It was only insofar as government could be made, in his words, a "business proposition" that it could hope to avoid the "waste, foolishness, and inefficiency" to which it was prey. He was not greatly interested in politics—admitting that he would "not be much disturbed" if prevented from voting in an election—and questions of ideology left him unmoved, convinced as he was of the self-evident validity of his own ideological beliefs.

Perhaps the flavor of his views is best given in his own words in excerpts from the *Stress Interview:*

> If the Government was run on a business foundation, it would be better. I think a lot of these loose ends and duplications would be avoided . . . The Government is in a position where they are constantly spending somebody else's money. Now that's the difference between the Government and Andy Mellon. . . . [Speaking of Russia] It could be just the form it is now, for that matter, if the right man was at the head of it. Nothing wrong with dictatorship if the right man is at the head of it. [You don't think a dictatorship in itself is a bad thing?] No. No. I think that if you've got the right man there, why a dictatorship is all

right. But it's so easy not to get the right man. I think that dictatorship
with the right man is a very good thing. I think that things can be
done quicker and a lot of good things can be done. Why, we wouldn't
have to be worried about votes or politics. He could really head the
thing up just like the president of a company can head a thing up. If
he's a good president, why you've got a good company. . . . [Pressed
on whether individual liberties would be possible under a good dictator]
If you have the right man at the top, you'd have your individual liberty.
[How would you control this top man?] Well, [laugh] after all, top
management's controlled too, when it comes to anything of a highly
important nature, by a board of directors.

Yet, when one probed his views on as extreme a matter as his "ideal
dictatorship" it became apparent that there were extenuating factors
which made his view "impractical."

I do feel that if we have the ideal type of man to run the company . . .
I mean, to run the country . . . that it would have to be an ideal man
to everybody, so you can see how far-fetched it is that everybody would
go along.

But that the "ideal" was attractive can scarcely be doubted.

Business ideology or the free enterprise system was not clearly defined in Charley's mind. It was, rather, a reasonable pursuit of gain
in a community of reasonable and like-minded men. We shall comment later on his approach to unionism. He saw no conflict between
business and labor that could not be worked out "reasonably" by
sitting around a table. Lanlin's view was that strikes were more often
than not the result of agitators and hotheads; "good business" was
an ideal that meant the good life for all.

But Lanlin resented a "moss-back reactionary." For to him, the
reactionary was as much the fool as the radical "agitator." A Republican, he was nonetheless a sarcastic critic of the "Old Guard" and the
"big interests" and considered himself to be a liberal. Though there
were elements in his political view which clearly stemmed from other
motives than business enterprise—thus, he was a strong supporter of
social legislation for the working man—he felt it necessary to square
these views with business practice. "Social security is a wise business
proposition."

In world affairs, Lanlin could best be described as an economic
nationalist. He saw the United States as the most advanced country
in the world—a judgment based on our material progress and well-
being. We had "technical know-how" (a favored term) and business
initiative. As he saw it, other countries envy us. Any country with
evil intentions toward us, principally Russia, both envied and feared

us. Our strategy, when others threatened trouble, was simply to take a firm stand and call their bluff.

A guiding principle behind Lanlin's views was a respect for our own and other nationalisms—provided nobody made trouble for us. Hitler, he felt, had been good for Germany up to the point where he made "a lot of demands that didn't make sense," the sin that Charley himself had learned to avoid early in childhood. "It's not our business to interfere with other countries. It's our business what we do and what we think is right and the same goes for the Nazis or Russians"— providing again, of course, that nobody makes trouble for us. Beneath these sentiments, however, was the conviction that there was not a country in the world, including Russia, who would not adopt our way if it had it in its power to do so.

Toward public affairs generally, Lanlin's view was strongly marked by gradualism and a rather unquestioning optimism. One finds scattered throughout his record statements of conviction based on the theme that Rome was not built in a day. He told us that his success on his company's labor-management committee—and we have reason to believe it was considerable—grew from his skill at getting to goals gradually. Both in describing his work with his union, in talking of the international scene, and in recounting his childhood relations with his parents he uses the expression "Don't make demands that don't make sense."

Finally, we must remember that Lanlin was a Catholic and that, in many ways, his Catholicism gave structure to his views on Russia. The precepts of his church he accepted quietly. Of his religion he said once, "What a tremendous big thing it is." The church also symbolized a relief from the tension of life. How firmly established in his personal life Catholicism had become, the extent to which it was related to his other values—even business values—we can judge from his own words.

> My faith grew stronger over the years. I don't say I wear it on my sleeve or anything like that, but I do say that I get satisfaction out of it. I do say that I get contentment out of it. I do get a sense of feeling good about it. I do get restfulness out of it. I can find. . . . It's an outlet and I can . . . I can go into a church. It makes me feel contented. I can kneel down and relax. I can seem to get things off my mind. Not only get them off but have a feeling of getting the answer to my problems. I have found it a consolation during times of stress and sickness, sickness of members of the family. For problems of business, things like that. Or it's an outlet sometimes if I'm bewildered by anything. I've found it good to go in and sit down and examine myself. No, my faith has become stronger . . . Well, when there's no service going on

is that part I like. Like some night, oh, say after supper or sometime when I'm reading, I'll say, "I guess I'll take a walk." I don't walk very far and on the way back I walk around and stop into the church for a while and sort of relax and come out and feel in a nice frame of mind, feel nice, I mean. You feel . . . you feel . . . I remember feeling good will toward everybody. You come out and have a nice viewpoint, a healthy viewpoint. . . . Ah . . . that's a nice viewpoint to have. It helps you. It helps you in business. If you can keep the way you feel at that time. . . . If you can keep that in front of you, if you could be that way all the time, you'd really be somebody. I mean, it's a nice way to be. It would be comfortable . . . in business. It would be helpful at all times. You wouldn't be impatient at any time. It'd be very helpful. . . . Patience and tact.

Lanlin on Russia

The very first words spoken by Lanlin on the subject of Russia in the course of his thirty hours of testing were revealing. Asked by the interviewer after a series of sessions on personal topics, "What about the outside world, the world at large? How do you feel about the situation there?", he replied:

Well, right off the bat, you'd think that Russia . . . you think that Europe . . . the dominating character seems to be what Russia's going to do and what not. As far as Russia goes, in my mind, I think that they've got an inferiority complex and they're trying to overcome it by talking big and making a lot of noise and arguing about . . . arguing more than they should to give the other fellow the thought that "we're not going to give in on anything unless we do a lot of talking." They don't seem to want to give in on something that doesn't amount to too much, no matter what it is. They want to argue about it. And they seem to take that . . . I think it's just to cover up their own abilities, or lack of abilities. I don't think they've got the abilities. I know they haven't got the abilities that the American people have, any way you want to look at it, initiative or thinking or ability to produce or anything at all, in any way. I don't think they've got what we've got, by any means. I don't think any of them have from any angle. When I compare . . . they're just doing a lot of talk, I mean this Communism business. Russia has been ballooned up, completely out of proportion. Oh, I don't mean that we shouldn't keep after them or sit them back every so often, but I don't think that . . . they're anything that we should be ascared of. I certainly don't believe in being easy with them. They're just a problem child that's got to be handled the right way. [You're not too worried about the way things are going over there?] No, there seems to have been sort of a restless mood. It's the people. The world itself is a beautiful place. It's beautiful. I think it's the people. Particularly the people.

The agitators tend to keep things in a turmoil. They seem to be the ones in the headlines and the ones who are agitated. They do so much talking about their agitation that they tend to grab all the headlines. I mean that certainly a person that was well-fed and contented, why he doesn't seem to be in the news. Nice fellow and pleasant to get along with, good companion and all that, but there's nothing about him that makes news. Whereas the headlines that we manage to see, the radio, that brings out the headlines. That type of person is hitting the headlines.

Here, then, was Russia—bumptious, making unreasonable demands, agitating, and somehow not in the image of the ordinary kinds of people who are not "hitting the headlines."

The central fact about Russia to Lanlin was her threat to world peace. What thinking he had done about the Soviet Union was by way of explaining, or rather explaining away this threat. In brief he saw Russia as a backward country of primitive people, "peasants" dominated by a powerful clique under Stalin. This clique, he felt, had by the end of the war come to be dominated in turn by the successful military men. These ruling groups, he believed, were bent upon depriving the Russian people of education on the one hand and religion on the other. The ultimate aim of Russian leadership was world domination which they could achieve only by keeping their people in the dark. If, Lanlin argued, the Russian people were allowed to learn about the United States in their schools, they would want to be more like us. And, indeed, if Russia's leaders had any sense, they too would try to develop their country's resources better to attain a decent standard of life. As for the prohibition of religion, its rationale was to keep people from the sense of individuality that would lead them to demand the rights and liberties they justly had coming to them.

In spite of these calculated efforts, the Russian people, Lanlin believed, felt friendly toward America. Indeed, it was clear from the context of his remarks that he found it difficult to conceive of any people not feeling friendly toward us even if they knew only a little about us.

We must pause for a moment here to note that while Soviet leaders were seen by Lanlin as having evil designs and a powerful will to dominate he nonetheless believed they did not want war. Partly this belief seemed to be compounded of his underlying, almost compulsive optimism and partly it stemmed from a half-formulated belief that they would work not by war but by "boring from within."

He said in one interview:

> Russia is trying to achieve control of the world by working from within. The Russians try to place men in positions where things will fall into their lap and they prefer this to trying to do it through war. They try to get other countries to rot from within rather than attacking them from without. To get their men into key positions. For instance, in the

Maritine Union and in companies like Ford and General Motors. We saw this when Germany and Russia signed their alliance. Workers in the United States stopped production. In this way they stopped our help to England.

The threat of such an approach did not loom as very serious to him, for, as we shall see in a later section, he was not at the time of our study ready to grant the possibility of defection in this country save by the very badly misled. But that is part of another aspect of his attitude toward Communism.

American counteraction to the threat of Russia, said Lanlin, should consist of calling their bluff and doing it boldly, without at the same time antagonizing them. He frequently cited in his interviews the fact that the Russians had a low standard of living and that they had no "engineering know-how," his favorite example being the way they allegedly left lend-lease equipment rusting in open fields because they did not know how to use it. With these handicaps, Russia would have to back down if we called her bluff. Asked if he thought this policy would bring the two countries together sooner or later, he replied:

> Sure, cause she's got to get together with us. She's got to live with us. She's dependent on us. She won't admit it but she's dependent on us. She has no hesitation in asking for a loan. She has no hesitation in wanting to know how we produce things. She has no hesitation in asking for machinery. She has no hesitation in asking for our guns and airplanes and the use of our men during the war. She still needs to get along with us. If we stand firm and say, "This is the way such-and-such a thing should be," and know in our minds that it's the fair way, subject to routine bargaining back and forth, we'll say, I think it'll work out all right. It'll work out all right. I mean, Russia will get back on her feet, at least where she was before. There's no reason why she couldn't get back in a matter of time like she was before. And if she wants to progress further than that, why there's only one place she's going to learn it, and that's here.

In the meantime, our subject counselled that we should keep our defenses: "maintain a large army and navy, send aid to Greece and Turkey, and don't take a single backward step." "We've given plenty of concessions; it does no good. All she recognizes is military strength. Then she'll make concessions." As in boyhood, Lanlin was convinced we could win the fights others started against us.

On the less belligerent side, Lanlin believed that if we could only get our way of life known to the Russian people, only educate them to the advantages of the American way and break down the barrier of ignorance, the Russian people would readily see the light. But he was not very optimistic as to the immediate success of such a program. Asked what he himself would do if he were head of the Russian government, he said, "Let them have religion. Let them have fair newspapers. Let them have education. Let there be an exchange of students between the United States and Russia. Their boys will see how Americans really think, and when those boys grow up and become leaders, they'll be broader people for their visit to America and Russia will broaden. There's very little you can do with the old leaders."

As for future policy, Lanlin firmly believed that if we followed a course of the sort outlined by him, there would be no danger of war with Russia. "She does not want to fight, particularly with an outfit as big as this country." The big danger was that we might grow negligent in the future and "proceed to leave Europe by itself gradually, attending to its own problems, depending on the powers that then come in. I mean, the people will start hollering about taxes and military budgets that reflect in your taxes. It hurts me to say it but I'm in favor of military training, a large army and navy and all that business. I'm very much in favor of a big club at all times."

Looking at this first differentiated aspect of Lanlin's attitudes toward Russia one is struck by several points. Compared with Chatwell and Sullivan, he saw very little by way of legitimate right on the side of Russia. Lanlin, unlike the other two, saw no ultimate conflict between Russia and the United States. Russia's leaders were bluffing, were out simply for selfish power against the best interests of their own people. To a large extent, as we have already noted, Russia and Soviet Communism came into Lanlin's thinking only because they were threats to a system which he took to be the true state of nature.

To be sure, he felt negatively toward Russia's curtailment of freedom and decried the slavery of the individual. But again, these matters seemed to concern him not for themselves but for the manner in which they affected our relations with the Soviet Union.

As for capitalism and Communism, Lanlin's interest was not really engaged, so convinced was he of the fraudulent "unreasonableness" of Russia's approach. "The Communists have nothing to offer the American worker. They represent only a noisy minority."

Indeed, only at one point did he give any evidence of considering Communism as a system of belief. The occasion was upon seeing the zeal of Communists in his labor union at a convention.

> Tremendous tenacity, tremendous zeal and devotion to their cause. They work on it twenty-four hours a day. I mean sleep is secondary . . . I admire their devotion. If they were only applying it to something more

constructive instead of that tearing-down business. . . . I've seen them
at work. I've seen them at union conventions. I mean your American
union man comes to a week-end convention and comes with a week-end
bag with a clean shirt and a shaving outfit, a comb and brush, a deck
of cards, a package of cigarettes, and maybe a notebook and pencil.
Your Communist comes with a brief case loaded with resolutions, pencils
and paper. He don't have any shirts or collars or neckties, shaving equipment. Or doesn't even have a room. That's the way he gets off the
train, just loaded down. And he proceeds to go right to work. He has
that brief case with him all the time. Their strategy is all laid out before
they go. They're interested in getting on all the key committees. . . .
They always have a nomination ready. . . . I think they've got themselves filled with this philosophy. They certainly punish themselves. . . .
I've heard of very highly educated ones taking a job pushing a broom
around in a factory in order to be in a position to expound their theories.

Though he saw these men as badly misguided idealists, he felt a
certain sympathy for them. But for "the very liberal thinkers who go
for the Communist front organizations" he had only scorn. "They are
being played for fools" and have no real appreciation of what they
have in this country.

At no point during his interviews was there mention of Communism
as an experiment or of the social welfare aspects of the Soviet state.
These were questions which had either not engaged his attention or
were written off as part of the sham façade behind which Russia sought
to hide her weakness.

In the course of the *Polling Interview* and the *Information Test* it
was apparent that Lanlin had little knowledge of the official Russian
views on marriage and the family which might have run counter to
his own, deeply held Catholic beliefs. Indeed, he knew they were
anti-religious and his explanation of the campaign against religion as
an aid in depriving people of their rights has already been set forth.
When we asked him to comment on the statement in the *Information
Apperception Test* about the government looking after the children
of working mothers in Russia, his response was immediate and negative. "I disapprove of all this for the very simple and evident fact
that it was not intended for women to spend their lives in those
endeavors but to be a home-maker and bear her children." And as if
the question had served to reintegrate other impressions, he went on
to condemn with moral indignation the "Russian women sharpshooters
during the war with medals row upon row across their chest proclaiming to an audience how many men they'd killed." On another item
which stated that divorces are more difficult to get in Russia than ten
years ago, he again showed a rather revealing indignation: "Deep

within their own minds they know that many cases of divorce undermine the stability of their country. But their motive isn't one of building up the home. . . . If the divorces are easy to get, it means shifting
from one woman to another which tends to put other things on their
mind, which Russia does not want. . . . The statement by itself I
approve, but the motive behind it, the selfish motive behind the words.
The ruling should be one of morals, but in Russia's case it has nothing
to do with morals."

Withal, though he reacted indignantly even when confronted with
neutral details of internal affairs in Russia and treated information
about Russia as proof of the immorality and ruthlessness of her leaders,
Lanlin concerned himself little with these matters.

We must pause here for a moment to examine the manner in which
Lanlin got his information about Russia and Communism. He did
not go out of his way to get it. One may distinguish two separate
sources from which he informed himself. From one, which we may
call his "line sources," he derived or had reinforced his basic attitudes
and valuations of Russia. From these, he formed the strongly stacked
hypotheses which he then "tested" against what may be called "filler
sources." In choosing his line sources he showed a high degree of
selectivity. They included such media as the Jesuit magazine *America;*
the diocesan weekly newspaper *The Pilot;* radio talks by Msgr. Ful-
ton J. Sheen. These and his parish priests were, in his words, the kind
that "don't seem to be afraid to sound off on the subject of Russia." In
one interview he said, "The Catholic Church don't intend to stand by
and let its religion or any other religion be destroyed." But though
the line sources were Catholic in origin, the evaluations of Russia
which emerged in Lanlin were not, as we have seen, religious in tone.
The Catholic speakers and writers to whom he refers provided him
with material for a predominantly secular point of view.

As for the filler sources, they were highly conventional and provided
information quite congruent with his line sources. On subways and
during slack times at the store, he read most of the Boston papers,
including such differing columnists as Stokes, Allen, Pearson, and Pegler, the last of whom he characteristically disliked as too extreme. On
the radio, his favorite was Gabriel Heatter, described by Lanlin as
favoring a policy of trying to get along with Russia. From the filler
sources, read with no great intensity of interest, he would take items
of a rather disconnected sort to confirm his strongly anti-Soviet point
of view. In the main, his opinions were more antagonistic to Russia
than those of most of the newspapers he read.

Lanlin scored near the bottom of our ten subjects in information about Russia. Where Chatwell made two errors on our 53 item *Information Test*, Lanlin made 19. In terms of the content of his information, he was quite lacking about those aspects of Russia that had only indirect bearing on her role in world affairs. On those parts of the test that dealt with internal Russian affairs—government, economics, science and letters—he scored less than 50 per cent correct. Given this lack of information, internal Russia served as something of a projective screen upon which he cast images which would be congruent with his dominant sentiment. The Russian people, gullible "peasant types," were more to be censured than pitied for their backwardness and the oppression under which they lived.

Let us summarize Lanlin's attitudes toward Russia in terms of our schema for describing an opinion.

Differentiated object of attitude. The "Russia" of Lanlin's opinions, his subjective definition of Russia, was that of a backward country of great resources and ignorant people, dominated by leaders of evil intent whose motive was world domination. It is interesting to note that while Russia was seen as threatening us, the threat was of a kind that could be contained by firm action on our part. For Russia was in the image of an unruly, obstreperous child, really dependent on us, but nonetheless making "unreasonable demands." This is about the sole differentiated aspect of Russia for Lanlin. He does not see other possible aspects such as her proclaimed experimental objectives and social welfare aims.

Saliency. In comparison with Lanlin's three major concerns—his work, his family, and his property—Russia and the problems of Communism did not occupy his attention much. In Lanlin's life space, Russia was not a vivid object.

Time perspective. The temporal mold in which Russia was placed was twofold. On the one hand, Lanlin saw Russia as something of a headline grabber—making a lot of fuss that made news. In this sense, the everyday events of Russo-American relations were seen as so many momentary disequilibria. Beneath this level, our subject saw a long-term plan of conquest contemplated by Russia's leaders, a plan premised on the assumption that if other countries were badgered from within and from without they would eventually fall into Russian hands. Yet this did not lead Lanlin to the view that threat was imminent. Pervading his time perspective—indeed, pervading his life—was an easy optimism about the favorable outcome of most events. He saw Russia getting her "comeuppance" by some eventual process of justice—if we would only be firm with her.

Informational support. The major outlines of Lanlin's information structure were supported by his dependence on Catholic "line" sources which he kept easily and well confirmed by a casual and somewhat haphazard reading of the daily press. By and large, his informational background on Russia was rather poor, considerably less developed and integrated than most of our other subjects.

Object value. The affective tone of Russia for our subject was negative in quality. He found Russia bumptious, "peasant-like," unreasonable, boorish, and troublesome. As for her threat value, Russia was seen as threatening, to be sure, but threatening in the way that a strong but unruly adolescent is threatening. Perhaps the threatening quality of Russia was somewhat attenuated by the fact that Lanlin also perceived Russia as dependent upon us in the long run for her betterment.

Orientation. Lanlin's orientation combined elements of approach, avoidance, and hostility. We must convince Russia of the rightness of our own way, for once she sees and understands American ways, she will adopt them. "Educating" the Russians was, then, an approach orientation. In terms of avoidance, Lanlin believed in keeping out of Russia's affairs so long as she behaved, having little to do with her. But if Russia overstepped the bounds of reasonableness, we must be firm and if necessary hostile. In sum, try to teach Russia sense and let her be if she follows the lesson. If she does not, "Slap her down."

Policy stand. This can best be summed up in Lanlin's own words.

> It looks as though, in order to avoid war, we've got to get away from isolation and take an interest in any place in the world where liberties are being threatened by outside forces. I think it would be too much of a problem at this stage for the U.N. to handle. In fact, I don't think the U.N. is going to mean a thing without Russian support. It's going to fall apart like the League of Nations.

Lanlin's Life and Enterprises

Charley's father had been a frugal, hardworking man. Lanlin, Senior, was born of poor parents of German extraction in New Haven, Connecticut, and family circumstances were such that he never went beyond grammar school. Over the years he worked his way up to the position of managing a food store in a suburb of Boston, to which city he had come in his teens. A regime of austerity and saving made it possible for the father to buy up some property, heavily mortgaged, on which were several small neighborhood stores. This property and its care soon became the center of his interest. By dint of great skimping, the mortgage was finally paid off until, almost as a climax to his life, Lanlin, Senior, owned "mortgage-free property." Rarely during his childhood, Charley told us, did the family leave home on an outing for more than the day—the primary obligation being "to look after the property." His father took upon himself the task, over and beyond his regular job, of repairing and refurbishing the property. In later years, he had the advantage of his son's help.

Charley, an only child, was born in Boston in 1906. His father was thirty-four, his mother thirty-one at the time of his birth and the family was fairly launched on the struggling ascent to middle-class life. The father, a highly controlled person, was the dominant figure in the home. Charley describes him as "calm, deliberate, and very much of a planner." As a child Charley would tag along with his father when he was engaged in the perpetual round of tidying up, repairing, and "looking after" the property but there seems during this period to have been very little real interaction between the two. His mother, we were told, was a quick-tempered, impatient woman but he nevertheless formed with her the major affectionate attachment of his childhood. Part of his mother's pattern of emotional lability was what Charley called "moody spells." These increased in severity and frequency as she grew older. It is of no small interest that his mother used Charley as a confidant to whom she might "blow off steam" about the excessive economies practiced by his father or about the frustrations of life in general.

Of the extended family we know little as there seemed to be scant contact with any relatives and certainly no frequent family reunions. We know of an old grandfather who used to soak his feet in a big bowl of hot water on the surface of which the very young Charley would float matchsticks. We also know of a maternal aunt and uncle from New York who, according to the report of Charley, brought a great breath of gaiety and conviviality into the Lanlin household on their infrequent visits.

His parents seem to have had no clear-cut idea about what Charley should become when he grew up, but one can infer they had in mind for him some rather vaguely defined clerical-administrative career in business. It was apparent in our interviews that Charley looked to his parents for the major decisions about his future and had no formulated ambition of his own. He attended high school and then, as we have said, took a year-long general business course at a commercial school, the latter specifically at his father's suggestion.

Charley rather resented the fact that his parents had not been more ambitious for him. He said once, "I wish my father had made a point of seeing to it that I went on in my education. Oh, he didn't stop me, of course, but he might have pushed me on further. What I had seemed a lot and was a lot in comparison to his own education, and I suppose the transfer to college wasn't very widespread then. But I do wish he'd pushed me a little further."

Father was the family disciplinarian, although it appears that little discipline was needed, for Charley soon learned "not to make unreasonable demands." Punishment from his father was rarely if ever overt. Rather, Lanlin Senior's position in the family was such that a firmly spoken word sufficed to bring Charley into line. On the whole, he was a "good boy" and gave his parents little trouble. We find in our various interviews with our subject no mention of any scrapes or escapades.

In his *Autobiography*, Charley stated:

> I soon learned that when my father said, "No," he meant "No" and any further discussion or attempts to persuade was a waste of time, but in my mother's case, I could generally prevail, *not through tantrums*, which neither would stand for, but by kidding her along, a little soft soaping, and she would laugh and give her O.K.
>
> My father never punished me, perhaps because, when he told me something he did not want me to do, he would leave a definite impression that it would be wise to follow his suggestions. If he saw me doing something which he did not approve, all he had to do was say my first name, and from the way he said it, and tone of voice was enough for me, because that tone was not used very often, but when it was "Stop"!! would bounce from one side of your head to the other. In my mother's case, she would take a good right hand swing, only one, and none ever landed, as I could see it was coming, and I would leave that spot pronto, and from there on, it would be a bawling out.

Eventually, the mortgage was paid off and life for the Lanlins took a new turn. This event had evidently been a climactic one for Charley's father. The year was 1924, Charley had just turned eighteen, his father fifty-two. The elder Lanlin retired from the food store—whether this had been a long-established plan, we do not know. The regime of economic austerity eased: a car was purchased, a washing machine, a radio. In the years following, the family went off for outings and occasional trips. The pattern of the father's life now became that of a working landlord; he gave his time to care of the property and the many tasks which such a conscientious man would find necessary in "keeping it up." His remaining time was devoted to the neighborhood Chamber of Commerce of which he eventually became Treasurer and President. By the time of his death in 1935, Lanlin Senior had achieved many of the things upon which he had set his heart. The property was his "free and clear"; he was a respected businessman in the community.

Early in adolescence, Charley began his work career with a job at a grocery store after school and on Saturdays. During high school years, he worked Saturdays for a department store where the chance of being recommended by his school for a Christmas holiday job spurred him on to more studying. Of his earnings, he said in his *Autobiography:*

> I turned all this money over to my father, who opened a savings account for me, but increased my allowance from his own money, in fact, after my father's death, I found tucked away amongst his private papers, a little envelope marked with my name and saying it was the first week's pay I ever earned. I still have the envelope and the large old fashioned dollar bills with his writing on it. So, that expression, which we often hear, actually applies to me, "He has the first dollar he ever earned."

As we noted earlier, his first job after completion of his business course was in a bank where the imposed atmosphere of social austerity repelled him. His next job was a significant experience for him. It was in a large manufacturing concern and he soon found himself doing time and motion studies which brought him into contact with men who resented his work. This incident, to which we have already alluded, is best told in his own words:

> The foundry help was composed of foreign nationality entirely. Only the foreman spoke English. They knew I worked in the Time Study Department and as soon as I put in my appearance I was greeted with a burst of boos, jeers, etc. I was surprised, and then the foreman tipped me off that the Time Study boys had cut the hourly rate of the men and asked for increased production as well. I put in a bad day. They had many tricks worked out in an attempt to get me to count many molds twice. This would result in many arguments. They could not or would not understand English. They spilled hot metal near me, altogether too close to be an accident. Upon return to the office at night, I found that that was my job from then on. I resigned.

His next position, with the household appliance company, came immediately after this experience.

> The business school where I'd gone then sent me to the Appliance Company where I now work and have worked 21 years March 1947. At the time I desired work in a small concern, my experience in large concerns giving me the impression of only being a number on the payroll. But the person who did my interview felt I was the person they needed and offered me more money than the average company paid for a novice.
>
> Nineteen years I spent in the Payroll Department doing general clerical work. As time went on, the work did not prove to be remunerative or satisfying in a sense of accomplishment. Office work in a large company

can be and is constant repetition, giving one a feeling of doing nothing constructive. I yearned for work in which I was paying my way by the work. I had a desire to do something constructive, to face new problems, to avoid repetition. And for years the answer was in front of me but I failed to see it.

The opportunity, of course, was the chance to sell, but to this we shall return later.

The course of Charley's leisure ran in conventional channels. As a young child, an only child, he played alone a good deal of the time. "Being an only child, I found it no hardship to amuse myself." He was rather proud of the memory of cowboy-Indian battles played alone on the rug in which he saw to it that "the other side won as many times as I did." After that, play turned toward fantasy baseball on the same, well-remembered nine by twelve rug. In his *Autobiography,* he told us:

> My ability to amuse myself on days when I was confined to the house would often prompt my mother to remark that I was never any trouble to her, and at times she would come into the room where I was playing, thinking I might be lonesome, but I would always be wrapped up playing at games, that she would marvel that I could keep so busy without bothering her.

Yet during this period he longed for the day when he could start public school for then he would not have to be by himself on rainy days.

In the period following, juvenile fiction and competitive sports filled his spare time. He lived across the street from a playground and his major hobbies were the seasonal sports at which he was better than average.

Teachers had little effect on him. He knew, along with the others, "which ones were fake and which were real" but their impact was at best transitory. One teacher "got them all interested in Shakespeare" by his sheer enthusiasm but, as Charley said, "I never read Shakespeare since nor do dramas of this type appeal to me, but with him it was a pleasure."

In high school, Charley blossomed out, made many friends, took part in many activities and was obviously well liked. He was still seeing many of his high school friends and recently was elected an officer of his class at a reunion—"of which I am very proud."

One thing Charley learned in school is best put in his own words:

> Fights I had plenty of, at least one a week, in fact, we all seemed to be good for one a week. After awhile, it dawned on me, that when I went looking for a fight, I was always accommodated, and would lose, whereas when the other fellow, no matter how good a reputation he

enjoyed as a scrapper, would torment me, I would come out the winner, so once that realization hit me from that time on I never looked for fights, and I let them come to me, which they did.[1]

Of his sexual development during these early years we know relatively little, for on this subject Charley was quite reticent. He assured us that he went to dances often but rarely took out the same girl more than a few times. "Sex did not worry me . . . neither did it tease or annoy me. It just drifted along in a gradual sort of way."

At the age of twenty-five, Charley was married to a local girl—a cheerful, outgoing person of whom he said, "She is a fine wife, a good mother and housekeeper, and would be my choice again." In their sixteen years of marriage, there have been four children, the eldest fourteen, the youngest four.

Perhaps the contemporary Charles Lanlin—or the Charles Lanlin of the five years preceding our acquaintance—is best described in terms of those major enterprises which give pattern to his daily life. In our *Interview on Personal Values,* we opened with the question, "What things really matter to you?" His answer is revealing:

> What things really matter to me? Well of course . . . ah . . . ah . . . marriage matters first . . . and children. Conditions at home. Their life, their education, their health. Naturally their mother, who should have been in the picture before them, and the same things apply to her. And then work . . . the ability to get along with people, the ability to get ahead. I can't think of much of anything else that goes on in this world besides your home and your work.

Family life for Charley combined cheerfulness, worry, and some exasperation. Practically all of his time away from work was spent with his family and he was much concerned that his children should grow into "normal, ordinary people." He both enjoyed and was anxious about the role of guide and father which he had undertaken. In discussing his philosophy of raising children, he said, "The first thing is to get to know your children." He made much of the point that one should do things with them—play or at least discuss the seasonal sports. The satisfactions one got took the form of "keeping young, keeping your mind active." That he derived a vicarious satisfaction from their lives was clear from this statement about his method of catching up on their doings:

> I like to hear them tell it; I want them to tell it. I ask them to tell it and pry into their thinking. What did they think of something; did they notice this or that. I tackle them all in turn. That starts from the

[1] Cf. M. Mead, *And keep your powder dry,* New York, William Morrow & Co., 1942, for an estimate of the generality of this pattern in America.

moment you sit down at the supper table. You've got one in kinder-
garten that has a million things to tell you. Another in the third grade,
she's got a lot too. Being a woman, she's got a volume to tell. And over
here is a fellow who holds back a little. He's got a kind of inferiority
complex. The oldest fellow, he's 14, he's got all the answers.

That his family regimen sometimes interfered with Charley's own needs
was clear: "Sometimes it's kind of a hardship when you're trying to
concentrate on something yourself. Evening they all buzz around with
conversation." He felt the strain of parenthood and remarked at one
point that it "shows up the next day, in your work, in your impatience,
in your tone of voice."

At a somewhat deeper level, we feel that Charley derived a feeling
of control from his self-styled "prying" into his children's thoughts.
He was concerned that they be "normal kids" and "right." His behavior
toward them reflected his own concern about being a "regular person."
If at times the task of controlling and "checking up" on the children
became too much for him, it was also true, as we shall see, that there
were times when his compulsive need to keep tabs on himself proved
wearing.

His relations with his wife were routinized and it was difficult to tell
whether there was a long period after marriage marked by great
spontaneity in their relationship. They discussed matters of family
and business together, usually at bedtime, and he reported that she
usually agreed with him. She was, he stated, a very hard worker, who,
of an evening, would bring her ironing into the front room after the
rest of the day's work was completed. Of a cheerful disposition—"she
sometimes laughs right out loud when she's reading the funnies to
herself"—she nonetheless exercised a conservative influence on our subject by reminding him, on those rare occasions when he may have been
tempted to consider a daring shift in employment from his irksome
clerical job, that a family man could not afford to take chances and
jeopardize his security. Her words of advice on such occasions were
more in the order of reinforcement of his own beliefs than opposition
to any considered plan devised by Charley. Sexual relations no longer
have a prominent part in their partnership: "with four youngsters it
doesn't play any part to speak of."

As for his hopes about his children and their future, he said, "Each
one is a little different. . . . Go according to their aptitudes." His
appraisal of their talents seemed realistic, if conventional. The second
oldest boy, an introverted child, puzzled Charley. He saw him as
rather miserly and somewhat selfish and had "not thought much of his
future." "Our children are normal in all ways."

A second major focus in Charley's contemporary life—if not the main one—was his work. The closing words of his *Autobiography* were: "Most important lesson I learned in life—get into work you enjoy." Charley, as we have said, was a salesman. His job was to sell appliances to customers in a lower-middle-class section where the store he managed was located. The process of selling gave him his greatest satisfaction. It was the shift from clerical work to selling that prompted the closing remark in his *Autobiography*.

Concretely his job served several important functions for him. Working within the framework of a large, well established company guaranteed seniority and retirement pay. He felt secure and safe. Although he entertained the idea of shifting jobs several times during his clerical period, his desire for a secure and stable job prevailed. "I didn't want to lose my equity in the company . . ." In the *Argument Completion Test,* characteristically, he favored working for a firm which was steady and reliable over another which provided the chance for quick advancement but which might be chancy.

The security of Charley's job was matched by its opportunities for recognition and a sense of accomplishment. Although his account of a typical day at work indicated a considerable amount of daily routine and monotonous inactivity on the job—inventory, setting things in order, waiting for customers—there was also evidence of great satisfaction involved in selling. Asked, in his *Interview on Personal Values,* whether he preferred selling to his earlier clerical job, he had this to say:

> Yes, that's right. There's a feeling . . . In selling the product you're making out an order and taking their money and making the notation that in replacing a competitor's product there's something constructive being done. In other words . . . ah . . . that thing that you have sold, the article itself, and the returns from the use of that article are constructive. You're earning your week's pay . . . the profit from it is even more than your week's pay.

And as for the status satisfaction involved in selling, he remarked:

> I like to be doing something . . . that I feel is constructive. I mean . . . if you're . . . if you're . . . I mean even top management is interested. I mean they'll always stop and talk to someone that is in that [selling] position. They're always interested in his problem. Always gracious . . . courteous. They want to talk. I mean if they had their choice of the bookkeeper or *you,* they want to talk to *you.* See? I mean they want to talk to *you. You're* the key. In other words if *you* don't do anything that bookkeeper isn't going to do anything either. He might just as well go home. If you don't transact enough business he's out. In other words, he's dependent on *me.* Now the President of the

Company . . . the Vice President, they're in an upper bracket. They're not out meeting the public, the man in the street. They're not out meeting him. They're up there at the top and actually they're dependent on you too. In other words, if you don't produce, why . . . they don't cut any melon either.

Charley, moreover, liked the dominance of the selling role. Advising people about the suitability of a product provided too a means of domination. He told us of the pleasure of fitting his selling technique to the individual case. With first generation Italians he acted one way —"shout right back and wave your hands"; with "upper bracket" people in another—"let them come to you." Charley detailed the mystery of selling: the gracious and prestigeful entrance in the name of "The Company," "not just some firm nobody heard of"; the approach of helping the user of "our products," and on through the list.

If knuckling under to the arduous and austere routine of keeping accounts brought out the acquiescence he had learned in dealing with his father, the job of salesman gave him the opportunity to develop the technique of "soft-soaping" and cajoling that had proved so effective with his mother. This was the easier life.

Lanlin probably saw himself at the peak of his advancement in "The Company." He was unable to give a coherent answer to a question on opportunities for getting ahead, replying with what was a rather drawn out account of the company's organization chart. Asked what he would be doing twenty years from now, he symptomatically committed an error in arithmetic to arrive at the age of 52, the age of his father's retirement. He saw too many complications and details in the future situation to hazard even a general guess.

To say that his work life was without serious problems would be to overlook at least one important, even basic, conflict in Charley's life. For all his desire to be active and "constructive," he also had a strong wish to be relaxed, to "let go." Asked about an ideal vacation with unlimited money, he said, "I'd go to the beach if it was July or August. You said I'd have plenty of money? I'd go to California and Florida— travel. Maybe go to the mountains. It would be fine. You wouldn't have to get up and go to work in the morning." But on his vacations now, which he cherished for their promise of fewer demands of conscience, he was not gone long before he started making lists of the things he must do when back in town: business, the property, the union, etc.

No description of his contemporary history would be complete without reference to Charley's active role in union affairs. He wrote of his union activities in his *Autobiography:*

In the course of events our company became unionized and I was elected by ballot at the Union Hall as a member of the Labor Relations Committee of our Local. I was elected and reelected and served eight terms on this Committee. It was the best education I ever could have had. It broadened my viewpoint on things in general and brought me to the realization that I had been in a rut mentally. This work brought me into contact with all types, and many a valuable hour I spent learning Labor and Human relations.

Soon I was elected to perform other duties for my Local, such as delegate to State conventions, delegate to the National Convention in Omaha, member of the New England Board of the Union, etc., as well as keeping up my own labor relations work in my Local. I would assist in wage negotiations for other locals in my field in New England, was member of the joint Wartime Labor-Management Committee, appeared at the State House on bills, was Company Chairman of the United War Fund Drive, and Company Chairman of the Red Cross Drive.

Such activities opened up my mind and I soon discovered I enjoyed extemporaneous and impromptu speaking, such as took place at union meetings, councils, and conventions. Being the labor relations man in any local is the most important job, and a job that involves plenty of hot debate at any meeting, both from management and my own membership.

It was through his activities on the War Fund Drive that Charley met a Vice President of his company who, apparently impressed by his good social presence, urged him to go into sales work after the war when selling would open up again. Charley saw this immediately as a natural, enjoyable, and "constructive" way out of the "mental rut" of clerical work. His shift into sales work spelled the end, with no ideological remorse, of his union phase. The sales manager pointed out to him that he would have to keep time clear, afternoon or evening, for sales follow-up.

I couldn't have arrangements on any union activities and then let [the sales] go by, because my sales work would be more important, naturally. I mean, basically, that's what I'm there for. So the general sales manager said, "I suggest you resign from the Labor Relations Committee because of the night work." . . . You can't very well run from one part of Boston to another and settle a dispute . . . and leave the store. So I resigned.

Asked whether he had any regrets, he replied, "No. No. I had it eight years. I went to a meeting last night and they were having a hot session. It was kind of hard to sit there too. I felt like getting up and saying something, but I didn't."

Charley's history as a labor union official might suggest that he changed his attitude toward labor unions over the years. Such was not the case. His election to office as a union official was virtually an accident and was not premised on an abstract interest in unionism.

He was approached by some men around the shop and asked if he
would run for office. Before that time, he admitted never having given
union matters a thought.

In his beliefs, moreover, he had always sided with the "upper
bracket" management. On several occasions, Charley made the point
that there was no conflict between labor and management, that "they're
both in the same boat." If business is allowed to earn unlimited profits,
a policy in which he believed and which he felt to be the national policy
of his union, then labor is in a better position to ask for higher wages.
Always a gradualist in his approach to labor-management negotiations,
and ever ready to see management's point of view, he appeared to have
been an excellent negotiator in a company which had no serious problems in dealing with its employees. "Most strikes are unnecessary," he
said in one interview.

One may ask what satisfactions Charley got from his labor activities.
They were many. Display and recognition were, of course, prominent:
"the opportunity for extemporaneous and impromptu speaking" and
the recognition accorded an official. He frankly enjoyed the raise in
status involved in sitting man-to-man at the bargaining table with
management: "they have some bright boys, management." There was
also much opportunity for self-improvement in his union work: getting
out of his "mental rut," getting to meet "all types of people," "learning
the way the company was set up from the inside." Finally, Charley
told us of the satisfaction he got from being in a position to help
straighten out grievances: "setting things to rights." That he must have
been good at it is attested by his eight terms in office.

One may conjecture, finally, that most of the driving force keeping
Charley active in unionism for nearly a decade has now been diverted
into the functionally equivalent job of selling, a job which provided
the opportunity for display, recognition, nurturance, and which, moreover, was more congruent with his basic social philosophy.

We have spoken of three major enterprises that had given pattern
to Lanlin's life in the five-year period preceding our study—the father
of the family, the salesman, the union leader. A fourth, also of central
importance, must be added: shall we call it the role of "property
owner"? For Charley was acutely aware of the benefits and the
burdens of the mortgage-free property left by his father. In one interview he said: "I'm in a better house than my father had and have it
easier than he did. The main reason is because of hard work he done
on the property." How deeply rooted is this feeling we sense from this
statement in Charley's *Autobiography:*

I never did actually ever become financially independent of my parents, always turning in all my money to my father, part of which he saved for me, part of which my clothes, board, and room came out of, and even now, though they died some years ago, the income-bearing property, which they worked so hard to own outright, still makes a big difference in my way of living. This was the way they intended it to be, as I also put in hours of work on the property, for which they were grateful, such as cutting grass, shoveling snow, taking off wallpaper, etc. No more than any child should do, but even in my immature mind I knew they were both hard workers, and my admiration for that attribute in them would always prompt me to give them first consideration. This consideration always delighted them, which was sufficient reward for me, as I felt I owed them both plenty, and under the circumstances I was rather limited in ways of showing it. I made it a point to keep out of real trouble, so as not to cause worries.

Charley saw to it that the net take on the "property" ($2500 to $3500 annually) should not be too reduced by extravagant expenses and repairs. But the property was kept painted and in good shape. At the same time, Charley, prompted as much by conscience as by economic gain, saw to it that his rents were at going market values. He remarked to one interviewer, "I own property and I really have to go to town there. I've been told my business ability is good by people who said it even though it hurt them. They said, 'You drive a hard bargain.'"

Socially, of course, the property gave to the younger Lanlin the same feeling of belongingness to the local business community that it had bestowed on his father. Characteristically, Charley had begun to take an active part in the affairs of the neighborhood Chamber of Commerce as his father had before him. External sign though this may be, psychologically it was for Charley further confirmation of his middle-class membership. But the property was not regarded as a stepping stone to higher things. It and the status it bestowed were sufficient.

Like his father, Charley also found the property a source of some anxiety. On one occasion, he went off for a vacation with his family right after one of the stores in his building had fallen vacant. By the time he returned to town, he had plans, prospects, and lists beyond his usual measure.

Charley thought of himself as a friendly, social man. His participation in his local town affairs served to buttress this self-image. He once said with feeling, "I love my community" and in its behalf had served in various local civic associations. Yet, withal, Charley had few, if any, really close friends. Friendship was rather more a quantitative than intensive thing for him. His activity in the community seemed to satisfy his needs for inter-personal relationship outside the job and family.

In closing this section on Lanlin's life and enterprises, we must finally have a more detailed look at the significant emotional relationships that affected his way of looking at the world around him. We know already of the important role of Lanlin's parents in the development of both his personality structure and his system of values. For our subject was a highly dependent, passive child whose energies from his earliest recall onward were geared to reaching his rather reserved and (to him) awesome father and "staying on the good side" of his more emotional, somewhat mercurial mother. It was in this early setting of the family that young Charley, the only child, learned first to master and then to repress his natural enough aggressive and destructive tendencies by a form of reaction formation that had "reasonableness" as its motto.

The major decisions and the main thread of his life were in the hands of Charley's father. Even now he felt, with a sometimes uncomfortable sense of obligation, that part of his good fortune was not his own doing, but his father's: the symbol of "the property" had lost none of its force. In the *Loose Ends Interview* Lanlin said that he felt as he grew older that he was growing more and more like his father. And, indeed, the pattern of values, the "business ideology" which formed so large a part of Lanlin's outlook, was a heritage from his father.

That there had been a strong fear of rejection by his father seemed likely. Father never had to punish him "because I was never bad." Or again, "his voice carried a veiled threat." It was in the *Thematic Apperception Test* that we found the most striking indication of what a psychoanalyst called Lanlin's "castration fear." [2] In one picture, a refugee boy is being deserted by his parents. In another, a young boy just out of prison is being counselled by his father. In another, an older man has just hypnotized a young man who has shown hostility toward him. It is interesting that the independent analysis of Lanlin's *TAT* record emphasized the restrictive and threatening role played by parental figures, particularly with regard to aggressive impulses.

The constellation of attitudes built up around the image of his father represents, we believe, a significant "first edition" of later attitudes related to public issues. Russia is in the image of the rebellious child. "She's dependent on us. She doesn't hesitate to ask for a loan." Her

[2] Our subject's Free Association Hour contained considerable material on fear of losing his health, his strength, and his good physical condition and it was this material that prompted this provisional diagnosis.

aggressiveness—which, as we have noted, was an impulse Charley had learned to repress when it had his father as an object—was bluff. The bluff could be called by a show of strength. "I'm in favor of a big club." Then, when we say "No" we can, like a father, really mean "No." By this means Russia can be made to act reasonably. And again, like the father, we had the "know-how," something the Russians, the uninitiated, wish they could get. In the end, the conflict was between an unruly boy and a strong man. The former could make noise, but the latter, if he would, could shut him up.

Where Charley's mother was concerned, the picture is somewhat more complicated. She was the figure of childhood with whom young Charley had the closest emotional relationship. He was confidant, outlet, and comforter to her and where Father was reservedly remote, Mother was accessible—and, perhaps most important of all, controllable by "soft soaping" and cajoling. It is not stretching the matter too much, we think, to say that Lanlin developed in his relationship with her his confidence in the efficacy of being a gradualist, a calmer of troubled waters and a negotiator. Yet, his mother could still punish, could still flare up in anger. We know that she rarely did, yet the degree to which young Charley avoided any provocation to hostile rejection by his parents was, we feel, a measure of his fear of it.

A word about the curious ambivalence Lanlin expressed toward mechanical skills is in order here. On the one hand he revelled in America's technical "know-how." On the other hand he was derisive about those who put engineering values higher than human values. Recall that Charley's father had skimped and saved and, at times, had made his wife's life miserable by devotion to the property. It was to Charley that his mother would "blow off steam"—the father was apparently sufficiently forbidding to preclude himself as her target. It is reasonable to suppose that the early version of "know-how" is embodied in Charley's father, in his success in getting the property free and clear. This forbidding quality, this competence he saw as characteristic of Americans as a nation, qualities he saw lacking in the Russians who are not even able to develop their own resources.

We may raise the question of why it was that Charley so early gave up any form of struggle or rebellion against his parents' authority, why he did not assert himself more. Considering the circumstances of his childhood, it seems to us most likely that rebelliousness was not stamped down ruthlessly in his earliest years, but rather eased out of him by degrees in a situation where as an only child he enjoyed and did not want to lose high gratification from his parents. In other words, his parents gave him enough, but his father was distant enough to buy conformity gradually, outbidding the rewards of rebelliousness. There may be another element too. Being the confidant of his mother, although rewarding, may also have developed in him an added feeling of responsibility. In asking for his sympathy, his mother was also asking for his support and help in "keeping things going."

The adult Lanlin, then, continued to identify strongly with quietly powerful figures, now transformed to the image of top management. Those aspects of the quietly powerful which suggested the "moss-backs" of the big vested interests, he rejected. And so too he rejected the heartlessness of the "engineering approach" although he held it in some awe. These were the figures that stood behind the system of values which he took to be the actual state of things and against which he saw the Russians fraudulently making their unreasonable demands.

Reinforcing his tendencies to conform to the perceived demands of his parents was the pattern of his childhood and adolescent peer groups. Team sports, clubs, school activities provided practice in adapting the conformist attitudes developed in the family to the demands of peer group life. The agitator, the rebel, the troublemaker, the Communist— these fit readily into a mold that Charley had early rejected.

The Personal Setting of Lanlin's Opinions

It would be well if publishing permitted the inclusion of transcripts of our thirty hours of probing, interviewing, and testing. For here we reach the point at which it is difficult to present one's analysis of a personality without seeming either omniscient or simple. Our object is to examine the personal dynamics of Lanlin's life as these may throw light on his attitudes.

Intellectual capacities. Lanlin, our tests showed, was a man of superior intelligence—his *Wechsler-Bellevue Adult Intelligence Test* revealing a full I.Q. of 120. At the same time, the subtests of the *Wechsler* as well as the *Vigotsky* and the *Rorschach* portrayed a man who used his endowment best in detailed, concrete, and ordered situations that did not require the handling of higher abstractions. Since this particular characteristic was, we believe, of central importance in Lanlin's approach both to personal problems and public affairs, we quote directly from the analysis of his performance on the *Vigotsky Test.*

> S displayed good observational ability and attention to detail, but was quite incapable of grasping the initial indefiniteness of the task and of formulating and testing general hypotheses. His responses were deter-mined by the similarities and differences of individual blocks and he dis-

regarded the overall aspect of the task to the extent of repeatedly forgetting that he was to produce four groups of blocks. He was always aware of what he was doing but hardly ever aware of the logical implications of his attempted solutions. He frequently repeated solutions which had not succeeded.

Further confirmation of the style of Lanlin's intellectual functioning was gained from an analysis of his *Rorschach*. There was, to begin with, a large number of detail responses in his record. His habit of rejecting a first whole response to a blot in favor of a detail response had the flavor of "getting down to the real work: details." His intelligence seemed ordered to the extent of constriction (F plus being over 90%). On the other hand, his movement responses, which were relatively numerous, showed a lively fantasy life.

Lanlin's strength was in the ordering of detail and often the ordering showed itself in the form of conjunctive rather than integrated plans. He was addicted, he told us, to making lists of "things to be done"—prospects to be seen, repairs to be made, minutes to be transcribed. But where long-range thinking was concerned, he either depended upon others for the pattern, as upon his "line sources," or was without one. He was unable, the reader will recall, to give any coherent picture of his possible job future, falling back instead upon a recital of the company's organization chart.

At the ideological level, we noted Lanlin's incapacity to grasp or even consider possibilities of conflict based upon abstract principles. In labor-management relations, for example, there were for him no broad issues, but only the gradual and "reasonable" working out of details through negotiation. Discussions of Russia and Communism were in the same pattern. From his "line sources," he had borrowed and modified slightly a rather disjointed formula of Russia dominated by ambitious and unscrupulous men. In his concrete terms, Russia was as an opportunistic bluffer who could be backed down by a show of strength. Beyond this he saw mainly incidents of unreasonableness each of which could be handled so long as we were strong. His reading of the news was essentially the learning of incidents. Either Lanlin over-generalized by the use of simple formulas or he operated effectively on details. He seemed to have difficulty bringing the two levels of cognitive operation together.

In regard to ability to make friends and to understand others, Lanlin said, "I like people, all types. I like to be with them. I make it a point to get on with people, even those who are hard to get on with—particularly those." His desire to please and his practiced tact were, as he saw it, part of the technique for getting ahead in the world.

There seemed, however, to be little impulsivity in his approach to people and, as we have mentioned, he had few warm friends. Yet his appearance of warmth and interest attracted people to him and this was a source of no small gratification.

The development of Lanlin's abilities to "make people like him" grew from deep sources of which we shall speak presently. It was threatening for him when he found himself, despite his best efforts, still disliked. And so it is typical of him when speaking of the Russian people, of whom he knew next to nothing, to operate on the assumption that they liked us. Being liked was no casual matter for Lanlin. His development of social skills, of a deep defensive significance, was of a piece with his belief that other peoples *had* to like us.

Finally, Lanlin, who so admired his father's mechanical aptitudes around the "property" and who rated "engineering know-how" so high in our national arsenal, judged himself to be poor in mechanical aptitude. Mechanical things did not interest him, "definitely, in no shape, manner, or form," and, indeed, for those in his company who viewed their products "strictly from the engineering" view and missed the human problem, he had contempt. There is here a curious ambivalence to which we shall return, for this is a subject better treated in connection with his attitudes toward his father and toward authority. It suffices to say that since the matter of "know-how" looms large in the way Lanlin distinguishes Russia and the United States, these more fundamental attitudes are related to his opinions on Russia.

Impulsivity and control. In terms of affective characteristics we already know Lanlin as a man who treasured "reasonableness" and "getting on with others." Anger and hostility in others did not release corresponding impulses in him. Rather, he made a point of trying to calm people down in business, at home, in the union. When anger did boil over, and it was not often, it was generally a response to a long series of minor exasperations, and these mostly in the bosom of his family. We may recall too that as a child he learned not to pick fights, that he could win when the other was the aggressor. His reaction to bad news was worry rather than sorrow. In sum, Lanlin had little readiness for emotional arousal. He was a man under control.

Since the rewards he obtained from "self-control" were so great, there was considerable compensation for any losses suffered psychologically through restraint. His place was secured; he was "loved and accepted." And the society around him provided such a clear-cut set of requirements for the "good guy" that Lanlin probably had fewer conflicts than many others in his group as to what responses were required of him.

Nevertheless there was evidently some suffering from the close control exercised over emotional response. Both in fantasy and in overt behavior, Lanlin found great satisfaction in those highly permissive situations in which he could let down his controls. He reported in his *Interview on Personal Values,* for example, that being in church, especially when there was no service and he could just sit there quietly, was a great source of relaxation.[3] Yet, on the whole, Lanlin was relatively free of disruptive anxieties. He characterized himself as a worrier and it was partly through his technique of worrying that unfocalized anxiety was prevented from arising. Characteristically, his worries were about details of business or of family life and he seemed not aware of any large-scale, amorphous concerns. His lists were a case in point, a means whereby he was able to morselize his problems into acts which had to be carried out. Perhaps the closest Lanlin had come to "worry of an order too large to cope with" was during the last years of his dissatisfaction with his clerical job. But the mild depressions occasioned by that situation were handled adequately by strategies of adjustment that we shall consider shortly.

When we speak of Lanlin's controls, we must bear in mind that they served in two ways. On the one hand, it was necessary for him to control any hostile impulses that might disrupt the smooth flow of his interpersonal relations. But equally urgent was the necessity for resisting his own urges to let down, to adopt a more passive role. The exertion of impulse control spelled out, at the same time, a straining against passivity. Perhaps it was the double function of his church visits to allow him to release control of his impulses and to indulge his passive cravings.

That the well controlled Lanlin should first have perceived and then reacted to Russia as he did should be no surprise. Russia, with its unreasonableness and its "demands that didn't make sense," represented the kind of impulsive and unruly forces that Lanlin had banished from his own life. The orderly and accustomed pattern of values

---

[3] Perhaps as much to throw light on the *Rorschach* as on our subject, we present the report on this test:

S experiences stimulation from outside quite vividly (VIII-X 40%), but he is capable of expressing the emotions to which these stimuli give rise only when they are congruent with reality and socially approved (FC 3, no CF). They are expressed in a hesitant or deliberate fashion, under a continuous, cautious testing of the reality situation. This deliberate approach to emotional situations precludes impulsivity, fosters objectivity and tact, and thus assures a smooth social adjustment.

to which he adhered—a kind of Protestantized Catholicism—rejected
such impulsive, aggressive behavior just as his own conscience could
not accept hostility and unreasonableness in himself. So Russia was
seen in the image of the trouble maker; a trouble maker, however,
who could be controlled by a kind of parental firmness to which we
turn next. On the other side, however, is Lanlin's grudging admiration for Communist activists in the labor movement who, so to speak,
"never let down."

Basic strivings. The psychologists' act of isolating certain motives
and holding them up for examination is an artificial one. For strivings, like a set of simultaneous equations, must be viewed as inex-
tricably interdependent. Thus, in Lanlin we find security needs tied
together with needs for recognition and achievement. In turn, we
find this complex of needs variously in conflict with passive dependent
cravings on the one hand and heavily controlled aggressive tendencies
on the other. Here was a man who needed the recognition and approbation of his fellows—but in the secure, prestigeful setting of a great
company and in a type of work where he could, in his own words,
feel "constructive." And here too was a man who worked hard for
his sense of achievement and for the recognition of others, yet craved
to let down and relax, to give up the struggle. And finally, here was
a man who, in order to ingratiate himself into a position of acceptance
by others, had to maintain a deep-seated control over his hostile
tendencies. If we bear constantly in mind this complex economy of
motives we are less likely to go astray when viewing its components
in isolation.

Looking at his strivings from a genetic point of view, the point of
departure is Lanlin's strong but passive dependence upon his parents,
particularly passive where his relations with the father were concerned.
In reviewing his childhood memories he said in answer to a question
on daydreams and childhood ambitions: "I don't think I wanted to
be anything in particular. I never thought much about what I'd be."
What decisions were to be made were made by the father with young
Charley and his mother acceding. Only with his mother could he
take an active part in shaping decisions and it was not his mother
who made the major ones. Even with her, he showed the kind of
acceptance of her guidance that made him in her eyes an "ideal," i.e.,
compliant son. On the *Argument Completion Test,* significantly,
Lanlin favored a young doctor going into private practice rather than
social medicine so that he could reimburse his father for the expenses
of his training.

If passive dependence brought him success and approbation in the limited and austere circle of his family, he was to find later that his transfer of identification to other parent figures required a more active role. He had later to strive for his recognition, to work even in monotonous drudgery in order to be part of his company. And to manage the property, the symbol of his father's achievement, again required considerable expenditure of worried effort.

The reader has probably noticed the extent to which the question of dependence enters into Lanlin's assessment of the world. In his new job as salesman, top management and clerical workers alike were dependent on him. In another connection we find Lanlin enjoying the status of parent in which the children are dependent upon him. In the same currency, the members of his union are dependent upon him for negotiating settlements with management, a task to which he brought his powers of reasonableness. In short, Lanlin, who was himself a dependent person as we have noted, was also a person who enjoyed having others dependent upon him. In many ways, this enjoyment served as a defense against his own feelings of dependency or helplessness. How better contain the threat of Russia than by seeing her too as dependent on us?

We believe that the key to this attitude toward dependence can be found in his role as mother's confidant. While he found deep gratification in his dependence upon his family, he early learned that there was a great deal of reward in love when others were dependent upon him, as his mother was. Receiving sympathetically the troubles and cares of others was a privileged position rewarded with warm returns of kindness and love. Perhaps it was because Charley used this image of dependence-rewarded-by-love that he was convinced that, *really,* the Russian people liked America and Americans and that, even secretly, Russia's leaders couldn't help but admire or at least envy our ways.

Lanlin's needs for recognition, gratified first by his union activity and currently by his salesmanship, seemed to have been the outcome partly of his dependence upon others for support and partly of his residual fears of rejection. It is significant that Lanlin was our only subject to use "acquaintance with fellow workers" as a reason for staying on an old job in the *Argument Completion Test.* Social-environmental support was crucial to him. To be accepted perhaps meant for him not only something positive but also "not to be rejected." One may conjecture too whether external recognition did not also serve as a means of keeping him going, helping him overcome his wishes to let down. Recall his *Rorschach* analysis and the emphasis there upon responding to outer stimulation in precedence to inner.

And so Lanlin has developed his "approach to people," smoothed his front, and worked out a highly adequate adjustment to his recognition needs. In David Riesman's terms, his "other directedness" served not only social ends but also gratified deep-seated inner need.[4]

The main relevance of these recognition needs for Lanlin's attitudes toward Russia is in the degree to which they made it simple for him and gratifying for him to hold the majority or "normal" view on this subject. His needs are to be accepted as one of the group, not as an innovator. In this sense, Lanlin's anti-Communism served its social adjustive function easily and smoothly.

Finally, concerning Lanlin's capacity for expressing aggression, we know that the circumstances where aggression was permissible were limited. In a figurative sense, what he told us about his fights at school was true of the grown Charley. Fights *he* started were not won. Fights *others* started, Charley won. Or in another setting, if the aggression were organized, competitive sports, he too could have good, aggressive team spirit. He had to be with the group. Toward the attacker, especially the attacker of the group, his hostility was permissible as long as the group was with him. Short of these requirements, hostility-provoking situations brought forth his well practiced defenses as he soon learned that the peace-maker is not without honor in our society.

Lanlin should show good capabilities for moral indignation toward any person or institution whom he sees as expressing hostility wantonly. At the time of this study, he did not cast Russia in this image: more a bluffer than a wanton aggressor. It would not surprise us to find him far more aroused today. Five years ago, Russia was a noxious adolescent. Lanlin's hostility was aroused, but not strongly.

On balance, Lanlin has done well in gratifying his strivings. The price he paid for his success may become more evident as we consider the adjustive strategies that made it possible.

Adjustive Strategies

Very likely the principal adjustive strategy of Lanlin as we knew him was his planning activity. It served both to bind his anxieties to tangible events and acts—the routines of family and work—and to help him avoid getting into situations where disorder and impulsiveness would disrupt him. His planning, we have already noted, was not of a strategic, but of a tactical, detailed order. Its object was to morselize his problems into segments that he could manage. This type

---

[4] David Riesman, *The lonely crowd*, New Haven, Yale University Press, 1950.

of compulsive defense, having as its object the control and binding
of anxiety by his own acts, had little transfer value to the field of
public affairs. The planful conscientiousness that led Lanlin to be
an excellent secretary-treasurer of a local civic association and to take
a highly detailed responsibility in union affairs never led him to inform
himself with any care about world affairs. The "world" to which
Lanlin's planfulness and conscientiousness pertained was the world of
family, work, and the "face-to-face" local community. More than most
men, he was his brother's keeper, but his brother was someone he
might be likely to meet someday. Basically, he felt there was relatively little he could "do" about more remote matters—like Communism—and in consequence he tended to be relatively indifferent and
unpolitical in the broader sense.

That repression was another prominent mode of adjusting to impulsive problems is also quite apparent. This was, of course, notably
the case with his aggressive impulses and passive tendencies which
were both under a stern control. That both could find occasional
release in circumscribed situations was a source of relief for our
subject. We have already discussed the bearing of this defense on
Lanlin's attitudes toward the "noisy" and aggressively expansionist
Soviet state.

And finally we feel that to some extent Lanlin's adjustment represented a successful form of reaction formation. Against his passivity
he had erected a structure of enterprise and activity in his work that
served as a basis for social recognition and reward. To cope with
provocations to aggression—a nasty customer, a local man who unjustly
and bad-temperedly accused his son of killing a chicken, an exasperated
ticket seller at the theater, a hot-tempered member of his local—he
responded by skillful techniques of calming the threatening aggressor.
The response had become natural and automatic. He was recognized
and admired for it. It is no surprise then that "reasonableness" had
become the yardstick by which Lanlin measured public matters:
strikes, Hitler, Russia's behavior.

There are, to be sure, many other forms of his behavior that could
be subsumed under the heading of adjustive strategies. For Lanlin's
problems of ego defense were extensive and the range of mechanisms
manifested was varied. Unquestionably, for example, his identifications with such powerful external institutions as the "business world"
and the Catholic Church aided him in coping with rejection anxieties.
In support of these identifications, moreover, he was capable of employing with considerable self-deception the maneuver of rationaliza-

tion which we shall illustrate in a later section in our discussion of opinion maintenance.

His capacity to use a form of denial in defense was well illustrated in his approach to the *Argument Completion Test*. Of all our subjects, only Sullivan exceeded Lanlin in the one-sidedness of his arguments. In this particular situation, he could give no arguments or rather poor and sketchy ones on the opposite side of the fence from his own preferred position. Lanlin was also quite poor at seeing any arguments on the other side of the Russo-American conflict, as we have seen. On the surface it would seem as though this kind of performance was at odds with Lanlin's real capacities as a negotiator, his skill at bringing opposing sides together. We believe that the contradiction vanishes, however, when one takes into account the fact that Lanlin operated in his characteristic negotiatory manner only when, so to speak, he was playing for stakes in a relatively face-to-face situation. An abstract task (like argument completions) or a general current issue (like Communism) did not evoke his creative talents. There were no rewards involved, no payoff in terms of the increased affection given him by the parties to a dispute. Peacemaking in Lanlin was a response to concrete, "real life" situations. It did not generalize to abstract situations.

Finally, Lanlin had a healthy capacity for restriving in the face of setbacks. It was the nature of his worrying that he would develop plans for action rather than rationalizations of defeat. An empty store on the property, for example, called forth a flurry of list-making and prospect-searching that invariably succeeded in setting to rights the manifest source of his concern, "the property."

So, while several psychologists who examined individual productions of our subject with no other knowledge of him diagnosed him as a man who must suffer considerable and disruptive anxiety, the fact of the matter was that what anxiety he had was well bound up in intellectualized worry and that, in the main, he operated very effectively. Had Lanlin been less well under control, it is likely that he would have found Russia a far more tempting target for violent hatred. His adjustive strategies worked so well that he needed no all-out scapegoat.

Opinion Maintenance and Furtherance

When a person holds opinions that reflect his personal adjustment but that are violently opposed by his social environment, he is forced to guard and nurture his opinions carefully. For Lanlin such was not the case. Maintaining a set of opinions that accorded with the views of the majority required no great effort from him.

We must distinguish first what might be called external and internal forms of opinion maintenance, the former being activities directed toward various sources of information, the latter being intrapsychic. Externally, Lanlin did not expose himself to media of information or people who represented a challenge to his views. Perhaps we put the matter too voluntaristically; the fact is that he had few opportunities for such exposure. On the contrary, the reading of Catholic periodicals on the one hand and the popular press on the other provided a varied enough diet of support to his loosely formulated opinions on national and international affairs.

That he was not accustomed to the work of internal opinion maintenance, the task of dealing with facts and opinions contrary to his own beliefs, can be judged from this comment by the investigator who administered the *Information Apperception Test:*

> The S had no apparent difficulty understanding the instructions. The interview lasted in all approximately two hours, which included a five-minute break after the first five items had been completed. The S was obviously fatigued at the completion of the interview. Nevertheless, the lack of spontaneity of the S, in the opinion of the interviewer, was not attributable to fatigue. On the several occasions when there was an apparent lack of attention, the S did not appear preoccupied. It was the interviewer's strong impression that the S had lost the thread of his thinking; that he was not able to pick it up; that he didn't know where to go from there, nor was he able to recall what he had just finished saying —literally blank.

Recall that this test required the subject to interpret aloud the meaning of various brief factual items about Russia, some favorable, others neutral or unfavorable. His performance was a constant though disjointed effort to cramp all the items into the mold of Russia as a nation whose leaders exploited and hoodwinked its people and sought power and dominance. In all save one instance he succeeded—even at times to the point of strain as when he commented on a statement about diverse nationalities and languages in Russia by pointing out that they were all under the thumb of the Central Government. The exception was the statement that factory managers in Russia earn as much as the equivalent of $10,000 a year. Obviously he was not used to thinking about Russia in terms of such details. He was touched at a sensitive spot. His answer follows:

> [Long pause] Well . . . factory managers and supervisors in Russia . . . are . . . classified in the . . . Russian upper class. To be manager

or supervisor they've got a technical knowledge that the rank and file haven't got. They are foremen of industry and as foremen of industry . . . they . . . the knowledge they have . . . is valuable to Russia because despite the fact that there is so many people, there isn't the per cent of technical-minded people . . . is very small. And because . . . the per cent is small . . . and they are so valuable . . . the general scheme of making Russia . . . mighty industrially. . . . They rate. They rate a good salary and good positions in society.

[Does this item make you think better or worse of Russia?]

No . . . I have no feeling on that. I mean, we assume if a man does know more . . . that he isn't there from a political standpoint . . . His work is . . . he should be paid. Apparently he must be. No, I have no feeling about their being worth $10,000 as foremen or managers of the plant. . . . If they were managers or supervisors in this country, they'd be able to live on a little higher scale than the rank and file do.

[How typical of Russia would you say the item is?]

The statement isn't alarming. The statement is alright. The factory managers and supervisors get up to $10,000 a year. That's alright. That makes sense. We assume the statements, as you say, are all true . . . that they do get $10,000. There's nothing alarming about that statement. No one would argue that they paid them a full week's pay. No . . . there's nothing alarming about that statement. $10,000 sounds like a lot of money for Russia to pay to anybody. But, if it's a true statement, they must be worth it or they wouldn't be paid. $10,000 strikes me as a lot of money to be paying out in Russia considering how they keep their lower classes restricted in money. It sounds like quite a lot. It certainly means that a shop supervisor is in a higher bracket financially and can indulge in a lot of luxuries that the vast majority of Russians cannot indulge in. I dare say that any of the supervisors are first OK'd by the government before appointment. Somebody certainly . . . would have to have that type of job and we assume that these people are fitted for these positions.

[Does this item interest you very much?]

The only point that interests me is the $10,000 a year. $10,000 a year interests me. That would interest me in any country. That would interest me right here. I didn't think they paid that much and yet I know they must. It must be a fairly important position. I know it's important to them industrially to have somebody there who knows how to produce machinery. But the fact that they have plant managers . . . that's standard practice. I would say that $10,000 is considerably above the rank and file . . . for a country that . . . that gives the impression of . . . everybody pitching in on the same level to get the final result.

Lanlin's "defense" of his opinion operated almost at a perceptual level. He did not perceive information or views contrary to his own for what they were, but rather as either confirming suspicions or as providing evidence of wrong-mindedness. Where Russia was concerned, blacks and whites tended to prevail and he was not adept at perceiving the grays of the case. Given this effective device and given the benign and confirming information environment, maintenance of his views was quite automatic.

He did little to develop and further his opinions on the subject of Russia. His news reading was casual, piecemeal, and haphazard. Insofar as one can single out an example of opinion furtherance, it was his regular reading of the Jesuit magazine *America* from which he gained much confirmation and some extension of his basic views. Where his positive values and opinions were concerned—his belief in and support of the prevailing system of values—he took an active part in business, union, and community affairs but these activities were less designed to elaborate his beliefs than to carry them into action.

Prediction of Lanlin's future attitudes is contingent of course on one's views of the developing national and international situation. Assuming that the future portends an armed stalemate between East and West, Lanlin's views should remain unchanged. In the event of war, he will in all likelihood regret that no better solution was possible, yet he will give his wholehearted support to the war effort and interpret war as a means of bringing Russia to her senses. Just as he had accepted sacrifices during the last war when the enemy was one in whom he saw *some* virtues, he would even more readily accept them in the future against an enemy in whom he saw no good whatever. Indeed, the force of moral indignation could be mobilized more easily where Russia is concerned than ever was the case with Germany.

A Functional Summing-Up

We arrive finally at the task of summing up briefly the manner in which Lanlin's opinions on Communism and Russia functioned in the economy of his personality.

Expressively viewed, his opinions were of a style with his general cognitive functioning. Resistant to abstraction generally, he characteristically avoided seeing broad ideological issues in the present conflictful international situation. Events followed from the malevolent activities of a ruling clique in Russia whose concrete acts and intentions provided the dynamism in the international situation. This highly controlled, concretely ordered, and modulated man found the behavior of the Russian state abhorrent. But it was of a piece with both his controlled approach and his preoccupation with local interpersonal relations that he should be relatively indifferent to an issue like Russia and Communism.

One other expressive consistency worth noting was Lanlin's tend-

ency to optimism. Whether by result of a "temperamental trait" or of
the smooth flow of his own childhood development, he faced the
world with the implicit conviction that "things would turn out alright."
So too with his opinions on Russia: stand firm and everything would
work out. "The world is a wonderful place."

Lanlin's opinions toward Russia and Communism were not of central importance to his everyday adjustment. This is not to say, however, that they did not reflect deeply important adjustive needs. For
most emphatically they did.

Most important of these adjustive needs was for social approbation,
acceptance, and recognition. We need not reiterate here the origin
of these needs in an early and unterminated dependency relation with
his parents. He was left with a predisposition to accept loyally the
economic and religious order of the dominant society around him: a
fusion of middle-class and Catholic values. We speak of such a man
as a conformist, but the term is superficial and fails to do justice to
the centrality of the motivational problems with which Lanlin had to
deal. Indeed, he was a conformist, he was "other oriented," but not
out of a conscious design to conform.

It was natural, then, for him to reject out of hand and fail to see
virtue in a system (for him, not a system but a clique) which could
threaten his own. So deep-seated was his aversion to anything that
brought his values into question that he could not fully take them
seriously, having to belittle Russia as "bluffing" or, better yet, as *really*
dependent on us. There could be no war, for they were dependent
on us and knew it. Charley had learned in his role as confidant to
his mother and later as negotiator, that those who were dependent on
one would not attack. Life had never taught him that dependence
could also lead to hostility.

In this sense, then, Lanlin's opinions served both in his *social adjustment* by concretizing his allegiance to the society with which he
identified and in making possible the *externalization of some of his
basic inner problems.* For the condemnation of Russia as the unruly,
demanding, aggressive, unreasonable nation was an affirmation of his
own early and continuing renunciation of "making demands that didn't
make sense." He lived by this formula, at a cost in tension, and who-
ever did not was a threat to his way of life.

His opinions or, better, his general view of Russia and of the motives of her leaders, served as a useful mode of *object appraisal.* Having personalized and concretized the issue of Russia in terms of the
motives of Russian leadership, there could be no real surprises. Whatever Russia did was comprehensible in terms of these motives. What

on the surface might seem like good deeds could now be written off as part of the bluff. Faced with an item on the *Information Apperception Test* that Russia was publishing large quantities of books including translations of Shakespeare, he could even write Shakespeare off as probably having something to do with a change in Russian line toward England. Evil acts he took for granted. On the whole then, the orientation to reality was of a form best designed to protect him from any reality contrary to his own. If his beliefs prove correct, he is well cared for. If not, he will be slow to change.

CHAPTER 8

HILARY SULLIVAN

A COMMUNIST in belief though not a party member, Sullivan held opinions about Russia that were fraught with much more personal significance than those of the ordinary citizen. His attitudes illustrate vividly how a person's creative interpretation of the external world can play a strategic part in making difficult personal problems supportable.

Just as the personal significance of Chatwell's world view casts no light on the present validity of nineteenth century Liberalism, so our scrutiny of Sullivan's Communism can tell us nothing about the tenability of the Communist position in 1947. As we have repeatedly taken pains to observe, psychological interpretation must be carefully disentangled from *ad hominem* argument. We must also agree with Sullivan that he is "typical" only of himself. The psychological sources of Communist ideology in general are outside of our present concern.[1]

Our functional approach does, nevertheless, lead to some expectations in regard to people like the Communists who hold intense attitudes, and defines a limited sense in which we assume Sullivan to be "typical" of them. Whenever a person feels strongly about a topic, we run little risk in inferring that it has important personal meaning

[1] For pertinent evidence on the characteristics of American, British, French, and Italian Communists, *see* G. A. Almond, *The appeals of Communism*, Princeton, Princeton University Press, 1954.

154

to him. The attitudes of a Communist should therefore provide unusual opportunity to trace out the adjustive functions that they serve.
Deviant and unpopular, the views of such a person inevitably encounter attack from the public media of communication and perhaps
from some of his circle of acquaintances. Unless he responds to such
attack by consolidating his position and building it firmly into the
structure of his going concerns, his dangerous opinions must succumb
to social pressure and he ceases to be a Communist.

Introductory Sketch

Hilary Sullivan was a 48-year-old, self-educated man, the son of
poor Catholic parents, who at the time of the study was making a
precarious living working on weekly newspapers and occasional publicity jobs. Newspaper work had predominated in his spotty and
variegated occupational career. His Communist beliefs were his most
salient characteristic, both to himself and to the interviewers. Born
a Catholic, he was no longer a believer. His physical health was good,
except for a shoulder injury that prevented his attempting heavy work.
Psychologically, he presented a history of claustrophobia and heavy
drinking with delirium tremens, and described himself as "kind of
nervous and high-strung." Nine years previously, his first wife had
divorced him because of his drinking. An abstainer since shortly
thereafter, he had remarried successfully five years before the study.

We got in touch with Sullivan through a person active in left Liberal circles whom we asked to suggest a pro-Russian subject. Sullivan
was not told, however, that the study would concern Russia. When
we explained over the telephone that we were studying "normal men,"
he insisted, to our perplexity, that he was not "normal," repeating the
same point in the *Enrollment Interview*. From the very beginning,
Sullivan was wary of our attempts to put him in a pigeonhole, especially any conventional one.

As he first appeared at the Clinic and we subsequently came to
know him, Sullivan was a rather large man, with heavy, well-rounded
physique, light hair graying at the temples, pink complexion, a large
mouth, and indistinct eyebrows that made his blue eyes seem small,
and his whole appearance rather that of a jolly piggy-bank. He
dressed neatly, usually in a gray business suit. His face was expressive,
ranging between joviality, deadpan pseudo-naïveté, and emphatic
(sometimes mock-serious) contortion. In gait, he was awkward and
a little confused, as though he might stumble over himself, while his
gestures were abrupt, large, and not graceful. In general bearing, he

gave the impression of being well-mannered, uncoordinated, and somewhat disoriented.

In talk, which Sullivan clearly enjoyed, he was prolific in disjunctive
outbursts. He often failed to complete sentences, and there were
frequent asides, self-contradictions, and immediately retracted paradoxical statements. While his grammar was good and his vocabulary
rich, the effect was occasionally spoiled by his unsureness about words
that he had more often than not employed correctly.

In his relationship with the members of the staff, Sullivan was warm,
informal, and witty. He actively tried to establish relations on a level
of informal equality. Often he seemed to be playing for an impression, waiting for the interviewer to give the appropriate reaction, to
which he would respond gratefully. Characteristically he insisted on
his own often paradoxical phrasing of his opinions; to the discomfiture
of interviewers, he would often reject their reformulations of his
meaning.

Sullivan's Values

Sullivan's attitudes toward Russia were part and parcel of his version of the Communist world view. We approach his opinions about
the Soviet state as he himself would wish by first examining in outline
the main features of his ideology and value system. The details will
emerge later on.

(1) Sullivan was a Marxist and a non-party Communist. His understanding of the Marxist position was worked out adequately on
the main points, but did not always embrace the details of doctrine.

(2) Through his Communist ideology, he consciously sought meaning and purpose in life.

> You're always seeking a stronger purpose for living. . . . I think we
> should justify ourselves.

Purpose was to be sought; it could not be taken for granted.

(3) The world was in flux. "We do not live in a static world," he
liked to state; "my philosophy, so far as I understand it . . . I don't
think . . . is a static thing." Education was therefore a "continuing
process" for him, and he made much of Lincoln Steffens' dictum that
schools should "teach the unknown," not the known. Experiment was
good. Life was a constant, rather grim struggle for survival. The
processes of historical change were inevitable and could not be evaded.

(4) The capitalist patterns were outworn, and fated to be replaced
after an inevitable interval of Fascism by developments along the lines
of the Russian experiment.

(5) Although historical processes were inevitable, the individual had the obligation to see the right and do his part, whatever its effectiveness. The highest virtues, valued by Sullivan in their own right, were intellectual integrity, "savvy," and the courage of one's convictions. These were best embodied in his ideal, the independent radical Scott Nearing.

> I would like to have . . . the . . . the savvy of men like Scott Nearing, I'd like to have their courage, their stick-to-it-iveness . . . their great faith in what they believe is right.

(6) However, people in general and himself in particular were to be excused when they fail to show these virtues. It was too much to expect a person to escape "the pattern." Not everyone could be Scott Nearing. People were basically trustworthy and good, and

> When they let you down, there's an economic reason. . . . I don't blame them. I blame the pattern.

Even ideological opponents in the Republican camp could be accepted in these terms. "They *are* good men, you know, according to their lights."

> Now this *J*, he's a splendid fellow. Marvelous fellow. He sees Communists under the bed . . . but he's a likeable fellow . . . he's got integrity. . . . Well, gee whiz, just because they don't agree with you . . . your social and economic beliefs. . . . There're other likeable things about them.

Communism was the second of two ideologies which Sullivan's life had encompassed. By his late twenties, some years before he was to embrace the Communist philosophy, he had gradually fallen away from the Catholicism in which he grew up, though most of his friends were Catholic. When we encountered him, he was neither religious nor anti-Catholic. He said:

> I appreciate those people who have the faith. They've certainly got something that we haven't. But I haven't got it and there's no use trying to kid myself that I have. There's nothing there for me to lean on. . . . I recognize the fact that everybody reaches for some spiritual thing and for some reason or other they think that there's something beyond . . . they reach instinctively for something higher. I know they do it . . . but I don't, and it's instinctive and there must be some reason for it. I don't know what the reason is. If there is a reason, it has not been explained to me in a sensible manner.

His account of the satisfactions that he found in religion emphasized forgiveness, dependence, and hope:

It was a solace. You'd go to church. Go to confession. You'd come out . . . forgiven. Now. . . . And this atmosphere in which they brought you up . . . when things were bad, you'd go and see the priest . . . have a calm talk and feel better for it. You'd pray, and hope. It's hope that they preach. And of course, life everlasting.

From the perspective of his second ideology, he looked back on his earlier faith as a "crutch."

We were quickly alert to possible equivalences in his two faiths, an interpretation on our part that Sullivan soon came to suspect and to reject vehemently. Contrasts in the personal meanings that Catholicism and Communism had for him proved most illuminating in regard to the functional grounding of his political views. To pursue this analysis, however, we need closer acquaintance with his strivings and predicaments. These topics will occupy us later after we have examined his views on Russia.

Sullivan on Russia

In the third session at the Clinic, Sullivan was explaining to the interviewer on *Personal Values and Religious Sentiments* how he became a Socialist. We break into the transcript at this point.

E: You'd call yourself a Marxian Socialist, would you?

S: Yes.

E: There're Socialists and Socialists and Socialists.

S: I'd call myself a Communist. That's what I'd call myself.

E: That must bring trouble on your shoulders, I should think.

S: I don't go out of my way telling everybody I'm a Communist, though. That's the closest. Like Scott Nearing. If somebody says, "Well, are you a Communist?", well, Scott says, "Not at the moment." You know.

E: Because he didn't have his card?

S: Well, no, because the Communist Party of America he'd disagree with, because he thought that they were the tail to the foreign policy of Russia.

E: And how would you feel about that?

S: I would feel exactly the way he did . . . that I was interested in the theory of the thing . . . as a revolutionary theory.

E: You don't care particularly about Russian Communism? You are interested in Communism as a general thing . . . to apply to. . . .

S: No. . . . I'm. . . . Here has been an experiment in Russia . . . a social experiment. Well, they made mistakes . . . the same as we in our social experiment made mistakes. In our Constitution we had chattel slavery. [Umhum] Well, we abolished it, but we killed an awful lot of guys off before we did. But the thing is, we did. Well, so they have made a lot of mistakes. So we, I think, are in an admirable position to profit by their mistakes. Well. Because Russia was a pre-capitalist state . . . ah . . . there are certain things in . . . in . . . that happened in the Union of Soviet Socialist Republics that wouldn't apply in our. . . . So I'm in favor of adapting these things. And I'm in favor of letting these people work out this alternative.

E: Umhum. How do you see the future in those terms? Do you think that some sort of Socialism or Communism will be a likely possibility in America?

S: Well . . . yes. Because I think we're the only [laugh] capitalist nation left.

E: What sort of a time-schedule do you see that taking place in?

S: Well, we will simply go on trying to make a system . . . an outmoded system . . . work and then the forces from the left will disorganize the forces from the right. And the forces from the right will rush in and you'll have Fascism as the last dying gasp of capitalism. [Said very forcefully and slowly with pauses between words.]

E: You think Fascism will be a stage that we'll have to go through before we have Communism?

S: Right. Yes.

E: And you're reconciled to that pretty much, then?

S: Yeah. I'm pretty sure . . . that's going to happen.

E: It's inevitable, so you think. . . .

S: I think it *is* happening.

E: What do you see as the thing to be done under that view of things, then? You don't think there's any hope to avert the stage of Fascism?

S: No. None.

E: So what is the thing which you find most important to do?

S: Well, the thing most important to do is to . . . preach a doctrine of one world, united nations, and that's sort of self-preservation, because if we don't have it, we're likely to be vaporized [laugh].

The *Open-Ended Interview on Russia* conducted the following week by the same interviewer formally broached the topic of Russia as follows:

E: You remember when we were starting out on this thing, I told you we were going to be interested in some of your opinions on current affairs as well as in who you are. And, at this point, I'd like to start in on that part of our project. We've decided to concentrate mainly on attitudes toward Russia, because we think that's a good hot subject that most people have opinions on as it's pretty much in the news nowadays. And we think it's important in itself to find out about. So that from now on you'll probably be hearing quite a bit about Russia—or we'll be hearing from you. To start out, this evening what I'd like is for you to tell us as much as possible in your own words just how you feel about it, and why. So, to start with, you can just start anywhere and tell me some of the things you feel about Russia.

S: Well, of course I feel very very kindly toward Russia as a country . . . and towards the Russians. I have a book on Russia [laugh] which I think I've told you about. And . . . it just occurred to me the other day I should probably go through it again. Well, I think the Russians have an alternative to capitalism . . . at least they are seeking an alternative. They're engaged in a great experiment and I think we should be sympathetic towards any people engaged in an experiment the aim of which is to benefit most of them. That applies to what you people are doing here tonight.

E: You see the Russian development as an experiment.

S: As an experiment. Now I know . . . or, I feel, I don't know . . . I feel this way . . . ah . . . They are enjoying a very great measure— I'd say GREAT, all caps . . . of success, because the press of this country is blowing its top about it and resorting to every means to discredit it. Well, I only can see from that the thing is working out very well, because if it wasn't working out, why get excited about it! On the other hand, they have told us prior to the war that these Russians were very very stupid people, peasants, left their tractors out in the fields, couldn't repair them—all that sort of thing—it didn't get anywhere. The kind of myth they gave me when I was a kid. And I believed them for a while.

E: You think that the existence of all these rumors about Russia proves that there must be something there?

S: Yes. Definitely. Yeah. Well, then came the war. And the Russians did know something about manufacturing, production. The rocket gun . . . I think they were very successful with that. And they captured more equipment from the Germans than we sent to them in lend-lease. So I think that destroys that myth.

E: You think that their war achievement is something that convinces you that they . . .

S: Well, of course, I didn't need convincing, because I liked them. I like Slavs. I like Lithuanians. I lived with them. I know. In other words, how could you tell me that a Lithuanian or Pole or a Russian was stupid when I lived with them and knew that they were pretty good mechanics.

E: You knew them as people.

S: Yes, as people. Because I lived in a polyglot—that's the word, isn't it? I lived in a polyglot community.

Here begins an historical account that need not be quoted. As these selections indicate, Sullivan's attitudes toward Russia formed an integral part of his central ideology.

While Sullivan knew and had thought much about Russia, the differentiation in his attitudes did not show itself in a pattern of praises and reproofs. Except for minor Russian mistakes in planning, which he admitted defensively but could not specify even under the pressure of the *Stress Interview,* he was favorable toward Russia in every respect. His attitudes were nevertheless highly differentiated in a cognitive sense; he reacted with discrimination to many facets of Russia, of which some were important to him while others he had to explain away. The basic formula was apparent in his initial statements. Elsewhere he stated it succinctly as follows:

> That it is a social and political experiment and that it is the alternative to a system that has had its historical purpose.

The principal guises in which Russia entered his ken can be summarized as (1) Russia as an experiment in social welfare, (2) Russian Communism as the only alternative to a moribund capitalism, (3) Russia as in basic ideological conflict with the United States, and (4) Russia as a temporary "police state."

Time and again Sullivan underlined Russia's significance as an experiment. "I see Russia showing us a way," he told us. "It's the only country where youth has any hope. They try to say that youth has hope in this country. I don't believe so." This social experiment he saw as enjoying a large measure of success, evidenced by Russia's war performance and by the violence of opposition to her in the rest of the world. The experiment extended to treatment of minorities, industrial progress, cultural progress, etc., etc. Even greater was the success he foresaw in the future:

> I also think that they are a strong people, and they have ideals and that they will see it through. And I think . . . of course to me it's the only hope.

Russia for him was the sole source of hope. The United States, once a strong and fortunate country, was already entering an inevitable stage of Fascism. There was no hope nor security nor real Democracy here.

> Everybody you talk to is worried about what is going to happen to them.

Sullivan saw the two countries in basic ideological conflict.

> E: What do you think some of the main sources of disagreement are between us and Russia?
>
> S: There is one main source. Ideology.

But Russia had been playing realistic power politics like the other great powers:

> I think that the Russians are having in mind what took place after World War I and their experiences in the League of Nations, which weren't very happy—but they learned a lot about world politics and diplomacy. And so they said, "This time we are at least equal to these boys and we'll not be tossed around." So they expanded their borders. For what reason? Just to bargain, because that's the way diplomacy and treaties are made. They're bargaining counters yet. I don't see why they should, but that's the way they have to be made. . . . Of course it's all right for us to do that. . . . [Gives example of U.S. obtaining Japanese mandate islands.]

The United States had its inevitable role cut out for it:

> I can't see where American policy can be anything else than what it is, being a capitalist nation . . . and the last one left [laughing]. I can't see.

The future was dubious, threatening, but somehow vague:

> Well, there's two great powers . . . there's Russia and the United States and their ideologies are at variance . . . they cannot accept . . . they cannot . . . their premises are simply. . . . So they will collide. The only thing that can prevent their colliding is that England will come in with Russia and therefore the balance . . . is . . . will be so great that it will probably stop a collision. At any rate, if that happens, we probably will not be vaporized.

At another point Sullivan made a different prognosis:

> The question is, if Russia is a strong power and surrounded by nations supporting her, will Uncle Sam attack her? I think not. However, there is one group in this country that wants war and they may go on anyhow.

Elsewhere in his immediate reactions to the Truman Doctrine he asserted that "this is the first phase of World War III."

> I happened to pick up the *Monitor* that night and there it was commenting on Truman's speech. And I thought, "There he goes [laugh]. He's moving faster than I thought. Gee, this is two years ahead of time." He didn't give me a chance to catch up with it. But I wasn't shocked or anything by it.

The relatively high degree of inconsistency or confusion in his thinking about the possibility of war, while scarcely peculiar to Sullivan, raises the question of personal determinants since it contrasts so sharply with the orderly progression of events that he envisioned at an historical level.

It was when he considered Russia as a temporary "police state" that

Sullivan came closest to qualifying his altogether favorable judgment, yet even here he could not see the cloud for the silver lining.

E: Some people have compared German Nazism with Russian Communism. I wonder how you react to that comparison.

S: Well, German Nazism was totalitarianism for the benefit of the few, not for the people. The present form of Russian government is a totalitarian government for the benefit of all.

E: You don't have any reaction against totalitarianism in itself?

S: Yes. Ah . . . I've been brought up to believe . . . and I think rightfully so . . . that we should have a measure of freedom . . . movement, speech . . . and all that sort of thing. But, as I've said before, there's a state of martial law. Now when there's a state of martial law, you have totalitarianism. And when that emergency is over and the thing is secure, then you go back to your Russian Constitution. I don't know whether you ever read it or not . . . but you'll see that it's quite an instrument. And you can see how it works. But, the thing that we forget is that they are in a state of emergency—a state of war.

E: That is something that would justify practically any emergency measures?

S: Yes. And that they were a feudal state, and they had such a gap to bridge, and at the same time had to contend with enemies from without. And also enemies from within, because they had the counter-revolution.

E: You think they really had a counter-revolution there?

S: Oh, yeah. Any revolution has a counter-revolution. Suppose you didn't believe . . . you know, in Russia . . . then what would you do? You'd work in the underground. In fact it's in every country. Do you mean to say that there couldn't be an underground in Russia? Of course there can be an underground in Russia. There can be an underground anywhere. There is an underground. Let's be realistic about this [laugh]. If there isn't an underground, why do you have the NKVD—the secret police?

E: You think that was a necessary thing, with the counter-revolution there?

S: Yeah. Well, yeah. The police state doesn't appeal to me very well. A police state. But it evidently is necessary. I don't know whether it is or not. But it evidently is necessary, because of the counter-revolution—the movement to overthrow the thing. And they had a plot and plans to throw the thing over, and they were taking every measure to protect it.

As soon as the pressure let up, he believed, Russia would become more liberal.

They know that they have to relax and give people civil liberties. Otherwise you have your underground.

Hilary Sullivan knew much about Russia and was favorable in every respect. A few of the miscellaneous aspects that his opinions took cognizance of may be noted briefly. None was of central importance to him.

Russia's role in World War II rated his strong approval. Russia had stayed out of the first phase of the war only to prepare herself better, Sullivan held, and when the invasion came, the Russians had done a "marvelous job." Self-preservation and the love of country had come before ideology in accounting for their splendid performance, but that was only natural.

Sullivan also approved of Russian religious policies.

> Well, of course, I think the Russians take a very very sane view on the religious issue. They, according to the Constitution and the Workshop book, say that you can practice atheism or you can practice Christianity . . . but it seems that what we object to over here is the atheism. In other words, organized religion over here can sabotage any group of people that might be atheists . . . and the same thing holds true for people who have some religious faiths.

Morality was no problem. Russian family customs are like ours, he said, except that nursery schools are provided that make families possible for working mothers.

Russian industrial progress came in for equal praise. "In ten years I think they'll leave us so far behind that we can't even hear the band." Similarly with the arts and sciences and virtually anything else an interviewer could bring up.

> S: Now . . . I think that in Russia the work that you people are engaged in would find a . . . a . . . readier sympathy and cooperation than in this country.
>
> E: You think they are interested in fostering research?
>
> S: Yes, and the arts, and all the humanities. And I think that by pooling all these things they're going to make them great. I think their leaders are sincere . . . and . . . I recognize the fact that they are revolutionaries . . . that they are. . . . I like their idea of agreeing on programs . . . and whenever they set out to accomplish a program, those people that get in the way or try to sabotage it, they get out of the way. I think that's very logical, to my mind.

Alienated as he was from the premises of conceivable American policy toward Russia, he saw little that he could do about it. Events would pursue their inevitable course. He had little hope that other Americans could be brought to share his goals:

> E: So it's pretty much a course of events out of control of the American people, whether we get along with Russia or whether we don't?

S: Yeah. Well, the American people, of course, if they *knew,* but they don't know . . . and the American people don't know how to think. They say, "Oh, this is the best country in the world." That's what they say, 365 days in the year. "This is the greatest country in the world. Why should we give them anything?" . . . all that sort of thing . . . over and over again. They'll go to the polls . . . and they'll vote wrong. Well, we have a record, according to one man. *They Also Ran,* by Irving Stone, which is a biography of the presidents who ran. It's pretty poor. Pretty poor.

E: Do you think there's any hope so far as educating the people to see things the way they really are?

S: No.

E: Just got to wait for the clock to run down.

S: Yes. I can't see any hope at all. Gee, I thought that after this war the boys would at least . . . going over across there . . . seeing those different things . . . having bull sessions . . . and it never affected them at all.

E: The veterans don't think any differently than they did before?

S: No, no. They join the American Legion and become a bunch of strike-breakers just like their fathers.

E: I should think you'd find this pretty discouraging, since you're trying to do something about all this, to find that you're just butting against a wall.

S: Yeah, but it's better to be doing something you believe in . . . Well, if you have an ideal to work for, it's kind of nice. You'd miss it.

Here was a man who had garnered considerable information about Russia in the service of his ideology. In fact, only Chatwell and Kleinfeld, both men with more formal education than he, equaled his score on the *Information Test,* 50 correct out of 53 items. Two of his errors on this test deserve special comment. One revised recent history in Russia's favor: he checked an item to indicate his belief that "Russia declared war on Japan shortly before [not after] the first atom bomb was dropped." The other revealed some ignorance of fundamental facts: he thought that "The present Communist government in Russia seized power from the Czar [not the Kerensky government]." But he could not have attained his high score without considerable knowledge of many facets of Russian affairs. Where had he gleaned his information?

Not primarily from books; he had read rather few books about Russia. On these, to be sure, he leaned heavily, but he depended primarily on newspapers, lectures, and pamphlets, and on much enjoyed conversations with friends who shared his sympathies. Unlike Lanlin, Sullivan did not habitually draw on "line" sources for hypotheses to test out against a wider array of "filler" sources. His line was internalized, and did not require direct reinforcement from without. He himself was the Marxist authority who told him the "correct" position to take. For keeping up to date, he much preferred the *New York Times* to the *Daily Worker,* which he did not particularly respect. The staff member who conducted the *Conformity Interview* summarized it thus:

> He does not even bother with the leftist press or magazine sources except for an occasional casual interest. His point is that from reading the *Christian Science Monitor* or the *New York Times,* with particular reference to the financial section . . . it is possible for him to arrive at his own conclusions which will be a solid Marxist analysis corresponding closely with what the *Worker* or the *New Masses* think. Naturally the Liberal magazines and newspapers are too wishy-washy to please him. He is from personal experience well aware of the way in which news distortion takes place.

Much of his time was spent in systematic reading of his favorite papers.

We may now summarize Hilary Sullivan's opinions about Russia in terms of our descriptive scheme.

Differentiated object of attitude. Russia for Sullivan was above all a promised land, living testimony to the possibility of a better world. The crux of his attitude concerned the contrast between Russia as a hopeful experiment in social welfare and the moribund capitalism of the United States. Other features of the object were highly elaborated, but for the most part secondary. Conflict between Russia and the United States was of more concern to him than to many of our subjects, but took second place to the ideological matters that Russia symbolized for him. The police state features of Soviet society, a source of some embarrassment to him, were relegated to the background.

Saliency. Sullivan stands by himself among our subjects in the central place accorded Russia and Communism in his scheme of things. With him, Russia was extremely salient, a continual focus of preoccupation.

Time perspective. Sullivan's hopes rested entirely on the long run. This well-elaborated historical perspective provided the justification he needed for Russia's momentary shortcomings; it also included grimmer expectations about the period of Fascism that, according to Marxist dogma, the United States must pass through before being able to follow Russia's lead. American relations with Russia in the shorter run, with the attendant possibility of atomic war, appeared more cloudy to him; he had settled on no single conclusion among the several contradictory guesses that he ventured from time to time with less than usual coherence.

Informational support. Diligent combing of the quality press and other sources equipped Sullivan with a rich background of factual detail in elaboration and support of a position that did not depend for guidance on his sources of information.

Object value. To an extreme degree, Russia appeared to Sullivan in positive guise. Differentiated as were the cognitive details of his picture, each facet shared in the positive affect that adhered to everything that the Soviet Union was and stood for. Whatever aspect might be brought up, he was certain to approve of it. The threatening outlook in Russian-American relations was an inevitable historical development detached from his feelings about the Soviet Union. If blame were to be assigned, it would go to the United States—but he hardly could blame even this country for fulfilling its historic role.

Orientation. Sullivan's orientation can only be called one of approach, but it was approach to an ideological ideal rather than to a source of events in the real world. For all the fervor of his views, Sullivan was not a Party member. Reading, talk, and revery were the primary avenues by which he "approached" Russia and Communism, though he had, to be sure, engaged in activities in support of Communist causes.

Policy stand. His stand on American policy could only be negative. Favoring support for the U.N. was the closest that he came to a positive stand, but this appears to have been more a random thought than a considered position. We did not believe that policy stand had much relevance to his attitudes as they functioned for him.

What manner of man had arrived at these singular views?

Sullivan's Life and Enterprises

Personal history. Hilary Sullivan was born in 1898 as the oldest son (and second child) of poor Catholic parents in Whitney, a Connecticut textile town where his father worked as a knitter. His mother was born in Ireland where she had some education; his father, native born, had only grammar school education but showed unusually broad interests for his background. There followed six younger children in the next twelve years, three of whom lived to maturity. Home life was not pleasant. Mrs. Sullivan sought to control the family by playing off the children against each other and against their father, showing traits that had recently contributed to her institutionalization as paranoid. Larry worshipped his father, and with the death of the latter from tuberculosis when Larry was fifteen, the beatification was complete. This bereavement was followed in a couple of years by the death of his younger brother, probably also of tuberculosis.

With his father's death, Larry's formal education was interrupted, after parochial school and not quite two years of high school. Although he had not found school rewarding, he had already begun to read omnivorously. Toward the end of the First World War he left his first full-time job as baggage-master at the Whitney station to join the Navy. He never saw sea duty, returning after a short but dreary experience to his railroad job. In 1920 he was back in the Navy for a brief period. From this first contact with the wide world, he was left with pleasant memories of European architecture and museums, but with a vast disrespect for the Navy and strong repugnance toward the shipboard homosexuality that he had witnessed.

After a brief and dissatisfied period of local jobs on his second return to civilian status, he took off with a reckless friend for four years of "bumming" around the country. This period of irresponsibility terminated in 1924 with the tragic accidental death of his friend. Back once more in Whitney, Sullivan worked periodically in the mills, escaping to New York for sprees when he would buy himself a hotel job and sell "booze" on the side. In 1925 he obtained a minor newspaper job, and was engaged, somewhat irregularly, in newspaper work until about 1933.

During his late twenties, Sullivan was troubled by claustrophobia in theaters and subways, and it was then and in his early thirties that he drank most heavily on his periodic sprees. His thirty-first or thirty-second year found him suffering from delirium tremens after such a bout.

When he was thirty he married a woman of similar social background who had been a factory worker since she was twelve. After eight years, his drinking led to divorce, and his wife obtained custody of their one child, a son. Meanwhile, his newspaper work had become a depression casualty and he was trying first in one way and then in another to make a living, by pursuits ranging from selling beer or Christmas cards to employment on the W.P.A. The divorce and the separation from his son left him at a nadir which had the virtue at least, as he put it, of allowing him once more to start from scratch. "I was trapped. . . . When the world topples down over your ears, it's better because you can start building again."

Following the divorce, his new life was marked by satisfying work on a W.P.A. Writers' Project. At the same time he gave up drinking permanently and moved into respectable quarters in Providence that symbolized his changed life. With the onset of World War II, he took

up, conscientiously, manual work in the textile mills, only to give it
up shortly because of his shoulder. There followed a succession of
war-connected jobs as guard, clerk, and investigator. At 44 he married a semi-professional woman, an "intellectual companion," who was
one of the last of his social group left after the reshufflings of the war.
Moving shortly thereafter to Boston, he returned in 1945 to newspaper
work of an irregular sort that left him much freedom but brought in
a fairly satisfactory income.

Sullivan's social ties in earlier years seem mostly to have been to
a succession of cronies who were his companions in drink and work
and play. More recently, he had cultivated a small circle who discussed politics and world affairs. His radical beliefs, which crystallized in the late 1930's, increasingly became the center of his life.

During his earlier years, he at first took little note of the soapbox
talks that were his first contact with Communism. Gradually, we are
led to gather, he began to take them more seriously. As late as 1930,
however, he had written in favor of Mussolini, who perhaps appealed
to his inner longing for a strength to bring order out of chaos. But
this peccadillo was hardly the expression of a coherent ideology. His
radical beliefs seem to have taken form about the time of the W.P.A.
Writers' Project. Among his co-workers were several avowed Communists, who would air their heretical views on the job. Sullivan
himself had been warned, when he was taken on the Project as a
political favor, not to get involved in political arguments but to "keep
his yap shut." This advice he followed, even to the extent of avoiding
the Communists after hours. Nevertheless, his own convictions were
taking form, and the prestige that the W.P.A. Project held in his eyes
doubtless served to invest with particular significance the opinions he
heard expressed there. In desperate need for a guiding philosophy of
life, Sullivan borrowed the appropriate ideas so auspiciously brought
to his attention. But his Communism was not adopted *in toto* by
conversion: it was, rather, a structure that he built for himself.

Present enterprises. The main areas of interest and endeavor that
stood out in Sullivan's current pattern of life can be listed, with some
overlap, under four headings: making a living, Communism, self-improvement and self-fulfillment, and friendship.

"My whole life has been concerned with getting a living," Sullivan
told us. Security could not be taken for granted. "The whole of life
is a problem: how to survive." And again, "I never use the gold
standard; I always use the hamburg standard." Starting with severe
poverty, he had never been economically secure, however much his
insecurity may have been of his own contriving. Although, like

Chatwell, he liked to daydream of the self-sufficient security of a farm, and more seriously considered seeking a municipal job, he had come to accept in practice a minimal level of security. The prospect of being on relief did not represent an unknown horror. For the most part, a job was simply a way of feeding himself, and when that was done he had little further interest in it. Speaking of the possible municipal job, he said:

> Well, if you have felt economic pressure all your life, then you simply have to take safeguards. That's a safeguard. Whether I'll take it or not I don't know. Now I'm enjoying myself with not too much work.

His first newspaper job and his position with the Federal Writers' Project, in both of which he took real pride, led him to depart from this point of view. At the time of the study, he still appeared to take considerable satisfaction in being a semi-professional man on the one hand, and a free-lance, for the most part his own boss, on the other.

Communism, we have seen, formed the pivot of Sullivan's coherent philosophy of life. In his daily life it provided the raison d'être for his favorite activity, reading and talk about political and economic affairs.

Ever since his boyhood discovery of books Sullivan had pursued self-improvement through the constant reading of books and newspapers and through seeking out intellectual discussions. In the last five years he had branched out into a new line, that of oil painting. Thus through his own endeavors Sullivan had achieved a culture that removed him from his working-class background. Far from mere rungs in a ladder of social success, however, his intellectual and cultural pursuits had become essential to his picture of himself. These attainments together with his sharp Communist perspective on affairs enabled him to value himself as an intelligent and cultured person who was "in the know" and, seeing the true nature of society, lived by no shams himself.

It was in the context of friendship that most of Sullivan's political and economic ideas were worked out. He valued highly the friends who dropped in for discussion and coffee. His present marriage appeared to be only another instance of this friendship pattern. Sullivan liked people, and said, according to his ideology,

> I feel that most people are trustworthy and when they let you down there's an economic reason. . . . I've always believed that and I always will!

Although intellectual friendship was his ideal, he fostered informal friendliness in whatever his environment might be. "If I'm going to work on a job," he told us in the *Interview on Personal Values*, "I'll make it as pleasant as possible for myself and everybody around me." With those who disagreed with him, he was likely to play the clown, a role about which he felt ambivalent.

S: I find it pretty hard to be cross with people, to maintain a grudge.

E: That can't be too much of a handicap, is it?

S: Well, no. If I insist on it, I have to laugh at myself. I feel ridiculous to myself.

E: You tend to view yourself with somewhat of a humorous eye?

S: Yeah. I see myself as a . . . character.

E: You like to see yourself in that role?

S: Well, no. I don't like to see myself in that role too often. Because that's wearing the cap and bells. And, you know . . . they say . . . "The fellow's a clown." Well, I don't want to be going around as a clown. But, if you're a character, they're liable to put the cap and bells on you. . . . If I talk to somebody whose mind I know is pretty closed, I just kid with him. And he kids back with me. I say, "Hello, Tovarich." When I go into a fancy restaurant, I say, "Anything for the workers?" [laughter] It's pretty hard for anyone to take offense.

On this surface level of his present activities some obvious sources of both satisfaction and difficulty may be discerned. Satisfactions came from the intellectual and cultural life he had fashioned for himself— from his perennial discussions over coffee with his wife and his friends, from his reading, from his painting, but also from the baseball games that he and his wife both enjoyed. Being a newspaperman still had its fascination and meant something to him for the semi-professional status it conferred, as well as for the inside view it afforded behind public personages and events. And, looking inwards, he could take satisfaction in the sophistication and integrity with which he saw behind appearances and forsook bourgeois "hypocrisies" for the hard but predestined realities as portrayed in the Communist ideology.

Yet there were also major problems facing Sullivan in his pattern of living. Some of them are already apparent. As it had always been, his source of income was still insecure. His commitment to Communism also entailed various difficulties. In a time of decreasing tolerance, his very opinions endangered his livelihood and his relations with others. His concession to economic pressures in not joining the Communist Party involved, in his eyes, a compromise in integrity that was only compounded by the "venality" of his job activities according to his Communist standards. Finally, the "cap-and-bells" technique he had worked out for getting on with people who differed with him sat poorly with his self-esteem.

Significant emotional relationships. We return for a closer look at Sullivan's early family relationships, which turn out to have been deeply influential on his outlook on life and on the Communist opinions that became so salient to him. Larry's father, whom he fondly remembered after thirty years, "didn't have any faults, except being ill, of course, always having a little touch of T.B." He was the

> finest looking man I ever saw . . . just handsome. A gentle person. . . . One of the earliest memories is entertaining us with all kinds of sounds of birds and animals, and songs. . . . Going up to meet him when he came home from work, and he'd take the youngest on his shoulders and two or three piling onto him.

> In a family of much confusion and disturbance, he was the center of peace and serenity.

> I'd say his strongest point seemed to me to be that he had a kind of kindly, calm philosophy. For example, when my mother was blowing off her top and sprinkling holy water on everybody from top to bottom in the house, raising Hell, my father would sit calmly and look out of the window. And he'd sort of try to calm things.

Although Mr. Sullivan occasionally punished with a strap, Mrs. Sullivan was the main disciplinarian. For the most part Larry got from his father a kind of warmth and comfort that children more usually find in their mothers.

Mr. Sullivan emerged from Larry's adult eulogies as a vivid, talented person of broad and contagious interests. "The minstrel type of Irishman," sensitive and humorous, he figured in his son's recollections as a great entertainer who could do imitations, recite Shakespeare, play semi-pro baseball, and take part in amateur plays in spite of having had only a grammar school education. Larry remembered being roused by his father in the middle of the night to see Halley's comet; the children were brought up to share in his lively interest in the larger world. In general, "he was just a marvelous man . . . and we could never get enough of him."

While the father was busy and tired and little available for his boys to confide in, Larry early became aware of his strong views on Trade Unionism, according to which "the lowest word in our house was the word *scab*." In fact, as Larry took pains to point out, Father was something of a radical for his day, who would quote from the early writing of Hearst and Brisbane "in great gobs," and once tried unsuccessfully to organize his plant.

The impact of his father on Sullivan's personality seems to have been large. The reasons for his particularly strong attachment must be sought in the total family scene. But in this attachment we may find the origin of most of his enduring interests and values, as well as some of his characteristic techniques of adjustment, including things as diverse as his interest in baseball, his "cap-and-bells" role, his intellectual curiosity and cultural interests, and an incipient radicalism. He believed that his father would agree with his contemporary views.

While Father was all hero in Sullivan's family drama, Mother was all villain. He may have overdrawn the picture from his present perspective, but there is no doubt that she created an exceedingly bad family situation. As matriarch and disciplinarian she commanded no respect. She was given to constant harangue and "mental punishment," rubbing it in how poor they were and how the children were bringing disgrace on the family. Her especially vicious technique, from Larry's point of view, "was to play one of us off against the other."

> She didn't force you to do anything. She was a person who got you to do things by guile . . . never gave me or anyone else any affection that I know of. I've asked and they say no. . . . Impressing on me how important . . . not "how important" but how *imperative* it was to bring home what I made . . . and that they'd starve and all that sort of thing. And she always impressed on us how hard she worked . . . always telling us that our father was no good . . . which was all a lie.

"The chief ideal in the home," Sullivan tells us in another connection, "was to be smart so as not to bring shame on the family." From his mother Larry felt a pressure to conform, to maintain appearances, for which she offered little recompense. Even at an early age, conformity had acquired unpleasant meanings for him.

To give Larry even more grounds for feeling exploited, she rankled his boyish pride by making him wear hand-me-downs, including girls' clothes. Later, after Larry's first return from the Navy to work in Whitney, she took all his savings to buy a new house, complaining afterwards to others that he didn't give her any money. In sum, Sullivan came to hate his mother vigorously and explicitly. On talking it over with his brother recently, they agreed that "when the O'Brians put her on a boat in Ireland they were glad to get rid of her." On probing, we gathered that he did not come to a full realization of this hatred until later years, but it must have underlain his childhood reactions.

Some fairly direct consequences of this miserable relationship to his mother may be surmised. One is the apparent lack of emotional depth in his marriages, and some tendency to reserve his stronger

emotional ties for men. A second is his frustrated need for dependent
well-being, perhaps at the root of his alcoholism. Thirdly, the guilt
and conflict that must have been aroused by his childish hatred may
have been a prime source of the burden of anxiety which he has carried throughout his life. Her carping criticism of his father continuing
even after his death ("He could have lived," he quoted her as saying,
"if he'd stayed up at the hospital but he wanted to come home and
give all of you the T.B.") contributed to Father's complete beatification. His mother had raised all the possible criticisms, and he rejected
them. The pattern has echoes in his later unwillingness to admit
Russia's slightest defect.

Through her part in a family situation that left Larry with serious
problems of adjustment, his mother had important indirect effects on
his attitudes. More directly, she also impressed him with poverty,
contributing to an underdog identification compatible with his later
Communism. One may surmise that it was from her, too, that Sullivan
first learned the meaning of exploitation.

In general, Larry's siblings were unimportant in his life. An older
sister, who subsequently died, maintained the balance in the family,
but he and the younger siblings did not confide in her.

> None of us confided in anybody. We just sort of talked things over
> among ourselves. We had pretty much the same things to bear—dis-
> cussed things, not very thoroughly. I suppose if you could say it, we
> tried to forget Mother. We accepted things as a part of existence. We
> were all a clan . . . and all of us survived. That's about all.

There was no important sibling rivalry that he can remember.

Perhaps his experience of sibling solidarity acquired special significance when, at a later time, his Communist ideology was taking
form. In his early family experience he had made acquaintance in
prototype with the leading characters in the Marxist *dramatis personae:*
the exploiter in his mother, the working-class martyr in his father, and
the union of the oppressed among his siblings. It seems to us both
idle and improbable to advance the sort of speculation that would
see in Sullivan's later Communism simply the repetitive elaboration
of his familial struggles. Much more plausible, we think, is the conjecture that in his family he acquired certain pervasive attitudes toward himself and others that found congenial resonances in Marxism,
more congenial ones than in his earlier Catholic solution to his problems.

The significant figures in Sullivan's adult life seem to have had
little direct influence on his sentiments or personality. In the past, his
important personal ties had all been with men his own age with whom

he worked, drank, or bummed around the country. The most conspicuous of these was the companion of his wanderings from 1921–24, whom he described as a reckless character who would try anything. The violent death of this friend was another devastating personal bereavement; he was not, however, a source of Sullivan's present ideas or sentiments. His present friends, who mostly shared his left-wing views, entered his circle only after he had arrived at the radical position. So far as we can tell from his account, personal ties followed and confirmed his radicalism rather than created it.

It is no longer possible to reconstruct clearly the meaning to Sullivan of his first marriage. As he described her, his first wife showed the traits of a compulsion neurotic. During the first few years of their marriage they got along "pretty well" though with little emotional intensity. The greatest blow from their divorce was the loss of his son, with whom he was maintaining intermittent and deliberately casual contact.

This was his account of how his second marriage came about:

> This girl has always lived away from home, never had a home and she's a marvelous companion. And the group we knew went away to war . . . broke up, so we were the only ones left. She was working in one place and she said . . . I said, "You've got a problem and I've got a problem; let's get married." And she said, "We will, some day." And we'd meet and meet and talk about it, and then we got an apartment . . . and so [laughs] we got married.

The bond between them, it appears, was their common problem of parental rejection. We may further surmise, as other information confirms, that their relation rested mainly on intellectual companionship. She agreed with many of his political ideas, though she would sometimes protest his exclusive preoccupation with them. Retaining her job and her own circle of friends, she was not dependent on Sullivan financially or otherwise.

The Personal Setting of Sullivan's Opinions

Capacities and traits. Taken together, our battery of tests showed Sullivan to possess a superior intelligence the functioning of which was considerably impaired. The *Wechsler-Bellevue Adult Intelligence Test* showed him to best advantage, with a full I.Q. of 128, a Verbal I.Q. of 134, and a Performance I.Q. of 118. His score on this test places him just within the "very superior" group, or the top three per cent of the general population, and leaves him tied for third place among our ten subjects. His *Wells-Alpha* score of 119, while not outstanding and in eighth place among our subjects, nevertheless supported the *Wechsler* in regard to his good intellectual level, particularly since he had had so little formal education. The *Rorschach,* however, revealed a "relatively low level of mental functioning . . . either consistent with an average endowment, or else due to an impairment by a disorganizing emotional factor," the latter interpretation being required by the other test results.

Though he was well endowed, his capacity for organized and abstract thought was limited. For example, his none-too-successful attempts at classifying the blocks of the *Vigotsky Test* were interpreted by the examiner (working in ignorance of other personality and opinion data) as follows:

> Although this performance gives no evidence of a high level of conceptual thinking, disorganization and blocking seem to be more outstanding features than the actual lack of abstract thinking. It is notable that S has some ideas about the required logical procedure; thus he realizes that categories once tried have to be "out," knows that he should be able to find the required categories by comparing the samples, and generally tries to find a "formula." His performance, however, does not conform to these fragmentary verbal expressions. . . . Yet the perceptual factor is not given free play either—S obviously does not feel right about just following the perceptual tendencies, and constantly strains for a more logical approach, which results merely in blocking. This pronounced discordance is probably typical of S's thinking in general. . . .

The *Rorschach* analyst, also working independently, described his approach to problems as "careless and superficial, lacking in organization and precision, as well as in effort," while the *Wechsler* report remarked,

> His generally poorer performance scores seem due to his tendency to overgeneralize and ramble, a characteristic more suitable to high Verbal scores but inadequate for Performance tests. Consistently in these latter tests he overlooked detail.

These intellectual qualities were manifest in Sullivan's attitudes toward Russia. His opinions, we have seen, showed a subtlety and elaboration that could only be possible for a person of his high verbal ability. Yet the discordant, over-generalizing, disorganized quality of his thought processes also left its unmistakable mark. Apart from the loose, disjunctive way in which he presented his opinions, his sweeping judgment that Russia was *entirely* good would come easily only to a person so constituted.

Sullivan's other abilities may be passed over quickly. He rated himself "poor" in mechanical and in business ability. In artistic ability he thought himself excellent; artistic sensitivity was an important part of his self-image. What he told us of his aesthetic bent was in keeping with scores in the 7th and 8th deciles for artistic, literary, and musical interests on the *Kuder Preference Blank*. While he enjoyed music and art without a highly cultivated taste, he painted quite well for a self-taught amateur. The other abilities on which he gave himself an "excellent" rating—social, entertaining, memory, and intuitive abilities —were all based, as he explained them, on his interest in people, liking for them, and real gifts at getting along with them.

Turning to Sullivan's temperamental qualities, we note that his emotional life was drawn in strong if somewhat blurred colors. In his behavior as we observed it, as well as in the interview and projective test material, substantial evidence pointed toward strong and impulsive emotionality that was rather inadequately controlled. His many bereavements typically left him distraught, and he mentioned instances of emotional outbursts and fits of temper. The intense affect of his attitudes toward Russia was therefore characteristic of him.

Perhaps the crucial underlying fact of Sullivan's affective life was the high level of his anxiety, indications of which pervaded his history and his behavior and test records at the Clinic. At times, it had been not only manifest but nearly overwhelming. Early in his childhood he had been troubled by dreams of being buried alive; later he was beset with claustrophobia and fears of falling from high places. The theme of being "trapped" ran through several episodes in which his enterprises were at a nadir, and recurred in his *Free Association Hour*. When his life pattern collapsed with his divorce, he felt completely disoriented and wondered if he were going insane. At the time of the study, he told us in an interview after the end of the regular series, he had occasional spells of extreme depression and disorientation, when he would get the feeling that he was the only person in the world, feel utterly lost, and shake all over as he began to come out of it. These brief attacks occurred irregularly, perhaps once a month. He felt that he had become able to cope with them, mainly by sitting down to write or sketch. Besides this catalogue of gross disturbance, to which should be added his former alcoholism, there is the indication of emotional disturbance on the *Rorschach*, and his general disorganization and lack of coordination. The resultant picture is that of a person with strong predispositions toward anxiety which for the most part were brought under control. The control, however, was neither entirely dependable nor very efficient; his disorganization and impaired test performance bore witness to the struggle. The closest Sullivan came to a frank realization of his plight was his paradoxical remark:

> My whole life is worry, so now I do not worry. I say, "What the Hell can I do about it!" I do the best I can.

Aside from his occasional sieges of depression, his prevailing mood of superficial, somewhat "slap-happy" joviality appeared to be a defense against his underlying distress. Alcohol was a means by which he once reinforced the euphoric component of this mood:

> It mellows and expands the personality to such a degree that I certainly don't want to go back to reality. . . . Then I fall asleep. Then I wake up, terrifically depressed.

The summary of the *TAT* analysis, done with knowledge only of the "face data," caught his spirit well:

> There is a Pagliacci-like tone about S's *TAT* stories. Beneath an exterior which makes him out to be a lighthearted, out-going individual who knows all about life, there is a tense, frustrated, anxious, and unhappy individual who is quite ego-involved in most of his pursuits and who has developed a role for himself in order to keep people from learning of his weaknesses.

His Communist attitudes, we shall see, were of great help to him in coping with his underlying tendencies toward personal desperation.

Basic strivings. The pathological cast to much of Sullivan's history points clearly to deep-seated conflicts. One cluster of his needs that we inferred from his interviews and fantasy productions centered around security and affection, including needs for dependence, friendship, and recognition. These needs were in partial conflict with aggressive tendencies and strivings toward autonomy.

In evaluating his childhood, Sullivan told us disjunctively that he would like to have had "a home where the semblance of security . . . a mother who gave me some affection . . . and where there was some serenity, which there wasn't." On the one hand, he often described his whole life as a quest for minimal security; on the other, security remained a dream that he had only rarely pursued effectively. Short of full security of relationship, he was wont to seek emotional response from his fellows with somewhat more success. So highly dependent was he on response from people that, as we have seen, he would clown, against his ideal conception of himself, to get it. More stable sources of security in a well-composed pattern of life had eluded him, and he had, indeed, so contrived his life as to achieve the opposite result.

Two probable reasons suggest themselves as to why he had done so. His bereavements and frustrations, to begin with, had led him to define security defensively in the minimal terms of the "hamburg standard." He may have learned in the thorny bosom of his family that the fruits of a responsible quest for security would be taken away from him; only immediate pleasures were safe. And as he had found, it was easier to do something about his life when he was at rock-bottom. The less complicated a structure he built, the smaller distance he had to fall. Much of his life may thus be seen as a kind of flight into insecurity, a defense by willing the inevitable.

> . . . I never had security, so why should I miss something I never had? I have no sense of insecurity; I never had it.

Besides his need for defining security in minimal terms—a need that may have found symbolic expression in his persistent phobia of literally falling—there seems to have been a self-destructive element in the chaotic middle years of his history. We detect in his escapades something of self-punishment as well as of flight from an intolerable burden of guilt that was very likely the by-product of the intense hatred of his early years.

His ideology and attitudes partly resolved this conflict around security. First the Catholic Church, then the church of Communism, provided him with havens of security not to be found in his mundane affairs. Sullivan well could echo Luther's sentiment, "Ein' feste Burg ist unser Gott." It is interesting in this connection to note that to Russia, the tangible guarantee of his faith, he attributed the same total perfection that he ascribed to his father, the only solace of his turbulent childhood. Both had been too important to him, and his inner resources had been too precarious, for him to admit the slightest flaw. To the seemingly unfair attacks on Russia in the mass media, he reacted just as he had learned to respond to his mother's attempted defamation of his father, with utter denial of the criticism.

Among the tendencies that conflicted with Sullivan's drives toward security and friendship was considerable aggressiveness. His paradoxical humor, directed at others and at himself, had hostile overtones. With the average person whose views he did not respect, he would veer between trying to shock and condescending agreement.

> I shock them, then I retreat. All they want to talk about is what a great man . . . oh, Taft, is. "He's wonderful. Wonderful man." And I could go right out and shoot the ass off of him. See? But I agree and they think I'm wonderful. If they say, "Today is Wednesday," I say, "I guess you're right. It is Wednesday. I just didn't happen to look at the calendar."

Both these tactics had an aggressive flavor. The sequence of frustrations in his life gave reason for much resentment, of which that against his mother became explicit.

His Communist attitudes served these aggressive tendencies in at least two ways. On the one hand, their extreme nonconformity gave

him a way of shocking people and disturbing their complacency. That
he was strongly moved to do so is indicated by the fact that he did
it against his wife's remonstrance and his own better judgment. But
his ideology also provided an acceptable rationale for his aggressive
feelings, so that he could tolerate them without undue disturbance.
Several times he stressed that "revolution is not fun and people will
get hurt," and he saw the new day arising from the total ruin of the
old order. As a revolutionary in fantasy, Sullivan cast himself in a
Samson's role; self as well as contemporaries were to go down in ruin
together.

His strong need for autonomy seemed related to his security needs
in a more complex way. We infer its existence from such facts as his
insistence on defining the relationships that he entered at the Clinic
on his own terms, his choice of a free-lance occupation, the loosely
integrated nature of his marriage, his preference for an inefficient but
laissez-faire employer in comparison with a just but authoritarian one
on the *Argument Completion Test,* and his hatred of bureaucratic
organization when it impinged on his own life. Seeking autonomy
may appear like a polar opposite of seeking dependent security, yet
we must probably conceive Sullivan's stress on autonomy as primarily
a defense against what he had found to be the dangers and frustrations
of staking much on dependence. It was a way out of the trap. In his
daydreams, he imagined a solution that would give him both: his
ideological mentor, Scott Nearing, again provided the model for his
reveries of a farm that would leave him secure to pursue his beliefs
independent of economic and social pressure. But what a different
dream farm this was from Chatwell's! There was none of Chatwell's
stress on productivity; none of the realism that led Chatwell to investigate the dollars-and-cents considerations in bringing his fantasy to life.
Both in conception and in psychological function, Sullivan's farm was
even more clearly a refuge of escape. His simultaneous desires for
autonomy and security, as our analysis of his daydream suggests,
entailed the evasion of mature responsibility that had been a salient
fact through most of Sullivan's history.

Being a Communist also served his need for autonomy. His espousal
of an unpopular ideology was as much a declaration of independence
as it was an act of covertly aggressive nose-thumbing. Moreover, he
was not actually a Party member. Very likely the rigorous demands
of Party discipline would have conflicted too strongly with his autonomous needs, and required of him a degree of responsibility that he was
unable to accept. His Communism seemed to gratify simultaneously
both his needs for autonomy and for security; security by aligning

himself with a world movement that he believed to be the wave of the future, and autonomy because his beliefs gave him a vantage point detached from society on the one hand and uncommitted to Party discipline on the other. In this respect, too, the independent radical Scott Nearing represented his ideal.

There are a number of indications from test procedures and personal history that sex created problems for Sullivan. Overtly, his sexual life had been normal though not particularly active. The exact nature of his psychosexual problems, while important to a full account of his personality, makes little difference here. We can safely assume that their only bearing on his attitudes toward Russia was through their possible contribution to his burden of insecurity, guilt, and anxiety.

Finally, Sullivan's strong need to understand should be noted. Following his father's example though probably for complex reasons, Sullivan early developed a strong intellectual curiosity, a desire to know the inside story. Marxist philosophy furnished a particularly inclusive pattern according to which he could interpret the world.

Adjustive strategies. The succession of bereavements and frustrating experiences that had been his lot, his conflicts about security, and his considerable anxiety demanded of Sullivan a well-furnished armory of adjustive or defensive techniques. In broad outline, they involved a twofold strategy. In the realm of his personal life, the scope of his preoccupations, hopes, and fears was narrowed to exclude his immediate and seemingly insoluble problems from awareness. Balancing this impoverishment was his highly developed world-view in the realm of safely impersonal ideology. In his personal life he often seemed to blunder rather desperately against odds that he felt were stacked against him. Although it was scarcely possible for him to imagine an encouraging future for himself, his broad ideological perspective seems to have provided a substitute for personal aspirations.

Sullivan characteristically did not attempt to solve his problems by long-range planning. Having little faith in the arrival of future goods, he was unwilling to renounce present benefits for their sake.

If I had butter, I'd use a lot, then eat plain bread for a while.

Only when these benefits had totally vanished as he hit rock-bottom was he able to bestir himself effectively to cope with his problems. More typically he avoided awareness of them. In the past drink had helped him to evade some of his critical difficulties; he currently appeared to use passivity and sleep to the same end. Frequently spending an entire day lounging in his pajamas with a newspaper, he would also retire very early in the evening. His restriction of awareness did not actually protect him from dangerous situations, of course. It was as if he had been forced to admit defeat beforehand, but shielded his eyes from the blow as a stop-gap measure to preserve his psychological integrity.

His restriction of goals to excessively modest ones was akin to this strategy of avoidance. To minimize frustration, he lowered his level of aspiration drastically, often directing his sense of humor at himself to aid in the process. One might describe this pattern as a defense in depth: he tried to be ready for the worst. Although he spoke of "hedging," his preparation was mainly psychological; he seemed to feel that there was little he could do to prevent the worst from happening.

There can be little doubt that Sullivan had *repressed* a great deal. His childhood memories began late, at the time he started school. The idealization we have observed in the portraits he formed of his father and of himself could only have been attained through repression. In an early session Sullivan informed the interviewer with great emphasis: *"I have been a Socialist since I reached the age of reason."* When the results of probing in later interviews made this statement incredible, he showed considerable disturbance in readjusting his account.

To make up for this defensive limitation of his personal life, there was his highly elaborated Communist ideology. One of its important strategic functions may be described as the *intellectualization* of his personal problems. The "pattern" of historic processes, for example, helped to absolve him from personal responsibility for his actions and their outcome. Foreseeing capitalist breakdown as inevitable, he could put his personally fearful expectations in a context in which they appeared as part of an unavoidable process—hence depersonalized, less threatening, and something to be accepted rather than struggled against futilely. His ideology thus protected him from catastrophic reaction without making impossible demands on him for actual solution of his immediate problems. His philosophy of flux, change, and the pursuit of the unknown, which we shall shortly examine, helped to justify the disorderly and unknown in his own life.

Finally, his ideology permitted him to *identify* with a source of vicarious strength—the Communist movement and Russia. His ideological sources of dependent security were less vulnerable than his personal ones.

A precarious stance such as Sullivan's required much *rationalization* to shore it up. He was too insecure, and his consciously formulated picture of himself and the world played too vital a role in his security system, for him to tolerate discrepant features in his images of self and world. We are familiar with his propensity to explain away all of Russia's possible limitations. This characteristic he showed in other realms, as on the *Argument Completion Test*, where his arguments were the most one-sided of all our subjects.

In this description of Sullivan's principal defenses, we have so far ignored the considerable degree of *effective restriving* with which, as we have suggested, he was most likely to respond when he felt that his back was against the wall. Particularly after his divorce, he set about deliberately and effectively to build a new life. That was the time that he managed to give up alcohol once and for all. Quite without the benefit of Alcoholics Anonymous or of religious or moral scruples, he held himself to abstinence, although we have no reason to assume that the problems originally setting him to pathological drinking had been solved. In all respects he managed to pursue a wavering but on the whole by no means unsuccessful course of life in spite of a bad start and more than his share of body blows on the way.

Nevertheless, it is fair to say of his principal adjustive strategies that while they had the merit of preparing him to accept the worst, they did not equip him to do much to forestall it. How to avoid "going to pieces" in the face of ill fortune—not how to achieve good fortune—had been his primary concern. Nor were his defenses very efficient: his impulses broke through, his repressions leaked, and his anxiety lurked near the surface. Yet he seemed to have stabilized his conflicts at a low level of security. His strategies did work at the level of his unambitious demands.

Opinion Maintenance and Furtherance

When opinions are as deeply embedded in important functions of personality as were Sullivan's on Russia and Communism, it should be no surprise that he guarded them carefully from internal contradiction and from the buffetings of the outside world. His well-developed procedures for maintenance made it especially difficult to investigate the development of his opinions. To questions about the evolution of his views, his first reaction was that he had always had them. Only relatively late in the course of our interviews and with difficulty was he able to say that he had once thought differently. He then became hypersensitive lest we interpret his Communism as a simple equivalent for his earlier adherence to Catholicism. He was never able to point with any certainty to the time when most of his present views took form. Repression and rationalization had created a picture of himself as a consistent Socialist, endowing his present beliefs with apparent timelessness, stability, and validity.

Not only did he iron out temporal inconsistency, but as we have seen, he also ruled out internal conflict in his present opinions by creating a mental picture of Russia that was uniformly favorable. This achievement was such a *tour de force* that we can assume that the mere possibility of conflict within his attitudes toward Russia was intolerable.

As a Marxist, Sullivan was sophisticated enough to discount readily the more reactionary sources of outside challenge to his opinions. As we have seen, he could move comfortably among Republicans, with little showing save an unruly tendency to shock them. His closer friends, it is true, put no challenge to his attitudes, since he had selected them in terms of their political and social beliefs, but he by no means limited his selection of news sources to ones that were favorable to his attitudes. The maintenance of his attitudes, then, depended on his interpretation of experience, not on pre-selection of the experience to which he exposed himself.

He had a variety of ways of dealing with experience that appeared to challenge his attitudes. Some of these were apparent in his justification of Russia as a temporary police state that we quoted earlier. When he could attribute the attack to manifestly reactionary sources, he could deny or discredit it without even feeling a challenge. Such "shrugging off" was typical of his reaction to the more virulently anti-Russian cartoons of the *Cartoon Stereotype Test*. A good example is his response to a Burris Jenkins cartoon showing the United States as Little Red Riding Hood being duped of her basket of atomic bomb secrets by the Communist wolf.

> Well, this is jingoism. It's against One World but very subtly—no, not subtly, but pretty good. I know Burris Jenkins. He used to be a sports cartoonist. The United States shouldn't give away the bomb secrets and shouldn't engage in disarmament conferences and give up some of its sovereignty. The hostile nation is Russia. Well, let's see. The little girl dressed to represent America has a basket of atom bomb secrets, in the position of Little Red Riding Hood—blithely and naively going to her doom, with the big bear waiting. That, my friend, is a lot of bullshit. The more I see of them the more I lose my veneer of so-called civilization. But Burris Jenkins—you can't blame him. Burris Jenkins is a member of the middle class, tied to the bourgeoisie. I'd do the same probably, if I had his job. If you're a newspaperman, you have to chop up your rationalism. Like Walter Lippmann. One of the Harvard boys. He sees

chaos so he takes his axe and chops up his powers of rationalism . . . rationalization.

His ability to discredit sources of challenge stood him in good stead when the challenge itself was more serious than those provided by Hearst cartoons. He used this as merely the first of a much larger defensive repertory in response to the sixth item of the *Information Apperception Test*: "*Russians have been arrested from time to time without knowing what their crime was.*"

> Of course, I don't know who made this statement. And . . . the conditions might exist. I have no evidence to the contrary. I believe that when you're arrested, that you should be told what you're arrested for. But . . . and let me put the BUT in caps . . . law enforcement officers very rarely tell you why they are arresting you. That's true in this country or in any country. According to the law, a United States law enforcement officer is supposed to tell you "I arrest you for a specific crime." They do not do that. My authority for that is their own word. Ask the next cop you see. If you know the law, you say, "No, I won't go." But . . . I would say that the condition probably did exist in Russia. I don't know one way or the other. It probably does exist because when you have a revolution and defend it against a counter-revolution . . . then you have to resort to a police state for a while until you make things secure. After the revolution is secure and the state is secure, then the . . . there is a relaxation of the police methods and civil liberties as we know them are restored. The liberties are given back to the people. That is the intent of the Russian . . . the Union of Soviet Socialist Republics. If their constitution is to be believed. [Does this item interest you?] The item doesn't interest me any more than it's a condition that exists because of this pattern of revolution and counter-revolution. Now, would I care to be arrested without being told? No. Would I like to see someone else arrested? No.

The quotation bears testimony, of course, to Sullivan's mastery of two other defensive measures: pointing to similar defects in the United States (the so-called "mote-beam" technique) and minimizing the importance of Russian faults by denying their typicality or relevance.

Elsewhere he managed to transform challenging information even to support his position. In the *Stress Interview*, further, he sometimes "played possum," pleading ignorance and refusing to argue when hard pressed. It is less notable that he used these techniques than that he used them so successfully, digesting all information that reached him to a form that agreed with his attitudes. So armed, he could be little disturbed by outside events. From the Russo-German pact to the Truman Doctrine, events were carefully fitted into their place in his ideology with little modification in its fundamental structure.

So much for Sullivan's campaigns in defense of his opinions. What of his behavior on the opinion offensive? Mostly, one gathers, it consisted of verbal exchange among the faithful. As *Weltanschauung*, Sullivan's Communism served its many adjustive functions without involving him in the unwelcome responsibilities and constraints of Party membership. One has the feeling that his need for action, to the extent that he had it, arose from his wish to maintain a self-image worthy of his own respect. Two considerations excused him from taking such feelings seriously. First, a literal interpretation of Communist doctrine assured him that the American Communist Party was bound to be futile during the inevitable stage of Fascism. Beyond that, he could down any nascent urges toward martyrdom by applying economic determinism (the compulsions of the "pattern") to his own case. Full integrity, he concluded, was only for the Nearings, while much "venality" would be forgiven the Sullivans.

While Sullivan may not have conducted as vigorous a campaign in behalf of his views as their salience might have led one to expect, he was as active as any of our subjects in the search for information on which to nourish them. We have seen how much time and attention he devoted to working out the current implications of his views in critical reading, thinking, and discussion. In spite of the stability of his basic ideology in recent years, he characteristically told an interviewer who inquired, "What have you learned that you'd like to pass on—that has been most important to you?": "Gee, I don't know. I'm always learning."

What could we predict for Sullivan's attitudes toward Russia in the eventualities with which we have speculatively confronted our previous two subjects? Outright war between the United States and Russia, we thought, would simply augment the detachment with which he was wont to survey the contemporary scene. While we would not expect him to lose his faith in Russia or to become swept up in any tide of patriotism, we think that he would not be a bad security risk. Forced to be more discreet than would come easily to him, he would, as far as possible, cultivate his garden and wait for the inevitable to unfold. These adjustments would involve a greater compromise in the direction of "venality" than he was making at the time of the study, and would probably require considerable renunciation of his favorite roles. Remaining, and crucial to his psychological integrity, would be his Cassandra-like perspective. There is little different to be said about his probable reaction to a prolonged armed stalemate, except to note that he would most likely show a marked defeatism. As the worst approaches, he will have accepted it already.

A Functional Summing-Up

Let us, finally, pull together the strands of our analysis of why Russia came to mean so much to Hilary Sullivan and why his opinions assumed their present form. First consider their *expressive nature.* We have seen how his high intelligence and his proneness to careless generalization were essential conditions for an awareness of Russia that was at once so complex and so grossly one-sided. His intense, impulsive temperamental endowment was a necessary though not sufficient condition for the colorful intensity of his opinions.

From the standpoint of their adjustive functions, his opinions had complex roots. For our other subjects, Russia was something peripheral, intersected here and there, to be sure, by the personal values in terms of which it was seen and judged. Not so with Sullivan, whose attitudes toward Russia were central to his ideology. Our first question must be concerned with how this broader system of values and interpretations of the world entered his psychological economy.

From the standpoint of *object appraisal,* Sullivan's Marxist world view served only the most general function of sorting out the flux of events into a personally meaningful order. Object appraisal as we analytically distinguish the function fuses in his case with externalization. The all-encompassing order that he rigidly imposed on events had its source in what we can only interpret as a severely neurotic inner predicament. Given his ideology, however, his opinions appraise Russia in terms of his values. The Russia that he saw, the embodiment of all that was new and hopeful, was furthering his values of justice, progress, and social welfare. The uniform, enthusiastic outcome of his evaluation is evidence that object appraisal was dominated for Sullivan by the use to which he put it in the service of externalization. His powers of discriminating judgment had been sacrificed. Yet Sullivan rarely falsified; he interpreted. His attitudes were therefore not very vulnerable.

Russia as an actual fact today and tomorrow had very little relevance to Sullivan's personal needs and interests. Only when involved in the prospect of war did Russia seem to impinge on his current enterprises; precisely here his opinions became incoherent. Russia touched his ideology, not his daily life.

The function of his attitudes in *social adjustment* was also complex. On the one hand, he shared the universal desire for approval. Life had taught him to be modest in this regard, however, and the approval that he sought for his opinions was limited to the rather small group of friends whose judgment he respected. More generally, he wanted

response from people, and his non-conforming attitudes led admirably
to this result. For those who did not share his deviant views, his
opinions laid bait for a reaction that was gratifying in at least two
ways: they would take notice of him and respond to him as a conse-
quential person, and, moreover, if they let themselves be shocked, he
could feel himself superior. In the role that his attitudes played in
his social adjustment, then, non-conformity appears considerably more
important than conformity.

It is in the *externalization* of Sullivan's very difficult inner problems,
however, that his opinions and Communist ideology played their most
essential role in his adjustment, a role that did not require him to be
a political activist. These attitudes put his aggressive tendencies in a
guise that was acceptable to himself, as well as affording some opportunity for their direct expression. Having espoused a movement of
protest, he could both contemplate the final day of reckoning with its
settling of scores and enjoy shocking the complacency of his contemporaries.

More than this, his attitudes enabled him to maintain an image of
himself that added to his resources for coping with his difficulties. As
a Communist, Sullivan became, to his own eyes, a person with "savvy,"
sophisticated in the back-stage deals by which the world operates,
scornful of the euphemistic Pollyannaism of bourgeois respectability.
Security and support came, moreover, from his identification with a
strong world movement.

Most important of all, it was through his attitudes toward Russia and
Communism that he was able to work out, in a comprehensive world
view, a strategy which though not a solution to his inner problems at
least served to keep them tolerable. In this sense, they became major
bastions of ego defense. They helped him construct a world in which
his life prospects did not appear catastrophic. They placed his immediate frustration and hopelessness in the impersonal context of historic necessity, and on this solidly pessimistic foundation—a foundation
less vulnerable than his Catholicism had been—offered him hope and
confidence in the well-elaborated time perspective of ideology. His
uncertain personal prospects were submerged in the inevitable pattern
of an historic future.

CHAPTER 9

THE OTHER SEVEN

THE accounts of the other seven men in our study will be given in much more condensed form. Enough of our method of analysis has perhaps been conveyed in the preceding chapters to suggest what lies behind these brief sketches. Each case received intensive study and staff discussion, and the reports that follow are based upon a consensus of judgments. It was our experience that up to the number of ten we learned something new and important from each additional case. In order to share this experience we present forthwith our conceptions of the personalities and opinions of the other seven men.

ERNEST DANIEL

At the time of the study Ernest Daniel was employed as a factory operative earning gross wages of about $2500 a year. He was recommended to us by labor-union people as a man who was particularly active in union work. He proved to be a short but sturdily built man of 38, of Irish extraction and Protestant religion, married and the father of three children. In his willingness to take part in the study financial considerations were not negligible, but he also valued the scientific goals and looked upon his participation as a community service. He addressed himself to the tests and personal interviews in a careful, businesslike, self-possessed fashion, showing neither curiosity about his performance nor a desire for personal help. As the sessions progressed he clearly received much gratification from the opportunity to give us his opinions on public affairs. He expressed pleasure at finding a place where, as he put it, "I can shoot off my mouth for a whole hour and you people will listen to me."

Daniel's father was a railroad engineer whose income was limited but who maintained his home in a respectable middle-class neighborhood. The two children, Ernest and his older sister, were given a fairly strict middle-class upbringing with emphasis on morality and religion. Parental solidarity was high with regard to educational ideals and standards of behavior, but there was frequent friction over the family's financial status with which the mother was much dissatisfied. In speaking of his mother Daniel tried to be fair, but he sharply criticized her ambition, her impulsiveness, her obsession about money, and her threats to leave the children when they did not please her, a maneuver that left them "just sick with worry." He also criticized his sister for having bossed and ridiculed him, rebuffing his attempts at friendliness. Although he voiced these criticisms calmly, placing the blame on mother and sister, it was plain that he had not escaped strong feelings of inferiority. The sister had been more daring in opposing the parents and had also persevered in securing training as an accountant, thus providing herself with professional status and good earnings. She was an excellent mathematician; Ernest came to consider himself a poor one—an estimate not supported by our tests.

Ernest's strongest positive relationship was with his father, an intelligent, gentle, somewhat embittered and remote man who was shy with his son though fond of him. It was typical that he delegated Ernest's sexual enlightenment to the mother, who accomplished the mission in a fear-inspiring manner. During Ernest's childhood his father, often away from home, seemed hopelessly remote, but later he became a source of some affection, though never as much as the boy would have liked. The father served, nevertheless, as a model and object of admiration; Ernest considered himself a "carbon copy" of his father, whom he rated by all odds the most important influence in his life.

According to his own account Ernest "breezed through" grammar school and three years of high school, learning without effort, wellliked by teachers and popular with his schoolmates. In spite of small stature he took part in rough, active sports and won recognition for his prowess. He formed no definite plans for the future and received no guidance from his parents in this respect, a thing he later came to resent. He had had clarinet lessons, however, and was persuaded by two musically inclined friends to leave high school and attend with them a local music school in preparation for playing in an orchestra. Two years of evening study convinced him that he was not good enough to make a living this way, and as his parents could not help him financially to secure other types of training he held a succession of miscellaneous jobs up to 1941, when with the assistance of his pastor he secured his position in the factory. He was then 32 and his third child had just been born.

The new job was by no means commensurate with his mental ability, which according to our tests placed him within the range of college students (*Wechsler-Bellevue* I.Q. 128). He performed a monotonous, mechanical task which yielded no rewards beyond his wages. In this job, however, he came into contact with an active labor union, and there was presently opened to him a whole new range of interest and accomplishment. His union work soon became the center of his life and its organizing principle. Starting as steward of his department, he rapidly worked up from one position to another, through one committee to another, until he held a vice-presidency in the state organization. As he himself put it: "I seem to have my finger in everything and more or less take charge." At the time of the study his mind was constantly occupied with union affairs; his extensive newspaper reading was guided by the desire to argue union policies and write letters to congressmen concerning labor legislation. He characterized himself as a "fanatic of unionism." It was his own belief that he had "grown in stature" as a result of his union work. He had learned to control his impulsiveness and his temper and to perceive important situations with calm objectivity.

In devoting himself to union work Daniel followed rather directly in his father's footsteps. Part of his satisfaction came from implementing an identification which he had long felt and desired. Further attraction seemed to lie in the feeling of security and strength he obtained from belonging to a group of people united for a common purpose. Although his own increased influence and recognition greatly gratified him, the group character of the enterprise was an essential element in his new feeling of worth. He also found growth for his hitherto fallow mental abilities in the exciting game of matching wits with management in collective bargaining. Much as he enjoyed this work, he was not fully satisfied either by his own progress or by that of his union as a whole. He was defeated in certain elections, and his aspiration to become a paid union official, as his father had been, was not fulfilled. Repeatedly observing an ignorant union electorate succumbing to power politics and letting popularity triumph over competence in the choice of leaders, he was forced to agree with his father's

remark that workingmen are their own worst enemies. His own identification was with union leadership, not with the rank and file, a point
of great importance in understanding his attitude toward Russia.

One of the most striking features of Daniel's personality was the
discrepancy between his energy and assertiveness in union work and
his ineffectiveness in bettering his personal economic position. In spite
of superior ability he had not, either in school or in the years immediately following, shown initiative and perseverance with regard to
making a better living. In retrospect he repeatedly complained about
the failure of his parents to push him. It seemed necessary to assume
the persistence of half-suppressed feelings of helplessness, inadequacy,
lack of will power, and need to be pushed, which feelings he had been
able to overcome only in the particular situation of group struggle
for betterment. The family atmosphere had been such as to generate
both hostility and feelings of inferiority. This apparently produced a
deadlock in self-confidence which was resolved only when the hostility
could be channeled in socially sanctioned union activity while the
inferiority was overcome by group alliance. It was noteworthy that
Daniel constantly minimized the aggression implied in his union activity. He perceived collective bargaining almost in the light of a friendly
game between contestants who were really working for the same goals.
Lifting the issues from a personal to an ideological plane was clearly
helpful in the freeing of his assertive energies. Nevertheless the
problems implied in his earlier helplessness were not completely solved.
Optimistic about ultimate progress toward greater social welfare,
Daniel looked forward to little improvement in his personal position.
He tried to give his children the friendly companionship that he himself had lacked, but he had little hope of being able to support them
in specialized training, and there were even times when he fell victim
to gloomy anticipations of failure and poverty in his declining years.

In Daniel's view of life there was a certain discrepancy between
optimistic and pessimistic sentiments. On the one hand he believed
that people are decent and kind, and that humanity as a whole can
progress to a happier, more secure life through rational cooperative
effort. On the other hand he seemed deeply imbued with a gloomy
"dog-eat-dog" conception of human nature in which relentless striving
for power disrupted all cooperative effort and in which ideals of
freedom and rationality were merely life-saving illusions. The evil in
human nature required the constant and forceful control supplied by
religion and morality, to which Daniel offered frequent verbal homage.
Although he proclaimed religion and morality to be the cornerstone
of his philosophy, his attitude toward them was somewhat passive:

he seemed to feel that his parents had completed the job by implanting in him religious beliefs and the knowledge of right and wrong, and that it was his turn now to impress them upon his children. His own strivings were enlisted rather in the cause of social progress as embodied in trade unionism. He subscribed to the ideals and policies of the C.I.O. which he defined as improving the general welfare through a program of social security, socialized medicine, and socialized education. In striking contrast to Chatwell, who had consciously subordinated the goal of security to that of freedom for maximum personal development, Daniel declared that "the most the average person can get out of life, or wants to get out of life, when you sum it all up, is security for themselves and family." As for free speech and civil rights, he was willing to call them "a big thing," but a big thing "that does not accomplish a lot." The capitalist system seemed to him full of faults, but he believed it could be gradually limited through legislative measures and peaceful collective bargaining. If his praise of the American way of life sometimes sounded a little hollow, he was nevertheless prepared to endorse democratic procedure as he found it embodied in labor unions.

Both the clear and the contradictory parts of Daniel's value system showed themselves in his opinions about Russia. To him the outstanding aspect of Russia was its achievement of a *social welfare state*. As he understood it, the Russian regime insured free medical help, free education, a fixed minimum on wages, no unemployment and no threat of insecurity. Every gifted person would be pushed by the government toward the professional goal that best fitted his abilities. Toward this aspect of the Russian experiment, corresponding so closely to the goals of his union work and obviating the frustrations that had been most intense in his own life, his attitude was cordially favorable. He voiced disapproval of the *limitations on freedom and democracy* inherent in the Russian regime, but considered them a temporary shortcoming attributable to Russian history. The *threat of Communism* to the capitalist system was certainly not to Daniel a strong ground for opposition, although he recited the usual objections to the abolition of free enterprise. He absolved Russia of any intention to interfere disruptively in our internal affairs. Going further, he absolved Russia of plans for *world domination*. All she wanted was her share of the material wealth of the world, and in expressing those wants she appeared to him less dangerous and less imperialistic than England. He favored getting tough with England before we thought of getting tough with Russia. But just at this point his darker views on human nature intruded to produce an inconsistency. Although he regarded

Russia as friendly and saw no danger of war, he did not favor cooperation to an extent that might jeopardize our security. We should not
give up our atomic secrets, he believed; we should take over war bases
and adopt universal military training. Perhaps this implied suspicion
of the Russians bore some relation to that aspect of their philosophy
which he most deplored: their attitude toward *religion and morality.*
Without the ideals and restraints provided by this source their behavior
could not, according to the darker view, be other than wicked and
self-seeking. Yet their building of a social welfare state implied,
according to the brighter view, that they had achieved rational cooperation. His favorable sentiment toward this achievement dominated his attitude as a whole and caused him to view shortcomings
with charity.

The understanding of Ernest Daniel's opinions about Russia must
start from an appreciation of the deep conflict of values to which his
life had exposed him. It would be a serious error to regard him as
simply continuing the trade-unionist philosophy of his father with its
emphasis on security and social welfare slowly achieved by group
action. Central as this doctrine had become for him, closely as it
agreed with his father's intellectual outlook, he was nevertheless a
late convert who had first tried to live his life the other way, on an
individualistic basis, and had failed. He had heard his mother clamor-
ing for more income, he had absorbed the ideology prevalent in the
public schools, he had listened to American Protestant teachings about
individual sin and salvation. He had seen his sister and doubtless
some of his schoolmates hammer their way to success, and he had tried
it himself, bitterly aware that his father could provide no help. He
had even adopted the aspiration that he would some day be able to
provide such help for his children. He was, in short, deeply imbued
with the ideal of individual enterprise and success. Both inner and
outer forces conspired to block his achievement, so that to the burden
of suppressed hostilities created by the atmosphere of his upbringing
he was obliged for a time to add those engendered by a sense of
personal failure. When at last he found scope for his abilities in union
work with its long-range optimistic ideology he became a zealot, but
the new outlook could not quickly obliterate the traces of the old.
He was an optimist on deeply pessimistic foundations.

The information environment in which Daniel maintained and developed his opinions was largely determined by union newspapers
and the conversation of fellow union officials. With these sources of
information he found himself usually in agreement, their picture of
Russia being tolerant like his own. He also read three highly con-

servative daily papers which he did not allow, so he claimed, to influence his opinions. He had talked with union men who were supposed to be Communists and had conceived a high respect for their constructive ideas. At the time of the study there had been no open split in his local between Communist and non-Communist factions.

Daniel's opinions reflected very clearly the need for *object appraisal.* In them he expressed his preference for an arrangement under which an unskilled workingman would be given the chance to develop to the top of his capacity, and would in any event be protected from financial insecurity. In the welfare state which he believed Russia had achieved it would be unnecessary for a man like himself to worry about old age or to feel inferior if he could not pay for his children's higher education. That Russia had accomplished the very purposes for which he labored slowly in his union work disposed him to judge the Communist system favorably and to minimize its faults. Collective bargaining here, and the Communist welfare state in Russia, offered rescue from feelings of helplessness and defeat that were inescapable in his earlier conception of reality. Needs for *social adjustment* played a definite though somewhat less vital part. His opinions served to reinforce the image of himself as a member of the labor class and to strengthen his identification with the labor movement. They were not, however, affected by any diffuse tendency to conform; disagreement held no terrors, and his views were held with sturdy disregard for what others might think. The *externalization of inner problems* affected his opinions in certain fairly apparent ways. His own passivity, with resentment that his parents had not pushed him, seemed responsible for the special praise he bestowed on the Russian state's pushing of its capable members into trained responsible positions. His feelings of dependence produced an overdrawn picture of individual security in Russia. Finally, the complex of feelings that included fear of his own aggressiveness, fear of the viciousness of others, and the need for firm defense and moral control, seemed to be externalized in his vehement criticism of Russia's attitude toward morality and religion and in his inconsistent advocacy of strong military preparations for a war that he believed unlikely to occur.

On the *expressive* side, Daniel's opinions showed the influence of certain deep-seated traits. In all his conversation he displayed, for example, a strong tendency to be deliberate and fair, an attitude to which he had trained himself in order to counteract his youthful impulsiveness. At the same time it was not always possible for him to implement his fairmindedness by real insight into other points of

view. There were limits to his flexibility, though not to his desire
to see things broadly and dispassionately. Another trait that appeared
consistently in test performances, conversations, and the discussion of
opinions, was a steady holding to his own lines of thought in the
presence of impressions that might have distracted others. Even when
interviewers wished to express appreciation or reassurance they often
found their remarks interrupted by Daniel's unswerving march to his
conclusions.

SAM HODDER

Although he was a factory operative and a union member, Sam
Hodder contrasted in almost every other respect with Ernest Daniel.
He was casual about his union participation, little interested in long-
range plans for social betterment, quite contented with his position
in life even though he earned only about $2700 a year. His education
extended only through six years of grade school, and his scores on
tests of intellectual ability were the lowest of our group, though still
within the "bright normal" range. His forty-eight years had been
spent in ways so diverse and helter-skelter that it was almost impossible to reconstruct the order of events. From fifteen to forty-five he
had used alcohol with great freedom, but for the last three years his
allegiance had been given to Alcoholics Anonymous.

Hodder provided us with our best opportunity to examine opinions
in a person little given to reading, reflection, or the more abstract
operations of mind. His speech was ungrammatical, disjunctive, full
of slang and profanity; the limits of his vocabulary often demanded
a rewording of instructions. Many of the verbal coins used in the
exchange of opinions were unfamiliar to him, so that we had to learn
his views without relying on such standard pieces as "Socialism,"
"Liberalism," "veto," and "isolationism." It was plain from the tests,
however, that Hodder was a man of better than average potentiality.
His performance on the *Wechsler-Bellevue Test* yielded an I.Q. of 113.
At a concrete level he functioned effectively, showing good common
sense and practical judgment. It was in the realm of abstraction that
his limitations were most marked. On the *Vigotsky Test*, for instance,
his performance was primitively concrete, and in the *Argument Completions* he found it impossible to marshal arguments, though he sometimes put forth a fairly sound overall conclusion. He never read books,
rarely listened to the radio, and did little more than scan such newspapers and magazines as came his way. Both his information and
his opinions were arrived at almost wholly through channels of conversation.

In all his contacts with us Hodder was completely at ease, good-humored and cheerful. After a brief warming-up period he obviously came to consider all the interviewers as good friends with whom he could have an enjoyable time, even when they involved him in baffling tasks or, as in the *Stress Interview*, unaccountably expressed nonsensical opinions. He took them as partners into each situation, pleasantly sharing with them his reminiscences, opinions, and reactions to the tests. He did not try to impress us, nor was he overimpressed by us. When his views were challenged he asserted himself vigorously yet without hostility. In the interviews he was almost always open and frank, conspicuously free of defensiveness. While acknowledging his educational and intellectual shortcomings with some regret and condemning his past life as a heavy drinker, he discussed these matters with little sign of sensitivity or guilt. His interest in our project was at the start purely financial, but he came to enjoy the sessions for the fun that he could get, and give, in social interaction.

When Hodder was three months old his mother, a dressmaker, turned him over to her parents for upbringing. From this circumstance and from his evasiveness when questioned about his father we inferred that the relationship between his parents might have been of the most transient character. Although the mother lived near the grandparents, she apparently had little contact with her child and was content to leave him in safe hands. Hodder described his grandmother with some warmth as a kindly woman who took good care of him, fed him well, and set him the pattern of a devout Roman Catholic. She was probably a most satisfactory mother during his infancy, but she got beyond her depth when it came to understanding and guiding an active growing boy. He remembered that she dressed him in clothes that brought ridicule and that she tried to keep him from playing with other children on Sunday. Her attempts at restraint soon became ineffective; he did pretty much as he pleased, getting out of school and church attendance and living largely outside the home. The grandfather, a shoemaker and a drunk, was equally ineffective. Though he sometimes attempted control and sometimes helped get Sam out of scrapes, he inspired neither admiration nor fear and provided no model after which, or against which, the boy could fashion himself. From the time Sam was six or seven years old his grandparents had no influence that could compete with that of the boys who roamed freely in the run-down neighborhood.

It was in the gang that Sam developed the main outlines of his present personality. Tall, lean, and strong, he met group standards as a fighter and probably exercised his share of leadership in the daily

program of adventure and mischief. Gang activities were a constant
source of pleasure and excitement, and his belongingness gave a solid
ground of security. Absorption in the activities of these groups together with the defiance of authorities prescribed by group mores contributed to his neglect of school. Against school authorities, truant
officers, and the police he learned to conduct a guerrilla warfare of
trickery, cheating, and defiance. The police were the enemies most
feared, but their influence and threat were effectively annulled by their
own attitude of joking and kidding between occasions of punishment.
The activities of the gangs changed with age. Games and mischief,
inter-gang fights and petty stealing evolved in the direction of more
serious delinquency, and the program was progressively enriched by
gambling, drinking, and sexual exploits. It is interesting to note that
the gang members themselves felt a certain parting of the ways during adolescence. A few members joined forces with older delinquents
and embarked on criminal careers; the others found employment and
began the painful process of settling down. Sam Hodder rejected the
higher walks of delinquency but postponed settling down in favor of
going to sea as a sailor.

After a few years at sea, having visited many parts of the world
and participated in many adventures, he came ashore again and supported himself by a succession of small jobs. For a two-year period
he had his own business delivering coal and ice. At the age of 32
he obtained a job with the company for which he has worked ever
since, a large and stable concern offering a considerable sense of security. Describing his work, he mentioned as its chief asset the pleasurable company provided by the team of fellow-workers, among whom
there was a constant exchange of banter and horseplay. He valued
also a certain sense of power over authority—the team could easily
make or break a foreman—and a feeling that the work was important
and responsible, inasmuch as carelessness might lead to the spoiling
of expensive materials. He had taken a part, though not a prominent
one, in the unionizing of the plant. According to his account, this
step was not stubbornly opposed by the management, which maintained the most cooperative relationship with the union.

Hodder believed that he was "about 25" when he married. He
"married for love" and in retrospect considered his marriage entirely
satisfactory. His wife, a woman of quiet tastes, kept the house well
and reared their daughter into a "splendid young lady." He gave his
wife credit for preserving the marriage in spite of his heavy drinking.
She was helped in this by the support of her mother who lived in
the same building, and by the fact that he never spent the housekeeping

money nor was violent toward her while drunk. Hodder spoke of his wife with kindness and affection, just as he spoke of his daughter with approval and pleasure, but we got the impression that his family life really meant less to him than the companionship of his numerous men friends. Even at the time of the study, when he had not been drinking for three years, almost all of his free time was spent away from home, sometimes in the activities of Alcoholics Anonymous, sometimes in other forms of community enterprise, sometimes even at bars where he took soft drinks and endured, perhaps even enjoyed, the jibes of unconverted drinking companions. Wherever he was, it was always in company.

In attempting to understand Sam Hodder's career we are probably justified in assuming an original basis of security laid by the maternal ministrations of his grandmother. It was perhaps his love for her and respect for her values that left him with an enduring counterweight against serious delinquency and hopeless alcoholism. His mother's rejection, which he probably dealt with by some combination of repressive and counter-rejective tactics, seemed very much a thing of the past in his mind but may have contributed to his forming no deep attachments to women, even his wife. The influence of adults early ceased to be paramount in his childhood; instead, an identification with age equals became the main source of his attitudes, goals, and ideals. This influence was reflected in his indifference to ideals of achievement, getting ahead, improving one's status, and in his accent on excitement, adventure, and the code of fair dealing and mutual help among equals. Perhaps the lack of absolutism and severity in his conscience resulted from its formation chiefly through membership in informal groups of equals. At all events it was in neighborhood gangs that he developed his main pattern of strivings: friendly sociability and companionship. The pursuit of these central satisfactions also served as a means of adjustment and defense. Sociability and companionship probably disposed of any feelings of weakness, inadequacy, and anxiety. We ourselves witnessed his skill in creating an atmosphere of friendliness and the consequent ease with which he met what might otherwise have been the frightening demands of our study.

It was in the light of this analysis that we tried to understand his alcoholism. Drinking began as a group activity at around 10 or 11 years, when some of the boys were hired to help on a beer delivery truck. Hodder continued drinking with sailors, friends, co-workers, and casual companions. He drank to excess and was hospitalized twice, once with a severe attack of delirium tremens. Marriage produced a moratorium of only eight months, and later, when prevailed

upon by wife or priest to take a pledge, he merely waited impatiently
for the time to be up. It is important to bear in mind that although
most of his spare time was spent in drinking he never drank alone,
never abused his family, always managed to keep his job, and was
able at forty-five to abandon the lifelong habit. He described himself
as a happy drinker, not one who sought alcohol to get over worries.
There was little evidence that his drinking served to narcotize anxieties
and provide satisfaction for repressed needs.   Its primary service
seemed to be that of reinstating the happy-go-lucky, irresponsible atmosphere of the boyhood gangs, thus easing the strain of settling down
to respectable middle-class adulthood.   Such an interpretation is supported by the highly social nature of the cure. He and his chief drinking companion both became worried about their health, his friend's
condition being somewhat ominous.   While in this frame of mind
they followed advice to make contact with Alcoholics Anonymous, and
their skepticism was melted when they realized that the woman who
greeted them knew all about drinking. They were soon involved in
the many social activities of the organization, which seemed to provide Hodder with an adequate substitute for the companionship he
had formerly sought to stimulate by drinking. He became thoroughly
identified with Alcoholics Anonymous and felt no danger of real re-
lapse.[1]

If we make explicit the beliefs that seem to be implied in Hodder's
disjointed conversations, we arrive at the following picture of the
world as he saw it. There is a Higher Being who has placed man in
this world and who tells him, through religion and church, what is
right and wrong. Hodder had either forgotten or felt incompetent
to discuss any specific teachings of the Roman Catholic Church, but
in spite of this paucity of content it was clear that religion had for him
the definite function of sanctioning meaning and order in the world.
The good life as he saw it had both an individual and a social aspect.
The individual man should be a thinking, orderly human being, who
tries to see where he stands in the world—not a fool who behaves on
impulse, who takes no responsibilities, who may even come to live
like an animal in dirt and disorder. This ideal of rationality and
order as the basis of human dignity was a value which Hodder had
doubtless entertained for some time but formulated more explicitly
after joining Alcoholics Anonymous. The social order he saw as re-

---

[1] For a fuller discussion of this feature of the case *see* E. Hanfmann, The life
history of an ex-alcoholic, with an evaluation of factors involved in causation and
rehabilitation. *Quarterly Journal of Studies on Alcohol*, Vol. 12, No. 3, pp. 405–
443, September 1951.

quiring people to give the other fellow a fair chance, not to be just out for themselves. This requirement did not exclude shrewd dealings, but it definitely put limits on them. Such limits he characteristically formulated not in terms of abstract moral principles but with reference to the behavior of the other person. If he himself were unfair, for example, it would be proper for others to cheat him. Most people, however, he considered to be decent, therefore deserving of decent treatment and of help when they needed it. A generally fair social system run by decent people he perceived not simply as an ideal but as existing, as "human nature," with only a minority not confoi a-ing to it. One can sense in this part of his outlook an extension of the code of fair dealing among members of a group which he had learned on the streets in his boyhood.

Hodder's genial, unambitious way of life allowed him to extend his philosophy to specific issues without finding many objects of bitterness. The friendly relation obtaining between management and workers in his plant, and his own sense of having been dealt with fairly, set the pattern for his acceptance of the American economic system. He wholeheartedly favored all social security measures, especially those designed to counteract the effects of unemployment. His image of the international scene emphasized trading and competing for material benefits, and though hazy about details he favored international cooperation and fair dealing with the help of the United Nations. Aside from a certain cautious attention to our own self-interest, inasmuch as some nations still demanded more than their fair share, his view of the world would have been remarkably benign except for one thing—the Communists.

To Hodder the Communists represented that small portion of humanity which is not fundamentally decent. The Russian people he perceived as just like people anywhere, but they were duped and enslaved by their Communist leaders, a small but powerful group which was the source of all evil. The real Communists, he said, were "ruthless people, out for themselves and down with everything," seeking all the power and wealth they could grab, unwilling to give the other fellow an equal chance. Rejecting the basic give-and-take of cooperation, denying the axiomatic value of religion, they functioned as a destructive force in all human affairs, local, national, and international. His ideas about Communists had been formed many years before when as a sailor he encountered members of the I.W.W. whose fanatical violence outraged him; later, he had met Party members in union work whose tactics of disturbance increased the antipathy.

Conceived in such a pattern, the Communists formed a living negation of all the values he held to be important.

Hodder's current attitude toward Russia followed from his basic idea about Communist intentions. He distinguished various aspects of the problem: the impairment of freedom, the economic system run for the benefit of Party members, the atheistic bias, the grasping international attitude, the ruthless methods; but he was against them all. His feeling was intense, and all aspects of Russia seemed to engage the same central values in him. His information was quite defective so that few contradictory facts embarrassed his forthright vehemence. That the Russian plans included a social welfare state, for example, was not part of his fund of knowledge, and he accepted a test item which stated that private property was restricted to Party members. For our own policy he advocated a vigilant firm stand, helping Greece, Turkey, and other threatened nations, opposing Russia wherever she created disturbance.

Ever since Hodder emerged from his thoughtless alcoholic days he had been trying to think rationally about the world and his place in it. His views on Russia formed a part of this recent attempt at *object appraisal.* He used the Communists as a way of explaining anything that seemed to disturb his generally satisfactory world. His own ambitions did not extend beyond repairing his home and perhaps earning a few more dollars a week; his daughter would soon be taken care of by marriage. His main desire was to find the world open, friendly, and fair-minded, a suitable medium for his central strivings. Contented as he was with his immediate world, he felt it to be not perfectly secure, and the Communists were his hypothesis, so to speak, as to the source of danger. It was not easy to estimate the extent to which *social adjustment* entered his views. In his largely Catholic milieu and in his not very radical union his opinions created no disharmony, but it was also true that discussion of opinions was not in his circle a particularly acceptable social technique. We exerted ourselves to overlook no way in which his sentiments could be thought of as representing the *externalization of inner problems,* but our catch was somewhat small. The drives he attributed to the Communists seemed either absent from himself—he showed little urge toward power and wealth even at covert levels—or so readily admitted by him, as in the case of aggression and trickery, that an assumption concerning defensive projection became superfluous. The one way in which externalization possibly functioned was that by picturing the Communists as really dangerous enemies of society he sharpened the contrast between them and his own career of less sinister delinquency, thus bolstering his none too secure position as an advocate of decent living.

Viewing Hodder's opinions in their *expressive* aspect it was easy to perceive the influence of his limited education, weakness in abstract operations, and lack of the discipline of reading and serious discussion. His intellectual shortcomings made it easy for him to focalize the evil in the world uncritically upon the actions of certain people. Because of his affiliative needs he could not attribute evil to human nature as such or to any sympathy-awakening minority, but because of his concrete thinking he could not place it in an abstract construct such as the economic order. A group of people defined merely by their greater selfishness and wrong-headedness satisfied the demands of his intellect and conveniently accounted for evil both at home and abroad.

CLARENCE CLARK

In all cases thus far described it was possible to mark off the life history into different periods of development. External events or the culmination of inner growth brought the person from time to time to a new level of achievement or established for him a new kind of equilibrium. Such highlighting was absent from the case of Clarence Clark, 41-year-old accountant, who quite early had been forced into a hard psychological bargain with life and had lived ever since within the terms of the contract. Adventure and experiment, the unplanned and the unforeseen, had no place in the agreement, the purpose of which was rather to guarantee security against the encircling threats by which early circumstance, upbringing, and economic problems conspired to keep him beleaguered. He had led his life according to a plan that allowed for little variation over the years.

Before his arrival we knew about Clark only that he was employed in the accounting department of a large manufacturing concern and that he had been with the company for 18 years. He proved to be a man of average height and slender build, neatly but inconspicuously dressed. His speech was clearly enunciated, his vocabulary good though colorless, his sentences well formed and connected, but it required frequent questions to keep him from falling silent. At first he was highly suspicious of the project, needing detailed reassurances that his anonymity would at all times be preserved. The force of his resistance caused the enrollment interviewer to doubt that he would participate, but after a while Clark expressed his satisfaction with our security measures and thenceforth became a willing though not garrulous contributor. At first his motivation seemed purely financial.

At no time did the scientific purposes of the study evoke signs of strong interest, but he did come to enjoy the attention paid him and the opportunity to display and confirm his most valued abilities. In appropriate connections he brought up problems of his children and his own feelings of inferiority, asking the interviewers for advice. When we expressed appreciation of his strong points and sympathy for his hardships we judged from his reaction that he was inwardly most grateful for these signs of esteem and understanding.

Clark's story was one of those in which social class and class aspirations played a crucial part. His parents had attempted to maintain middle-class standards on a lower-class income. The father, who had only a grammar school education, was for most of his adult life night janitor of a school building, on duty 84 hours a week, so meagerly paid that he sometimes tried to eke out his income with part-time day jobs. According to the son's account he was industrious, never smoked or drank, and observed the highest moral standards. His lack of vocational advancement, and the inordinate attraction exerted by a pension which in fact he never lived to receive, thus probably bespeaks a trait of extreme cautiousness and self-distrust. In spite of low income the home was maintained in a lower-middle-class neighborhood, and when Clarence was 8 the family moved to what was considered a better neighborhood. The mother, of middle-class origin and with a high school education, followed her class tradition of keeping house and not looking for outside work. When Clarence was 13 he began to work in a store during his spare time. Part-time work continued without respite until he completed his two-year training at a business college and took on a full-time job. It was a stiff grind, but it resulted in his having, at 41, a secure white-collar position in a stable concern, with a salary of $3500 and a home for his wife and two children in a "better-than-average neighborhood." Nevertheless, the margin of security remained narrow: in one of the interviews he said, "My one ambition in life is to get my bills paid up."

Clark's upbringing was such as to emphasize single-mindedness in bettering one's social and economic position. His parents agreed that getting an education was the crucial step. His father's "one ambition," said Clark, "was that I should get an education, and he'd go without a shirt in order to pay my way in school." His mother added a further specification, quoted by the son as follows: "You go ahead and be a hail-fellow-well-met and you'll get along in the world." Other traits in the mother, however, tended to undermine her espousal of purposeful extraversion. Although she taught Clarence to be tidy and punctual, she found it difficult to let him go out and play rough games with other children, supporting her oversolicitude by a theory that his bones were brittle. Clarence's sister, his only sibling, three years older, was the mother's favorite and received preferential attention, a fact about which he assured us warmly that he felt no resentment. He played a good deal by himself, absorbed in his toy trains and erector set. His father when available at all was so taciturn that Clarence felt him to be an almost complete stranger. In retrospect he estimated this as the one great lack in his childhood. "My one ambition," he said, "is to be a companion to my son because I was denied it." It is hard to assign a rank order to this "one ambition" and the other one of keeping his bills paid. Both were important and were pursued with great seriousness.

Both parents administered discipline, the father being regarded as the higher court. That the parents were making sacrifices for Clarence's welfare and education gave them a strong moral hold on the boy. The father especially played on sympathy: "He'd talk to me very seriously and say that I was worrying him and my mother . . . and I'd just decide I would improve." This atmosphere of sacrifice and moral claim probably started Clark on the way to his compulsive conscience with its emphasis on neatness and order and its spurning of idle pleasure. Clark felt himself to be very like his father and bemoaned his poor success in meeting the maternal standard of hail-fellow-well-met. When at 29 he married a hearty, easy-going woman who liked people and readily established superficial friendships, he was probably influenced by a sense of completing his own personality by taking on someone who could fulfil the maternal ideal and create the human contacts which it was difficult for him to achieve alone.

In Clark's current life the two strongest preoccupations seemed to be his job and his son. In his job he had risen to be the head of his department, with three men under him. He had reached the ceiling of probable advancement and sometimes thought of looking elsewhere, yet he felt rather certain that the lure of greener grass would not pull him to the extent of moving his children out of their present favorable neighborhood. He found satisfaction in his precise work with figures and in the overall view it gave him of the operation of a large company. He also enjoyed the opportunities for friendly and sometimes covertly aggressive banter with fellow employees at rest periods and in connection with company-organized sports. But he complained of having to work under pressure and of receiving little recognition from the company, and he was unable to take satisfaction in directing his subordinates, really preferring to do the work himself. He was, in short, dissatisfied with those parts of his work which too deeply stirred his ambivalences in human relationships. The company, exacting in its demands and niggardly with its esteem, not always responsive to his contributions to the suggestion box, repeated the emotional deprivations of his childhood upbringing. Nevertheless, he did not intend to do anything that would imperil such security as he enjoyed. His role as a faithful subordinate was hard for him to accommodate in a pleasing self-picture, but no freely operating motives urged him toward greater power or greater responsibility.

Clark's relation to his 7-year-old son and namesake was colored by his desire to provide the companionship lacking in his own childhood. The upbringing of his other child, a daughter of 10, he relegated entirely to his wife. With young Clarence he played games and spent considerable time. He took very seriously the duty of molding the boy's character and did not spare the punishments he considered necessary to this end. Signs of dishonesty worried him greatly, as did the child's reading difficulties at school, suggesting not only trouble for young Clarence but also the reflection of discredit on the older Clarence. If the intended companionship seemed sometimes marred by Clark's embedded insecurity and punitiveness one could only reflect that he was doing the best he could to make the world a happier place than he had found it.

When one has mentioned these two areas of interest, the job with its casual social accompaniments and the family with its special emphasis on the son, the story of Clark's current life is virtually complete. He had little social life outside of company activities, knew his neighbors hardly at all, and had come to avoid most movies and radio programs, especially those that made a disturbing appeal to emotion. He took his family to the Roman Catholic church regularly every Sunday, but otherwise his spare time went mostly into puttering around the house and keeping his bills paid. His future outlook was expressed almost wholly in financial terms, partly no doubt an occupational habit but partly a reflection of his tendency to depersonalize his picture of life. Thus the children's education he discussed purely as a financial problem, and one of his few excursions into fantasy took the form of a statement that he would like to have a million dollars.

In attempting to formulate the psychological dynamics in this case we concluded that the central pattern of strivings, hidden beneath the character armor, consisted of dependence and a need for acceptance and recognition by others. Clark depended on others to assume responsibility, provide guidance, and make him feel important and lovable. The history of this pattern we traced to lack of companionship with his father, his mother's preference for the sister, maternal oversolicitude, and a physique ill-suited to command the respect of other children. The strength of his dependence and passivity made it hard for him to build a satisfying self-image, and his craving for recognition represented a constant need to have this image bolstered by others. Short rations for his central needs resulted in aggression which had to be kept under the most rigid control, having vent only in petty criticism and the finding of faults in others. The difficulties created in this wise hindered the outflow of interests and made it necessary for him to carry burdensome defenses. Within a planful and orderly life he could achieve some slight measure of freedom, but security demanded tactics of avoidance, self-restriction, and even repression to cope with anything that lay outside his tested routine. We felt that Clark's adjustment was probably quite stable. His adjustive mechanisms worked in such a way as to protect him most successfully against experiences with which it would be difficult to cope. He had to endure feelings of inferiority and dissatisfaction with himself, but he was not prey to disorganizing anxieties.

Clark's performance on tests reflected clearly the organization of his personality. He told us that school work had usually found him at his best. He liked clear-cut tasks where there was always a right answer; thus he excelled with figures but was somewhat less fond of languages. In accord with this he made an excellent showing on the *Wechsler-Bellevue Test,* his I.Q. of 125 placing him in the top 4 or 5 per cent of the general population, but in the less structured *Rorschach* his stereotyped, constricted performance might have been given by a person of no more than average ability. His one fault in the *Wechsler-Bellevue* was the occasional making of hasty errors, a consequence of his eagerness to show up well. Imaginative tasks, in contrast, found him hopelessly at a loss, often seeking guidance from the examiner. He did not, as sometimes happens, attempt to reduce his bewilderment by a precise use of details. He sought rather to approach each stimulus with a rigidly conventional statement about its most obvious features.

Of all our subjects Clark was the least interested in discussing his values and opinions. The pattern of restriction that characterized his personal life reappeared in the realm of opinions. Having small resources for outgoing interests and attachments, he ruled out large areas of public concern which did not directly touch his daily life. About world and national affairs he cared hardly at all. Things were bad but you couldn't do anything about it. Even community affairs drew little of his interest and were largely handled under moral categories. Bound to conventionality, he clearly found it hard to maintain a sentiment in conflict with his group, yet his difficulties in assuming responsibility made it equally hard to come to a firm conformist conclusion. No enjoyer of controversy, he simply failed to make up his mind on issues likely to provoke argument.

The things about which he felt strongly were money and morality. He offered no criticism of the existing economic system, his one desire being to make for himself a secure place in it. The desire for money and the sentiments associated with it represented the channeling, by no means unrealistic, of his dependence and need for security. His strongly held moral sentiments sprang from a different source, his strenuous superego. Decency and respectability, foresight and diligence, and a good upbringing for children needed constant affirmation; their opposites merited frequent criticism and condemnation, providing a legitimate outlet for aggressive feelings. Clark could allow himself to experience "a grand feeling" at Mass, but when he came to expound his religious beliefs he framed them in the form of a contract with God, who will reward us if we adhere to clearly stated stipulations of right conduct. Religion was for him the basis for morality, and therein he found its chief importance.

Russia was too remote from Clark's daily life to evoke more than the most sketchy opinions. For the most part he was indifferent, though not more so, perhaps, than a fairly large segment of the American public in 1947. He was the least well informed of our ten subjects. "All I know," he remarked, "is what I see in the paper," a statement which we would expand only by adding what he heard from the church. We judged that he exposed himself as little as possible even to such information as was readily available. His opinions about Russia were all unfavorable but of low intensity and little differentiation. It is of interest that he perceived threat from Russia at precisely the two points of greatest concern in his personal value system: money and morality. The Communists constituted an international threat because of their greed, leading them to grab territory with its materials and man power and thus strengthen themselves at our expense. They also constituted a threat because of their atheism, under which heading Clark managed to include their wicked belief in dictatorship rather than democracy. His thinking on the whole topic seemed little more than a repetition of unexamined stereotypes, and his ideas on the course of future relations with Russia showed neither serious reflection nor a sense that the question was of real importance. Many aspects of Russia—for example, the attempt at a social security state—simply did not enter his awareness. He perceived Communism as a great evil—but very far away from the accounting department of

his company and from his home in the better-than-average neighborhood.

As might be expected from the foregoing, Clark was not clear-cut
as regards specific policies. He favored telling the Russians our policies, offering to trade with them, disclaiming designs on the lands
around them, and saying to them in effect: "You go ahead and see what
you can do with your country and we'll do what we can with ours."
Along with this cooperation we should get tough wherever necessary
to call Russia's bluff, as in Greece and Turkey under the Truman Doctrine, and if war seemed inevitable he favored having it now rather
than later when Russia would be stronger. Characteristically, the only
participation he envisaged for himself consisted of silent inaction:
talking about war made it more likely to happen, so his one contribution would be not to talk about war.

Clark's opinions about Russia, like his general values and like his
test performances, stood as striking *expressions* of more or less enduring
features of his personality. His lack of interest in the whole topic
reflected his general constriction and his tendency to exclude whatever
was disturbing, threatening, or hard to formulate. Reflected also were
his general insecurity and ambivalence, forcing him to timid indecisiveness on controversial issues and passive acceptance of ideas from
authoritative sources. The conventional and rather stereotyped approach which he made to our test materials reappeared in his use of
stereotypes in discussing opinions, while his preference for clearly defined right and wrong answers disposed him to cast the Russian Communists in a pure black role. This pattern of characteristics was expressed consistently in everything that Clark did for us.

On the *adjustive* side, his opinions about Russia were but little
implicated in his *object appraisal*, where his urge was to exclude rather
than to understand and take sides upon questions that did not force
themselves into his daily routine. His dim sense of personal threat
from Russia required only that he pick up a few readily available
stereotyped attitudes. With respect to *social adjustment*, the direction
of his opinions served the vital purpose of conformity with the people
among whom he moved, while his indecisiveness allowed him to avoid
the disturbing angers and inferiority feelings generated by argument.
Nothing in his opinions would have outraged either the majority of
Catholics or the majority of white collar workers at the plant, and nothing in his way of holding them would have invited contest from the
few who might have different views. *Externalization of inner problems* could be inferred in the special emphasis he laid on Russian
greed and Russian suspiciousness, tendencies over which he had to

exert definite control in himself.   A thwarted and threatened need
was responsible also for his idea that if he went to Russia, where most
of the people were "the peasant type," he would be "quite a big man—
the average Russian person would kind of look up."   In comparison
with other subjects, however, Clark's opinions about Russia played a
relatively small part in his economy of personal adjustment.   They lay
outside the arena in which his fortunes were being wrought.

BENJAMIN KLEINFELD

The opinions about Russia held by our next subject bore a certain
resemblance to those of Ernest Daniel, the factory operative and
ardent trade unionist described first in this chapter.   A simple polling
procedure would have made the two men seem much alike.   Both
were somewhat friendly toward the Communist undertaking, praising
in particular its social welfare side and the program of free higher
education.   Both criticized the lack of personal freedom and the hostility of the Communists toward religion.   Both men also took a charitable attitude toward Russian expansion while expressing serious distrust of our own motives in international affairs.   Yet in spite of many
resemblances in outlook Ernest Daniel and Benjamin Kleinfeld were
strikingly different people.   Their outwardly similar opinions were
nourished from different personal roots and played a different part
in the economy of personal adjustment.   Only by examining this personal context could one make sense of the divergent conclusions drawn
by the two men from what looked like the same premises.   Daniel
favored aid to Greece and Turkey under the Truman Doctrine, while
Kleinfeld opposed it.

It was through channels of chance acquaintance that we were able
to enlist the services of Benjamin Kleinfeld, 34-year-old Jewish shopkeeper who operated a small independent store in a shabby part of
Boston.   He proved to be a man of short stature and personable
appearance who presented himself in a quiet, neatly pressed suit
with white shirt and who spoke in an unexpectedly cultured voice.
Throughout the sessions he was always obliging, usually deferent,
rarely tense or defensive.   He showed strong motivation on the tests
and was eager to know how well he had done.   The *Rorschach Test*,
however, he found disquieting; he hastened to consult books in order
to learn what kind of secrets it was supposed to reveal.   We came
to sense in Kleinfeld a strong need to improve his understanding of
himself but at the same time an equally strong reluctance to let this
understanding get out of his own hands.   He did not ask for help,

but he very much wanted new tools for self-help. This was probably his strongest motive for participating in the study.

Kleinfeld told us that his grandfather had been the scholar and sage of a small Russian town. Kleinfeld's father learned the trade of book-binding, but gave this up when he came to the United States and found that it would require him to work on the Jewish Sabbath. Instead he opened a small store in a partly Jewish neighborhood and took up his abode in quarters over the store. Here he brought his bride, an immigrant from another part of Russia, and here he raised his family of two sons and three daughters. From an early age Benjamin was accustomed to helping with the chores and running errands for the store. When he finished high school his father sent him to a distant state university where the tuition was low, but this venture lasted for only a single year. Benjamin then worked in the store long enough to learn the business, whereupon his father helped him to set up a similar shop of his own in a much more prosperous neighborhood. He continued there successfully for nine years, but when at the age of 30, still unmarried, he was drafted for military service he sold the shop. He was in the service four years, seeing active and hazardous duty as an aircraft gunner in the South Pacific theater. When he returned to civilian life he looked around for jobs likely to be more congenial and lucrative than small shop-keeping. Circumstances, however, forced his hand: his father suffered an incapacitating illness, and Benjamin was obliged to take over the old family store which provided the only immediate means of supporting his parents.

The family atmosphere in which Benjamin grew up reflected the inevitable difficulties of overlap between Old World and New World cultures. "My parents," he wrote, "have always lived according to the teachings of Moses and the Bible, very simple, humble, and dignified lives. Their respect and eagerness for knowledge and culture and their disdain for physical prowess and materialism is characteristic. It was in this sort of atmosphere that they brought up their five children." In the midst of the jangling slum their home was, as he put it, "an oasis in the desert," where books were read and talked about and where music was played and assiduously listened to from the phonograph. The father was distinctly the head of the house and its cultural leader, the mother being cast in the role of efficient and nurturing homemaker, though sometimes perforce a helper in the store. Unlike the neighbors who let their children go regularly to the movies, Mr. Kleinfeld went first to any show he thought might be worth while and took his family only to those pictures which passed his moral and aesthetic censorship. Much as Benjamin admired this pattern of

family life, he realized how troublesome it had been for himself and
his siblings in modeling their own homes to harmonize with the American pattern.   Nor was Mr. Kleinfeld unaware of possible difficulty.
Though he preserved his orthodoxy, kept a full kosher home, and was
devout in his religious observances, he gave his children to understand
that they were free to do otherwise, apparently not wanting them to
carry an encumbrance in the upward march to professional status that
constituted his aspiration for them all.   The humble but dignified life
of the Bible required reformulation in the face of New World opportunities.

We have seen that Benjamin, still a shopkeeper at 34, showed little
sign of fulfilling the parental aspiration.   This fact gains overwhelming
significance when we compare him with his siblings.   At the time of
the study the girls were all married to professional people, the eldest
sister having besides an important job of her own.   The elder son,
two years older than Benjamin, had gone through a large university
and an outstanding medical school and was well established in practice and research.   From the beginning the relationship between the
two boys had been fraught with difficulty.   The brother was considered
frail, whereas Benjamin was usually in the most vigorous health.   As
a consequence the brother was pampered and excused from irksome
tasks, while Benjamin remembered himself as constantly delivering
packages or running errands for the house.   There were memories
of being bossed by the brother and of fist fights which the father
sternly interrupted.   During adolescence the relationship steadily improved, so that at the time of the study Benjamin felt quite close to
his brother as a person, but the projective tests convinced us that the
embers of early rivalry were still aglow, and in any event our subject
was fully aware that the discrepancy between his and his brother's
achievements continued to gnaw painfully at his self-respect.   That his
brother was a successful professional man, while he himself was behind the very counter where his father had stood for so many years,
acted as a constant stimulus to his feelings of inferiority.

To explain Kleinfeld's relative failure offers a difficult diagnostic
problem.   Quite early in his school career he fell behind his brother's
standard of grades, which from the start was a very high one.   Nevertheless he did well enough so that he was promoted to the city's best
high school, but here his difficulties increased and he was for a while
in imminent danger of failing.   He told us that he studied hard to
overcome poor preparation, but his parents thought he should work
even harder.   Gradually he accepted the judgment that he was not
a brilliant student like his brother.   When it came time for college

his mediocre record limited his choice to a school that did not have formidable standards. He made a good enough record, but the depression had arrived and his father was no longer willing to continue a dubious educational investment, preferring instead to set him up in business.

This was certainly not the kind of educational history from which one would deduce a serious lack of native ability. The I.Q. derived from the *Wechsler-Bellevue* was 123, and while we would guess that Kleinfeld's brother might score better in this test the discrepancy would not necessarily have to be a large one, nor would it necessarily signify any difference in initial endowment. It was clear, however, that the brother got off on the right foot with high marks at school and that thereafter his mental ability was a constant source of gratification. Perhaps because he was naturally less quick, but perhaps from some emotional or even fortuitous cause, Benjamin made a less distinguished start, and thereafter the gap could only be widened by its emotional consequences. Our evidence shows that there was early rivalry between the boys, that Benjamin felt injustice in the circumstance that his superior vigor could not be used for physical triumphs but only caused him to be saddled with extra tasks, that the father became impatient and sometimes angrily told Benjamin he would not amount to anything, that Benjamin bitterly resented discipline from the father he could not please; in short, that the prescribed pathway to success meant giving in to the unjust father and playing docile second fiddle to the brother. The truth can easily be read between these lines from his autobiography: "For many years I was the black sheep of the family, always destructive and inattentive at school. This up to the sixth grade, when through the influence of an understanding schoolteacher I became a model pupil at the head of the class." Not finding a similar teacher in high school, he was never again able to suppress his resentful distaste for school studies. Thus quite involuntarily he lost whatever chance he had of fulfilling the parental aspiration, which must, after all, have been in a most real if beclouded fashion his aspiration for himself.

Kleinfeld's adjustment to his position as a shopkeeper was an uneasy one. He meditated on escaping from the shop and utilizing his veteran's benefits to resume his college education. His father died during the time of the study, but with his wife to support and a child on the way he felt that another educational gamble would be too risky. He found increased satisfaction in the Old World portion of his parents' philosophy which emphasized the simple upright life dedicated to the higher things even in the midst of sordid necessities. In this attitude he was fortified by his wife, whose professional status had not prevented her from marrying a shopkeeper and who valued being a "real person" above external success. Unlike his siblings he continued to keep a kosher home. His less visionary hopes for the future included increasing his current income of around $3300 a year only to the extent that might be necessary to establish a better shop in a better neighborhood, live in pleasanter surroundings, educate his children, and have enough freedom from tiring work to enjoy music and reading.

It was probably natural that Kleinfeld, who had felt himself a black sheep in his own family, should have been intensely sensitive to his position as a Jew in a predominantly Gentile society. Not that he lacked reason: he told us of several embittering incidents, especially one at the state university which he felt ruined his whole year there. Nevertheless he seemed unusually haunted by a constant irritated yet anxious awareness of the problem. It had in fact played a significant part in his military service and in the disillusionment and pessimism that shrouded him after the war. Selling his shop in 1941 and going to fight the battle of Democracy and tolerance against the Fascist anti-semitic dictators signified for him the lifting of his life from a hum-drum to a crusading level, one goal at least of the crusade being ex-tremely close to his heart. When we saw him in 1947 this inspiration lay in shattered fragments. The army of Democracy had not been free from antisemitic incidents nor from the injustice of strutting in-competent officers, and the policies of the victorious allies as regards Palestine convinced him that a new day had yet to come. He had tried to do something for a great cause; he had learned how slowly great causes move and how little an individual can do to push them ahead.

The outstanding emotional problems in Kleinfeld's life centered around aggression and the feeling of worth. In the passions and jealousies of his childhood he had learned how little could be accom-plished by aggressive behavior. The same lesson had been driven home to him again as regards antisemitism. Although in earlier in-cidents he had sometimes responded with angry violence, he realized that this usually made things worse and had resigned himself to swal-lowing his feelings and avoiding a scene. Thus his whole experience, both at home and outside, had contributed to a feeling of helplessness combined with simmering resentment. His suppressed aggression made him irritable. Driving on crowded streets he was constantly enraged at the behavior of other motorists; behind his counter he was on edge for signs of ill-will and competitiveness, feeling satisfaction only in those customers who showed trustful dependence. Yet his very irritation added to his burdens and lowered his interest in group participation. In turn, his failure to participate in community and political affairs, his inability even to keep up with things and fulfil the role of well-informed citizen, hurt a cherished image of himself and made him feel all the more insignificant and ineffective. It was heavy work to maintain a tolerable level of self-respect, and we were not surprised that he felt life to be a burdensome strain.

In his outlook on public affairs Kleinfeld described himself as a "cynical liberal." He had outgrown the extremes of Communism and anarchism which had appealed to him at different times during adolescence, and was willing to settle for "lumbering democracy" and a basic free enterprise provided the interests of labor and small business were protected from the big fellows and monopolists. He hoped for the socialization of utilities including coal-mining and medicine. He was inclined to see a propagandist in every woodpile, viewing with cynicism all public utterances and believing that selfish if not vicious motives lay behind everything that was done. Nothing in his experience seemed to justify a belief such as the one held by Chatwell that Americans could be trusted to intervene abroad without covert plans for power and conquest. How could the United States, he demanded, talk of idealism and pretend to moral leadership in the world when its own house was not clean? The mistreatment of minorities and the selfish policy as regards Palestine came to mind as instances of the dirt in our own house.

Like Ernest Daniel, Kleinfeld was favorably impressed by the *social welfare state* in Russia. He strongly endorsed Russia's aim of providing education and medical and welfare services for all. The equalization of wealth he believed to be on the whole a good thing. Toward *limitations on freedom and democracy* his opposition was stronger than Daniel's. He saw no excuse for the restrictions imposed upon private citizens and felt that he himself could never endure this feature of the regime. When it came to *religion and morality*, Daniel's strongest ground for criticism, Kleinfeld took a somewhat milder position. Although angered by the ban on the Hebrew language and the policy of restricting religious observances, he was in general not ill-disposed toward Russia on moral and religious grounds. He was probably most concerned about Russia's desire for *world domination*, and what he judged to be the imminent threat of war. Unlike Daniel, he did not excuse Russia's expansion nor doubt the seriousness of her imperialistic designs, but he agreed with the idea that American motives were just as bad. Yet it was at this point that the two men differed most widely in their views on policy. Daniel advocated military preparedness and a not-too-soft stand in Greece and Turkey, which he felt Russia would respect. Kleinfeld believed that the only way of averting war was to give Russia no provocation in Europe or Asia, even if this meant that her expansion continued to the Atlantic and Mediterranean. Though not an isolationist in principle, he perceived intervention at the moment as a suicidal step toward war.

It would take long to explain fully the divergence between Daniel and Kleinfeld on this point. It seemed to us, however, that the key could be found in their histories with respect to self-confidence and the feeling of being able to fight for one's cherished values. In his union work, supported by the group, Daniel had learned to fight, had achieved some success, and had become identified with the democratic process as he found it in labor unions. Kleinfeld, in whose outlook the problem of antisemitism constantly bulked large, had learned the hopelessness of fighting an enemy which always seemed stronger, and had been disillusioned about the motives of those on his own side even in the successful fight against Fascism. As regards actual information about Russia's strength and intentions we could not see that the two men started from a different basis. Their differences sprang rather from pictures in their heads, pictures which had been painted by the brush of personal experience.

The information environment in which Kleinfeld formed his opinions was partly derived from a cursory reading of the daily press and casual listening to the radio. His cynical view that everyone was grinding an ax caused him to feel that none of the sources was reliable. Hearst papers he refused to look at, but otherwise he balanced his fare between what he called the "Fascist" papers and *The Daily Worker*, noting with interest the divergent accounts given of the same events. His parents had lived in Czarist Russia but had preferred to leave, and they were not disposed to believe that the Revolution had done away with all the evils they had known. An important source of Kleinfeld's knowledge was conversation in the circle of his relatives and their spouses and friends. He was minutely informed about Russian policies with regard to the Jewish minority and with regard to Palestine, and this vital theme played a large part in his whole picture of Russia.

Kleinfeld's opinions about Russia were clearly a part of the larger task of *object appraisal*. As a small independent businessman who valued his right to run his shop in his own way but feared the hazards of bigger competitors and business fluctuations, he favored a policy a little to the left of center, where freedom and security were compounded in a blend most advantageous to men like himself. Admiring the security provided in the Communist prescription, he could only deplore the absence of the ingredient of freedom. He believed that his goal of fair treatment for ethnic minorities was properly enshrined in Communist ideology, but much of the good was cancelled in fact by Russian persecution of Zionists and disfavor toward the Jewish religion. Thus several of Kleinfeld's opinions about Russia were parts of the general value system formed at the behest of his major interests. As regards *social adjustment,* his daily strategy was characterized in the main by a cautious withholding of affect and an equally cautious withholding of opinions. In high school, however, he had been transiently identified with small nonconformist groups in which opinions were of major importance. At the time of the study his chief membership group, the circle of his relatives and their friends, supported his conception of himself as a liberal, intelligent Jewish American, and in this circle his political outlook was shared, although in other matters he was not altogether averse from taking an unpopular stand. Of the *externalization of inner problems* we have already mentioned the most prominent instance. His difficulties in meeting hostility, his struggle to control counter-aggression, his fear of this aggression in himself, his sense of helplessness against external force, conspired to magnify in his mind the danger of opposing Russia and led him to advocate appeasement. We also felt that his childhood situation and his minority status had attached all his deepest sympathies to black sheep and underdogs, making it peculiarly difficult to identify with his own country in its post-war top-dog position. It seemed likely, in addition, that his strong espousal of personal freedom sprang not only from his clear interests as a small shop-keeper but also from a lasting rebellion against anything that recalled the authoritarian restrictions of his childhood home.

The analysis of Kleinfeld's opinions as expressions of enduring traits brought us first to a characteristic attitude with regard to knowledge. One might almost describe as gluttonous his appetite for information and his desire to support opinions with facts. As a result he was among our better informed subjects in spite of little time for reading and little deep interest centered on the topic of Russia. Another enduring characteristic was the pitching of his discussion at a high level of deliberate, cultured conversation. While at appropriate moments he displayed a variety of emotions, he preferred to discuss things with philosophical detachment. No doubt this trait was given extra prominence by the university surroundings, but we judged it to be an enduring consequence of strategies for the control of affect, strategies encouraged by the home atmosphere of veneration for learning. We felt also that a certain passivity and mildly toned pessimism had become sufficiently habitual and far-reaching to merit inclusion under this heading of our functional analysis.

ALBERT ROCK

Certain curious misconceptions led to the enrollment of Albert Rock in our study. His name was suggested at a time when we were trying to balance our group by securing some less educated subjects. The person who proposed him claimed to be well acquainted and said that Rock, a local contractor and active church worker, was a man of only grammar school education. The facts proved to be that he had completed not only high school but four years of college, two of these years being in engineering and two in a business curriculum. As we became better acquainted with Rock we could see the ground for his friend's mistake. His plodding course through college had been completed in fulfillment of a parental ideal, in preparation for a practical occupation, and without the striking of sparks or opening of unforeseen vistas. Interested primarily in a moral life and a practical one, sympathetic with the poor and eager to bring them the benefits of the Roman Catholic Church, he was not in the least identified with either upper-class or intellectual ideals. It was interesting to contrast him with Benjamin Kleinfeld, who felt a strong though frustrated identification with professional people and whose manner of speech suggested an education he did not have. Albert Rock, earning a much larger income and scoring a few points higher on tests of intelligence, talked like a man who had not gone through college and cherished the role of friend of the common people.

A second misconception lay in Rock's own mind. Apparently he did not grasp what was implied in a study of personality, thinking that only opinions and values would be discussed. He agreed to participate when he found that the schedule could be arranged to get him out of his home on the evenings when his wife held a sewing circle. His motivation turned out to be barely sufficient. Though his feelings were kindly toward most of the interviewers, and though for a while he found pleasure in expanding on his less personal attitudes, he was easily the least interested, least cooperative, most hostile of our subjects. Toward the university and clinic his feelings beforehand were probably somewhat negative. They became more so when the personal interviews, especially those having to do with family relationships and sex, convinced him that he had fallen into a hotbed of indecent "Freudism." Finally he reached the conclusion, blurted out under the pressure of the *Stress Interview*, that the questioning on Russia indicated a war-mongering desire on the part of the staff. With all these doubts and hostilities, with no financial incentive, burdened often by fatigue and worry about conditions at home, he nevertheless stayed with the project to the bitter end—strong testimony to a basic conscientiousness in completing what he had undertaken to do.

Albert Rock was a tall stocky man, clear eyed, strong featured, gray at 45 but erect and confident in bearing. His speech was calm but firm, his whole attitude composed. The range of his preferred relationship to interviewers included dominance, kindly interest, sometimes condescension or glacial reserve, but never dependence and almost never open hostility. His talk contained occasional mistakes in grammar and pronunciation but otherwise proceeded in what seemed like a quite orderly and connected fashion. It proved better to hear than to read, for the transcripts showed much recourse to phrases like "I mean" and "I mean to say," and his sequence of ideas was more often maintained by emotional than by logical ties. This way of using his mind proved to be not simply careless but deeply ingrained. When pressed for logical connection he was as likely as not to veer off into a collateral topic.

Rock was the youngest child of a large family. His father, of Scotch Protestant background, went to sea after finishing grammar school, but then came ashore to establish and build up the contracting business which later fell to his youngest son. Marrying an Irish Catholic girl, he was converted to her religion, but he carried into the new faith a considerable alloy of the Protestant ethic of hard work, self-reliance, and individual enterprise. One of his special characteristics was an interest in the poor and a desire to help their condition. Rock's mother hoed a hard row, never gaining ground on the demands of children and housekeeping, and she was the chief victim of the father's policy of investing his profits rather than bringing more money home. On this subject there were serious quarrels between the parents. Young Albert frequently found himself serving as mediator in domestic strife. "I'd try to patch up the difficulties between them," he said; "I was the confidant of both of them, and I think I can say that I was never a child because of it." On one occasion the mother, her nerves unstrung by a particularly sharp quarrel, packed a bag and left for their camp at the beach. Albert, then about eight, was sent after and stayed with her "until she got on more peaceful terms with everybody and came back home again." He well remembered how anxious he became over these quarrels and how moody they sometimes made him.

To his anxiety about his parents was added the infuriating dominance of his eldest sister, who tried to step into the maternal role and inflicted such insults as making him wear an apron while wiping dishes. Rock's general avoidance of outspoken aggression did not prevent him from airing to us the sentiment that older sisters should be drowned or chloroformed. The other siblings seem to have played a less exasperating part in his development. In one way or another they all managed to disappoint their parents, leaving school early and showing little interest in making a good living. This left open for Albert the role of the good child who conformed to parental desires and aspirations. He more than accepted the role: he tried to figure out what would please his parents and to do more than they asked. So successful was he that the father eventually made Albert, the youngest child, executor of his estate, a situation which created bitter feelings in the brothers and sisters.

The path of conformity was a hard one. The father, though often companionable, was a stern disciplinarian who permitted no visible disobedience. Rock, who later took over the business, administered the estate and showed a strong interest in the poor, gave every sign of having identified strongly with his father, yet his role in parental quarrels showed that his sympathies were divided between the parents. Another side of him took his mother's part, and his need to bring the quarrels to an end seemed to have been overwhelming. We may speculate that parental quarrels contain a peculiar threat to a child who is building his life around conformity. To the fear of desertion that would assail any child is added a sudden breakdown in the pattern of excellence he is attempting to emulate and an all too strong appeal to the aggressions he is attempting to repress. Once the storm is past the motives to conformity become stronger than ever, but also more compulsive and fear-ridden. At all events Rock as we knew him, while obviously a man of strength and stability, showed the lack of zestful enthusiasm that goes with an overstrict conscience, one that still holds wayward impulses in the bondage of childhood moral standards. Conformity was hard, and this perhaps explains the difficulties he had with school work, a part of the parental goal toward which his siblings had been particularly negligent. His progress through school was marked by a strain and effort hardly to be expected in the history of someone whose *Wechsler-Bellevue* score gave an I.Q. of 126 that placed him in the top 4 or 5 per cent of the general population. There were occasional attacks of nervous vomiting when some crucial test had to be met; there was one time when the hiring of a tutor proved necessary to avoid failure. Application to studies continued to be distasteful, and it was on this basis, as well as his father's antipathy toward college professors, that he violently rejected theorizers and impractical intellectuals.

There were three chief zones of interest in Rock's life at the time of the study: his business, his family, and his church work. His business as a contractor was not large, calling for the employment of at most twenty men. Profits fluctuated greatly, depending on the contracts obtained, but the previous year, an unusually good one, had yielded him an income of $20,000. Although the chief meaning of his business for him was to provide support for his family, it brought sufficient intrinsic satisfactions so that he never wanted a vacation. He enjoyed the variety of his work, was given "itchy fingers" by a good set of plans, and took pride in his small labor turnover and good relations with his men. Drawbacks lay chiefly in the competitive nature of the business and the real danger of being squeezed by large firms and large suppliers. With considerable foresight he had specialized his business in a field where a reputation for good work counted to offset low bids in awarding contracts.

The family was a more central value in Rock's life but a more dubious source of satisfaction. The first decade of marriage had proved that his wife could not carry children, and the memory of these years was anything but happy. When hope was finally abandoned they began providing themselves with children by adoption. This gave both of them a welcome sense of achieving the purposes of a home, but it did not solve all problems. Rock found satisfaction in creating a regime that emphasized, like his father's, strict moral discipline together with individual initiative. He found satisfaction in improving on the old regime by giving his children more companionship and helping them with their lessons. He also ended all overt bickering with his wife, but covert dissension still played an important part in his life at home. His wife's frequent claims of illness forced him into much housework even when he felt she was only babying herself. We judged that the theme of the misunderstood great man, which appeared persistently in his productions, derived from the position he fancied he held in the household. It seemed likely also that his fear of dropping dead from heart disease, an annoying though not crippling fear which he himself regarded as irrational, might be the final common path jointly chosen by anger, guilt, a wish for surcease, and a desire to be missed.

Rock's third area of interest seemed to be a source of unalloyed satisfaction. He belonged to a Catholic society the chief purpose of which was "visitation." The object of the visits, conducted always by two laymen, was to animate interest in the Church, bring erring sheep back into the fold, and put those with misfortunes into contact with agencies which might be of service. The agreeable combination of kindliness and dominance represented in the visitor's role had enlisted Rock's full power of learning. From his first-hand experience he was able to give us a description of the process of interviewing that reflected many of the insights contained in the books on our shelves. At the time of the study he was spending two evenings a week regularly on visitations.

It has been mentioned that Rock's general values drew inspiration from both Catholic and Protestant sources. In the spirit of a pious medieval Christian he believed in the Holy Catholic Church and the life of the world to come, viewing with pessimism man's imperfect nature and prospects in this world. Yet he also believed in the value of hard work, in a "liberal-minded" philosophy of live and let live, and in the world as a "pretty good place" except for the power-drunk chiselers who were responsible for most of its trouble. There seemed to be real conflict between complacent feelings toward this world and a pessimism that could be borne only by hope of the next world. Rock's standards of logical precision did not require that he should reconcile such conflicts in a wholly coherent system of values. It was clear that religion, which defined the moral order and one's goals in life, was his central and ruling value. The sacredness of the home, unsullied by divorce and blessed with children who could be guided along right paths, took precedence over other goals. His attitude toward community affairs followed the same pattern. He undertook to promote betterment by paternal guidance of the poor toward religion and toward reasonable measures of self-help. In the larger sphere of nation and world his humanitarian sentiments caused him to favor legislation that looked toward social security. Generally pessimistic about the motives of business men and politicians, he nevertheless believed that an occasional leader such as Franklin Roosevelt could tinker beneficently with the social order. Government regulation of business, however, appeared to him generally a bad thing into which Roosevelt was misled by college professors. Freedom of enterprise was important to him in spite of his views on chiselers.

Rock's attitude toward Russia was almost wholly antagonistic. His strongest opposition was directed at Russian policies with respect to *religion and morality*. The Communists rejected God, morality, and

the family, the very heart of his own system of values. He was glad
to learn that divorce was not easily arranged in Russia, but he saw
in the nursery school program an attempt to sabotage family life. His
second main ground for opposition, Russia's threat of war, evoked
feelings hardly less bitter. Here his outlook was somewhat tempered,
however, by uncertainty as to what should be done. While he favored
a firm stand, he was not pleased by the prospect of aiding "those awful
countries," Greece and Turkey, nor by the possibility that this very
aid might provoke hostilities all the sooner. He was also convinced
that certain groups in the United States were selfishly motivated to
create a conflict; he even began to fear that the Clinic staff might
represent such a group. Rock's third ground for disapproval was the
Communist government's *restriction of personal freedom.* He saw
Russian citizens as chained to their jobs and oppressed by rulers who
had no regard for human life nor the sacredness of the individual soul.
So strong was his general opposition that it spread even to those aspects
of Russia which might have been expected to evoke more sympathetic
sentiments. Thus *Russia's part in World War II* had won his respect,
but the good was cancelled by his judgment that "we gave them
everything that enabled them to live and they showed no gratitude."
Again, the *social welfare state* brought forth hardly any of the approval
that might have been anticipated from his views on social security and
help for the poor. As regards universal education, for example, he
believed that the American system achieved equally good results. On
the whole he was much more impressed by—and better informed about
—the oppression of the common man in Russia than by what was
attempted in his behalf.

There was one interesting departure from Rock's generally hostile
attitude. Russia was not far removed from its day of revolution, and
"revolutions," he believed, "don't always bring out the best in any
country." Clarifying this sentiment, he said, "We can't expect too
much from a country which has suddenly found itself with power in
its own hands. I look at Russia as a baby, a big baby that is in
process of developing. And they haven't learned how to live with
other people." It seemed to give him a certain pride to step out of
his usual involvements and take this detached historical view. Besides
taking some of the heat out of the issue, this outlook permitted a
limited sort of optimism, inasmuch as the United States had once been
a brash revolutionary state but finally developed along acceptable lines.
When we remembered the apron-clad young Albert at the sink under
his sister's sharp eye, and when we noted that he explicitly mentioned
using the historical argument with his wife, for whose sake he must

still stand at the sink, we felt less surprised that Rock found a way to
be charitable toward revolutions. By and large, however, his attitudes toward Russia were little softened by his capacity for occasional
detachment.

For the most part, the information environment to which Rock
exposed himself was not such as to mollify his views. His two preferred magazines and the two newspapers of his choice were notori-
ously conservative in outlook. From church publications and from
conversations with priests he was kept constantly briefed on Russian
atheism and immorality. Rock told us, however, that he sometimes
read papers and listened to commentators less disposed to criticize
Russia; he seemed perfectly aware, furthermore, that his usual sources
of information reflected almost entirely the interests of the church and
of business. "You have to discount an awful lot of what you read,"
he said, "because every one of those fellows is working for some
interest, one way or another." This bit of cynical sophistication
sounded like Benjamin Kleinfeld, but its effect on Rock was considerably less disturbing. Admitting that "what you read and what you
hear is the basis of your opinion" and that "certain types of publication
have a tremendous influence," he remained confident that his own
values and moral standards would serve to "sift out what's good and
what's bad." Rock preferred sources with which he was in general
agreement, but he was quite prepared to screen all information through
the stout meshes of his own value system.

When Albert Rock's opinions about Russia are considered in their
expressive function they can be seen to reflect an intellectual procedure
that is more emotional than logical. His different opinions corresponded to the way he felt about each topic, and he was not strongly
impelled to free the whole result from contradictions. On the topic
of Russia, which aroused very strong negative attitudes, his feelings
spread in all directions without encountering strong logical dikes. His
opinions reflected also a tone of pessimism, suspicion, and lack of
positive enthusiasm which was by no means confined to this particular
topic. On the score of *object appraisal* the plan and needs of his own
life caused him to favor a religious and moral interpretation of the
world. He had striven hard and sacrificed much to become a good
man, and it was still not without suffering that he maintained high
standards of behavior in his life at home. The affirmation of moral
values and of faith in an ultimate reward was for him a cornerstone
which the Russians were trying to knock out of the universe. The
religious and moral conception of life in his case dominated the social
and economic. Beneficiary of both his father's and his own business

acumen, he saw freedom of enterprise as a privilege which no mere sordid government should have the right to abridge. His strong humanitarian sentiments were channeled into the conception of helping the poor, a thing he found congenial to do in his church work. Social security legislation appealed to him in this light rather than as part of an economic program to change the distribution of wealth. None of the three main interests in his life—home, business, church work— were regarded with favor in the Communist system, to which he was therefore unalterably opposed. Yet the very blackness of his picture of the dangerous enemy caused him at times to need the saving thought that Russia might eventually grow up and learn to live peacefully with her neighbors. *Social adjustment* played a probably strong but silent part in forming and maintaining his opinions about Russia. His views represented no marked departure from those of parents and church; conformity to these standards was obviously crucial both in Rock's development and in his life today. He told us, however, that a number of his views were not in harmony with those of the people he met in his work and that he generally preferred to avoid arguments on heated topics. The *externalization of inner problems* produced certain visible colorations in his outlook. His struggle to control annoyance with an ailing, demanding wife, to be patient with his children, indeed to execute the whole cherished role of inspiring but kindly head of the house, required efficient use of repression and reaction-formation. In defense of his own defenses he criticized with particular warmth the Russian attempt to weaken the home and family. His sense that his activities in the home were not appreciated caused him to select for special censure Russia's lack of gratitude for our wartime help. Only in his rare moments of historical detachment did he find it safe to sympathize a little with the forces of evil, choosing the ground that they might represent youthful rebellious tendencies which maturity would rectify.

GRAFTON UPJOHN

Grafton Upjohn was the only one of our subjects whose family was in economic and social decline. Born into the upper class of an old New England city, where both grandfathers had become wealthy men with distinguished friends, he lived at the time of the study in what he considered a dreary middle-class neighborhood and supported his family with a government salary of $5100 a year. This was a drop from the standards of his parents and a real tumble from the affluent state of the previous generation. For the first eight years of his life Upjohn had lived amid economic plenty. Then began a series of financial reverses and retrenchments which pushed him from private to public schools and from vacations to summer jobs. Though his financial plight in 1947 was not acute on an absolute scale, it was nevertheless felt as acute in his subjective scale of needs and expectations. At the age of 48 he still hoped to make a financial "last spurt" which would give his three children the opportunities he felt they deserved. Yet he knew that the hope was ill-founded: he had neither the initiative nor the ability to achieve such belated success.

Upjohn was a man of short stature and rounded physique. He held himself straight, smiled often, and talked freely in a voice that was soft yet with an underlying rasp. His attitude was generally compliant, though he refused to lie on the couch in the two sessions in which this was suggested. He told about himself with apparent openness, but was the only subject except Clarence Clark who needed reassurance that the material was confidential. In these ways his behavior reflected what we ultimately perceived to be a characteristic organization of personality: a friendly and somewhat garrulous technique for presenting a favorable self-picture, but, underneath, a great deal of uneasiness about his real worth and a considerable capacity for resistance and aggression. In agreeing to participate in the study he responded willingly to that part of our appeal which emphasized a hoped-for public service. It was clear that he also enjoyed the prospect of association with members of an institution with social prestige, in whose company he expected to feel at ease and at home.

Upjohn remembered his father chiefly for his handsome appearance and fine manners. Apparently the father had little real contact with his children, serving rather as a remote but splendid picture of a man who knew how to enjoy life. Somewhere along the way Upjohn became aware of important weaknesses in his father: a lack of business acumen and a fondness for expensive luxuries, both of which traits he later perceived to be strong in himself. The mother also was remembered in her social role of entertaining well. To a surprising extent his portraits of his parents seemed like conventional fashion plates. The recalled instances of affectionate display almost always had something to do with giving and enjoying food. The young Grafton felt, however, some closeness to his mother and to an appreciable extent became identified with her. His early care was largely entrusted to a nurse of whom he became very fond. He spoke of himself as the pet of his parents, a role which he was also able to maintain with the nurse in spite of the presence of a younger sister. This role did not endear him to his older brothers, who picked on him and bullied him even though they allowed him sometimes to share in their escapades. He seemed to have striven without success for their acceptance and respect. Their superior sexual knowledge was a particularly sore point, especially when his own puberty was delayed until his sixteenth year. Thus his early home life established two enduring patterns of conduct. He could be deferent and ingratiating, willing to be helpful and at the same time making openings for the return expression of sympathy and affection. On the score of masculine assertiveness, however, his deep doubts drove him to strain for an acceptable self-picture, giving listeners a sense that he was preoccupied with building himself up. We ourselves witnessed many alternations between these patterns, and we judged that his lack of close friends, which he mentioned with regret, might spring partly from the difficulty of responding coherently to such rapidly shifting roles.

Upjohn never did well in school. He was sometimes on the edge of failure and usually squeaked through by a fairly narrow margin. As in several of our cases, the test results suggested potential capacity for a much better school record. Upjohn's I.Q. of 127 on the *Wechsler-Bellevue* was not consistent with an inability to pass grammar school and high school subjects. There was no substantial evidence of anxiety or other emotional interference with intellectual functioning. "Although he shows good conceptual ability," one examiner observed, "he may not always use it to full advantage, reverting on occasion to a trial-and-error approach in an attempt to get a hasty solution." After studying the test results we found little reason to depart from his own judgment that he was lazy. Good school grades did not have any meaningful relation to the kind of life he expected to live. College was a necessity, but only to the extent that one must get in and stay in long enough to graduate.

The financial pinch became severe just at the time when he expected to go to a private college preparatory school. He went instead to the local high school, where he developed a strong interest in athletics. During this time began the unfamiliar and somewhat humiliating experience of shopping for groceries and carrying them home. He was obliged to take on a variety of summer jobs which brought him into contact, intensely distasteful to him, with lower-class people of foreign backgrounds. Through a benefactor he was finally able to have two years at an excellent private school. Then followed a short stint as a second lieutenant in World War I. After that he entered college, and though he failed at the school of his first choice he worked hard to secure admittance to the small but well-respected college from which he presently graduated. He enjoyed especially the social and athletic features of school and college life.

At 24 Upjohn began to earn his living. Both the family fortune and the family business had vanished. He turned to selling, and for the next nine years had spotty employment in a variety of promotional schemes none of which worked out successfully. In retrospect he judged that he was a satisfactory salesman but generally poor in all other aspects of business ability; this confession came only after the examiner pressed him to support an initially higher self-estimate. In taking some of his jobs he evidently climbed aboard sinking ships without fully realizing their perilous condition. Support of his growing family was a constant problem, though this did not prevent him from resigning from one of his jobs when he realized that the business was dishonest. At last, and just when the depression was reaching its severest point, came a windfall in the form of an administrative post at the preparatory school from which he had graduated. Here he found security and contentment, though no great wealth. His work did not require the making of policy, for which he could gratefully lean on the school officers, especially the congenial headmaster, but it did require organization and detail work to which he proved more than equal. It also required numerous contacts with the students. In this paternal, or, as he more often called it, maternal role, he discovered in himself an unsuspected sympathy and skill in dealing with young men. He also enjoyed the school community and made his home the scene of good though not lavish entertaining.

Shortly before the outbreak of World War II a change in the headship of the school removed from Upjohn a strong emotional prop though it did not imperil his position. Without reluctance he reentered the service where first as a personnel and then as an executive officer he continued on a much expanded scale to practice the skills he had developed at the school. Some of the work he successfully accomplished called for great skill in planning, administration, and the effective handling of reassigned men. It is of interest that he reached his top level of performance when serving as second in command. When circumstances made him in effect commanding officer he suffered a good deal of tension and checked with some difficulty his tendency to make hasty and impulsive decisions. It was in such circumstances that he developed occasional attacks of gastric disorder and also feared that his sexual potency was failing.

He closed his military service with the rank of lieutenant colonel, having seen three and a half years of service at home and abroad. Deciding against returning to the changed conditions at the school, he found his present job in the government service and, with much difficulty, the home in the disagreeable neighborhood. His work yielded some satisfactions and called forth some of his abilities, but he detested the political atmosphere of the office, the uncongenial associates, and the lack of future prospects. The financial "last spurt" seemed ever more remote. His proven abilities, though substantial, were not of the sort that would promise success in the kind of business enterprise which alone could now fulfil his economic ambitions. For the most part he felt that he had reached about as good a position as he could get, but acceptance of this fact violated a cherished dream, seemed unjust in comparison with what he had once expected, and was a constant source of nagging discontent.

Upjohn pictured his present home as an island of social grace in the midst of drab uncouth inferiority. He regretted his wife's careless housekeeping, which he tried to rectify by a swift campaign of cleaning up on Sundays, but he found her a source of security and pleasant companionship, sympathetic with his interest in food, drink, and hospitality. He tried to run his home the way he thought it ought to be, which included bringing up his children according to strict standards of honest and well-mannered conduct. Apparently his methods put quite a strain on the household. It appears a significant clue that when he went to the war his eldest son, then 14, took over the paternal role and soon had the family so disturbed and terrorized that Upjohn was called back to set things straight. Furthermore, his method of dealing with the upstart head of the house consisted of browbeating him into submission. We gained the impression that impulsiveness and temper, which he restrained in positions of military command, were often not restrained at home. At the same time there was strong and genuine fondness for the children, pleasure in their accomplishments, and pride in what he considered the successful reclaiming of "that adorable little gangster," his eldest son.

Upjohn had moved a fair distance from what he had come to consider the "false values" of his parents. He well knew that their parasitic dependence upon accumulated riches and their insulation from the tough realities of life were anachronisms in his own and his children's generations, and that many of the associated values could have a dangerously enervating effect. He preserved the code of good manners, hospitality, and a taste for the niceties of life, but he wanted his children to have in addition a capacity to participate in the rough and tumble of the business world. His sense of public duty, service, and helpfulness, was much greater than that of his parents. Yet the effect of his early dwelling in a Garden of Eden was deep and lasting. Long enough to establish his first and basic estimate of life, he had lived where things were plentiful, where much that was uncongenial could

be avoided, where long-range plans were superfluous, and where be-
having like a gentleman was the only required task. That his fortunes
had turned out so differently left him with enduring resentment.
Fantasies of sudden wealth still lived in his mind, and may have
influenced the unwise decisions of his early business career. The hope
of a financial "last spurt" constantly gnawed at him. Furthermore,
we found evidence for covert fantasies that he was entitled to take by
force what was not granted him by providence. Just as Kleinfeld
could accept only half-heartedly his disappointing status as a shopkeeper, Upjohn was inwardly divided in recognizing his middle-class
economic status.

When it came to specific beliefs, we had the impression that Upjohn
tried strenuously to meet the requirements of the study by expressing
opinions but that he had given little thought to public affairs and
formed few stable guiding values. He said repeatedly that he was
uninformed, had not kept up, and was accustomed to blow hot and
cold. Though a Republican, he had voted for Al Smith as a protest
against anti-Catholic bigotry, and his attitude toward Roosevelt had
shifted back and forth several times, for reasons he could not formulate.
He favored limiting the profits of big business, called Communists the
gangsters in the ranks of labor, liked the idea of a firm strong diplomacy
rather than action through the United Nations. We found it impossible, however, to integrate his beliefs into a consistent pattern; moreover, on some issues it proved an easy matter to shift his position by
argument. He resembled Clarence Clark, though for different reasons,
in his lack of informed interest in public affairs.

One of his opinions, antisemitism, was more stable and carried so
much personal meaning that he was likely to push it forward in almost
any company. His attitude toward Jews had been built up in the
course of his life, as a result, he claimed, of his personal experience.
The complaints he made against Jews resolved themselves into these:
first, a group of qualities possessed, such as self-seeking, upward striving, shrewdness, and unscrupulousness in business dealings; second, a
group of qualities lacked, such as a sense of public duty, physical
bravery, good manners. The second group consisted of qualities possessed by Upjohn and valued by him, which were not, however, proving
effective in bringing the status and wealth to which he felt entitled.
The first group of qualities corresponded to his covert fantasy of grabbing what he wanted, and therefore awakened an envy and a resentment which overtaxed his capacity for objective judgment. Attributing
his position and prospects to his own shortcomings, he did not blame
the Jews for injuring him. It was rather that he secretly envied but

at the same time hated anyone who played the game with gratuitous assets of brains but without the restraints of honesty, duty, and good breeding. He had focalized this pattern of traits on the Jews, and he was vehement in his vocal complaints, but we did not find evidence that he thought of any policies except social discrimination. The psychodynamic purpose of discharging aggression and fortifying self-respect seemed sufficiently achieved by talk, especially when others confirmed him. We were reminded of Hilary Sullivan's deep need for Communism as a belief but lack of urge to take political action in its behalf.

Upjohn's opinions about Russia showed the same poor differentiation and lack of stable goals that characterized his value system as a whole. Not himself interested in ideologies, he seemed to overlook this feature of Communism and interpreted Russian *expansion and threat of war* simply as an attempt to get greater power. He viewed the revolutionists as peasants who had suddenly come into power and now, their "noses in the trough," wanted more and more. Rude and ill-mannered, grasping like any parvenus, they also would derive from war the benefit of more easily welding together the heterogeneous elements in their population. He strongly opposed Russian expansion, believing that we should fight strength with strength, aid Greece and Turkey, preserve atomic secrets, and sidestep the United Nations. This strong attitude he expected would prevent war, but he was not disconcerted by the prospect of war if it failed. His own success had reached its peak in the service, and he felt that he could be of some use again even if too old for active duty. He was but little disturbed also by the *threat to the capitalist system*. Much as he cared for the possession of wealth, he had never been identified with the active business world nor indoctrinated with its special hostility toward Communism. *Restriction of freedom* he strongly opposed, but without the deep preoccupation that characterized, for example, Albert Rock. He seemed to have no conception of Russia, or any other country, as a *social welfare state*, doubting most of the items on this subject that were put before him, and showing interest only in full employment. He himself thought that his objections were strongest to Russia's policies with regard to *religion and morality*. Though a Protestant, he had much of Rock's concern for the family, and was rather pleased by his own remark that Russia's moral code was simply "prostitution sanctioned by the government," even though he recognized that this was an overstatement. On the positive side, his admiration for *Russia's part in World War II* was unqualified. He thought well of *material progress* under the five-year plan and of full employment. On the whole, however, the objections greatly outweighed the virtues, and he was opposed to most of what Russia represented.

Upjohn's information appeared to be derived from conversation with friends and acquaintances, scattered reading of a few papers and magazines, and casual listening to news commentators. For the most part he chose conservative but not extremely reactionary sources. It was evident that he gave no more than fleeting attention to material on serious current issues. He characterized different commentators less by their views on political questions than by the entertainment value of their programs. His memory retained the "juicy gossip" of some of the broadcasts better than the serious implications of the day's news.

Upjohn's opinions about Russia can be seen as *expressive* of several traits. They were put forth, in the first place, in a most disjunctive fashion, sometimes with obvious contradictions. His lack of interest in anything theoretical was shown in his leaving out of account the Communist ideology. Primarily a man of action rather than reflection, he was clearer about our specific policies than he was about the general issues involved. But the same uncertainty which made him do better as second in command than when he was fully responsible for policy was apparent in his lack of stable goals and in his inability to discuss possible lines of action other than those already publicly proposed. Upjohn's *object appraisal* was colored chiefly by his interest in comfortable, refined living, in the possibility of obtaining a high income and accumulating wealth, and in warm stable family relationships as a source of security and pride. What was going on in Russia could only be a threat to these values, though he did not conceive it as an imminent threat. His successful military career, and the success of United States arms in two wars, had attached a certain value to the taking of strong, confident stands. Upjohn did not want war with Russia, but he was less frightened by the prospect than most of our subjects. Needs for *social adjustment* influenced the content of his views, and they were an important force behind his having opinions at all. This was especially apparent in relation to the staff, where in order to maintain the valued relationships he felt obliged to express opinions well beyond the realm in which he was interested and informed. To the extent that he had formulated anything about Russia it was, we felt, at the behest of social needs such as those mobilized by our study. The gentlemanly role with which he was identified required that he be able to converse intelligently about public events. The *externalization of inner problems* put a strong stamp on some of his views, notably his antisemitism, but we could not see that the topic of Russia rendered him much service on this score. His own covert desire to grab the wealth and status that had been denied him probably influenced him to emphasize power-grabbing and the nose in the trough when thinking about Russian expansionist policies, while his need to control the ungentlemanly and dangerous fantasy led him to reject the Russians as rude peasants. We felt also that his admiration for courage, physical strength, and the taking of strong stands were compensations for an early timidity and sense of physical inferiority, compensations which he had achieved with no little success but which still might be doing some service of inner reassurance.

DANA OSGOOD

The last of our subjects was a man of 38, a partner in a small real estate and insurance office in South Newton. His somewhat fluctuating income had reached $10,000 in the previous year, when business was particularly active. With his growing family he occupied a pleasant home in the prosperous suburb where he himself had grown up and where now his office carried on most of its business. An outstanding characteristic of his life was its dedication to community service. He was on so many boards of so many useful and charitable community organizations that only one or two evenings a week were left free from engagements. The motive of service was largely responsible for his willingness to participate in the study. Generally satisfied with his position and happy in his personal associations, he nevertheless sometimes thought that his life had merely drifted along instead of being pointed toward definite goals. Some discontent on this score, together with a strong need to feel acceptance and respect, probably accounted for his marked curiosity afterwards to know what we had made of him.

Dana Osgood opened his written autobiography with the following sentence: "I was one of those children born to parents who were in a position to send me to private schools and college and to give me the advantages of dancing school, music lessons, and all the things that go with a 'correct' bringing up." This sentence, including the quotation marks around "correct," forms a good starting point for the understanding of his personality. The economic and social status occupied by his parents came to his mother by inheritance but was achieved by his father only after an early career marked by ill health and frequent changes of occupation. It was in fact when recovering from an illness several years after his marriage that he drifted into the real estate business which finally brought him financial success in his own right. The home in which Dana and his sisters grew up was never without servants, including a nurse when the children were small. In this respect one is reminded of Grafton Upjohn's childhood home, but in spirit the two families were poles apart. The Osgoods cared little for entertaining or displays of affluence. They were loyal and active members of the Universalist Church, pillars of the community, much interested in providing a good home and sound influence for their children.

Osgood remembered his mother as completely dedicated to her children. No outside activities interfered with their needs, and she seemed to be "always there" when they wanted her. He praised her qualities of patience and kindness, but well remembered also her firmness on issues such as wearing rubbers or telling the truth. Memories of the father included certain genial moments, as when he told exciting stories about a western ranch he had visited, but there were also incidents in which Dana's desire to be helpful came to grief because of the father's high standard of orderliness in whatever he undertook. The atmosphere of the home was well-mannered and high-minded. Standards of conduct were clear, and the expectation that they would be met was so compelling that Dana remembered very little actual punishment. For all their devotion, the parents were felt to be somewhat unapproachable. Dana could not imagine confiding his troubles to them, especially to his mother who always seemed "far above" such things. Neither parent ever spoke a word to him on the subject of sex. This blend of devotion, high expectations, and reticence created certain difficulties for Dana in the management of rebellious impulses. Overt hostility achieved poor results, while the covert form left feelings of guilt. The parents sometimes used a technique of silent disapproval and seemed always to have difficulty in making their positive feelings explicit. Thus there was a shortage of reward for the expected good behavior, together with an all-too-good chance to magnify one's feelings of wickedness and inferiority. In a curious father-and-son story on the *Thematic Apperception Test* Osgood made the father watch his son's accomplishments with silent admiration; when at last he expressed his feeling, the boy received the praise "ruefully," for he was not happy in the work and had really been wanting to do something else. As a boy Dana was often uncertain as to whether he was pleasing his parents and as to whether he was pleasing himself.

Although the home involved certain difficulties, Dana found opportunities for a more adventurous life among his friends in the neighborhood. His happiest memories were of times spent with his cousin, a boy a year younger about whom he said, "We always used to click, no matter what we did. He was a little bolder than I was, a better athlete than I was, yet I seemed to be steadier than he was and we balanced each other beautifully." He sought companionship wherever it could be found, sometimes straying outside the neighborhood approved by his parents. Repeatedly he emphasized that he was not outstanding in groups: "just another player" in sports and "fumbling" with radio sets, for example. Apparently he got from the other boys what he got from his cousin: acceptance, encouragement to do "bad" things like breaking windows on Hallowe'en, and in general an initiative and zest which he could not muster from his own resources. Meanwhile his piano practice went badly, and at dancing school he was not only awkward but became, at about 12, extremely shy with girls. His parents struggled vainly to prevent the dwindling of his more formal social life. Feeling that something had gone wrong with his local adjustment they sent him away to a boy's boarding school.

The first venture from home resulted badly. Dana felt inferior to the rich boys at the school and was humiliated when his parents came to see him in a Model T Ford. His shyness persisted even when the other boys urged him to go out with girls. But when he went to a small college many miles from home he suddenly came into his element. Here his economic position was not inferior, he knew no one, he was on his own and had his own way to make. In his social life he at once began to make up for lost time. His dancing and conversation improved with remarkable speed. He threw himself energetically into a round of campus activities. Studies were merely a "great chore which had to be done," and they were done so carelessly that he finally needed an extra term to graduate. When his parents protested he replied, feeling his oats a bit, with the well-chosen argument that if they did not like his grades he would leave college and look for a job. This threat of downward mobility brought his parents into line, and in the end his father rescued him from all financial miscalculations by sending him whatever funds he requested.

After this period of freedom and happy development he returned home and began in random fashion to look for an occupation. Eventually he was offered a position in the office which had been his father's, though by this time his father had sold his share in the business and was in no way responsible for the offer. Osgood thus followed in his father's footsteps, but he was able to feel that his progress in the office was the result of his own efforts. From the start he enjoyed the work. Disliking routine application, at which he continued to be somewhat careless, he took pleasure in the constant variety and flexible hours of his business day. Above all, he found major satisfaction in meeting people, talking with them, helping them to find the kind of homes they wanted, and receiving their gratitude. "I enjoy people

immensely," he said in an interview, and later, "I don't think there's
anything quite as pleasant as to have people thank you ever so much
and send their friends to you and so on." He became an anchorage
point for clients new in the neighborhood, who often called him to the
rescue if anything went wrong with their houses. He liked this trouble-
shooting and found that he got "particular satisfaction out of helping
older people." He had, in short, fallen into a kind of work which gave
him contentment: "I'm very happy where I am and I expect and hope
to stay in my present position."

Osgood was married at the age of 32 after a long and somewhat
stormy engagement. His wife fitted into his background and shared
his ideals; harmony reigned in the establishment of a home in which
the children would be given love and a chance for self-expression yet
not allowed to dominate the household or render it unfit for adult
habitation. In her devotion to the children Osgood saw a similarity
between his wife and his mother. In relation to himself, however, he
emphasized especially her zest and capacity to make him feel more
deeply the experiences of everyday life. He took pleasure in the
children and also valued his home as a place of rest and as a place
for genial social gatherings. Home life was interrupted during World
War II when Osgood, having been rejected in attempts to enlist for
officer training, became subject to the draft. At the very top of the
age range, he was pleased to discover that he could take the rigors of
training, even though he lost much weight in the process. He was
not sent overseas and regained his weight quickly when returned to
domestic life.

With the exception of Sam Hodder, no subject in our group cared
so much about his friends as Dana Osgood. His friendship with his
cousin was only one of several childhood attachments that continued
into adult life. He had made new friendships along the way, generally
with men of considerable ability whose company he found stimulating
and exciting. In the Army, for instance, he developed a warm feeling
for an alert and brilliant Jewish refugee who showed him new beauties
in music, pictures, and scenery. Besides this quality of stimulating
him above his usually placid level, the friendships always involved
mutual esteem and appreciation. Osgood felt liked and respected by
his friends. He felt free to exchange mildly aggressive banter, which
he could both give and take without creating hard feelings.

Osgood's work for community organizations constituted another
major source of satisfaction. Like his parents he was active in the
Universalist Church, but otherwise his participations were of his own
making rather than the continuing of family traditions. Part of the

satisfaction came from being with people, but "more than that," he said, "I feel that if you are living in a community you are duty bound to belong to social agencies." Out of his experiences he had developed a general ideal of service, embodied in his statement: "I'd like to devote my life to helping others." As his career of service lengthened he began to receive certain outward marks of distinction, but it was evident that community activities appealed to him mainly for other reasons. Here he could work for clear and concrete goals, associate with others in enterprises of indubitable worth, and receive the thanks, always implicit and often explicit, due to those who give their time in unpaid public service. In community work he could be certain that he was pleasing people.

We would overlook the creative element in Osgood's life if we charged his devotion to service entirely to the conscience generated in his childhood home. We were careful to note, as was he, that both his vocation and his community work, close as they lay to lines of parental interest, were substantial achievements of his own. To a large extent they were the heirs of his campus activities at college and his group activities with the boys of the neighborhood, neither of which had enjoyed particular parental blessing. Indeed there was reason to believe that his conscience itself, admittedly a strong contemporary guide, had been partly shaped by his interest in being accepted by the boys who served to counterbalance the restraints of his home. Most of Osgood's submission to strictly parental goals showed earmarks of half-heartedness. He practiced the piano badly, danced clumsily, suffered shyness with girls, got poor school grades and groaned at the "great chore" of college studies. On those of our tests which most resembled school tasks he put forth a limited amount of energy, impressing one examiner as a "not too conscientious" worker. We judged that this withholding of energy had been the one possible mode of resisting parental pressures. As an adult he regretted some of the things he had not learned and not accomplished, wishing in particular that his father had been more strict and prevented him from feeling that everything came easily. His failure to work hard for parental goals was the basis of his idea that his life might have had more point and less drift. But through his friends, through his way of handling his business, and through his community activities he had achieved a way of life which was certainly not a piece of half-hearted conformity. The claims of conscience had come to be satisfied in a setting of gratifying social relationships.

In order to understand Osgood's general values it is necessary to bear in mind that he had little personal reason for wanting a change in the social order. It was natural for him to hope that his children would have the same advantages and economic security that he and his parents had enjoyed. Social and economic change would be likely to have only an adverse effect on his personal situation. Within the existing framework he was by no means an enemy of improvement. He attached great importance to the liberal and independent tradition of his church. He was interested in bettering child training and in alleviating the condition of the poor through community enterprises. But in politics and economics all his sentiments were conservative. He called himself a "dyed-in-the-wool Republican." He felt threatened by government interference, the trend toward Socialism, the power of labor, and especially the threat of inflation. When pressed he conceded that government ownership was in certain respects desirable, but for the most part he automatically rejected the idea. His interest in public affairs outside the community was rather small. Calling himself "not an original thinker" on such topics, he had borrowed his views first from his father, later from his immediate associates. One could properly say that he had a collection of views rather than an organized philosophy, and the collection had been made largely through such personal channels as lunch-time conversation with his business friends.

As regards Russia Osgood classed himself among those "optimists" who believed that war was not inevitable. Peace could be maintained if we took a strong stand against Russian expansion and at the same time aided the democratic governments in Europe. He found two things to praise about Russia: her stalwart *part in World War II* and her rapid *internal development* with respect to manufacturing, agriculture, education, and improvement of the condition of the poor. These strong points were badly outweighed by things which he could only deplore. Russia's *role in international relations* he believed to be inspired by a wish for expanded influence and power, the spreading of Communist doctrine being merely a secondary consideration. Her statesmen knew what they wanted, were playing a close hand, and in trying to achieve their power goals would stop at nothing except a counter display of force. Her *methods of spreading influence* received his vehement condemnation. He believed that a small number of dangerously fanatical Russian agents were responsible for our most serious labor troubles. *Restriction on individual freedom* he considered highly undesirable, causing a decay of individual initiative and responsibility and reflecting an attitude that human life was cheap. He was particularly outraged by Russian brutality in killing off political opponents. As regards *religion and morality* he was poorly informed, but what he knew he perceived as a threat to the family: the "foundation of any country," and as destroying a person's right to freedom of worship. When it came to specific policies he did not like the Truman Doctrine but nevertheless considered it inevitable: conditions required that we participate in Europe and show strength toward Russia. He admired the tough line taken by Secretary of State Byrnes and favored our maintaining superiority in crucial arms and in productive capacity. Along with this we should not relax our efforts to demonstrate the superiority of democracy, nor should we overlook any opportunity to proceed by peaceable means.

In examining the *expressive* character of Osgood's opinions about Russia we noticed first, as in several other cases, that because of a lack of interest in theory and abstraction he took no account of Marxism as an element in Soviet policy. For him the activities of the Communists were motivated by a desire for power uncomplicated by any interest in doctrine; this made it difficult for him to see any difference between Communists and Nazis. Another characteristic of his opinions was their lack of sharp definition. When confronted with a topic he was apt to give a series of sentiments without feeling impelled to resolve the contradictions that usually appeared. He was also wedded to a kind of fairminded detachment which in the end sometimes obscured his viewpoint. Though occasionally downright on specific questions, in extended discussion he typically began with mild and noncommittal evaluations which later seemed scarcely representative of his true feelings. These two traits, the mild detachment and the lack of sharp definition, we thought reflected his habitual mode of social interaction. As one who aimed to please, he had no urge to form harsh-edged opinions and little practice in forging weapons for altercation. His opinions were designed to avoid strife, in form as well as in content.

As already remarked, Osgood's *object appraisal* was dominated by a desire for as little social-economic change as possible. He was a beneficiary of the economic order, and everything in which he was interested —home, neighborhood, church, real estate business, community services —was predicated on the continued existence of considerable private wealth. This caused him to see no good in the Russian system except the points of resemblance to our own country: internal development of economic and educational resources, and a stout fight against Nazi tyranny. His poor opinion of Russia did not cause him to think war inevitable, but he felt that only a counter display of strength would check Communist imperialism. Osgood's *social adjustment* was an important and successful part of his life. It was not, however, an assertive adjustment, nor did argument nor even the taking of clear stands play an essential part in the kind of relationship he generally sought to establish. Although he accepted the social responsibility of having opinions on important topics, he took pleasure in agreement, and the few issues on which he showed vehemence were those on which we felt safe in deducing that his chief business associates were vehement. His views on Russia were in full accord with those of the people around him. We judged that he would need them to be so even if circumstances had not made it happen almost as a matter of course. Osgood's opinions about Russia did not strike us as being strongly colored by the *externalization of inner problems.* Only two points deserve mention. His dwelling on Russian brutality and his focussing of criticism upon it suggested the problem of repressed aggression, for which some of our material offered independent evidence. His admiration for strength and assertiveness, whether displayed by America or by the Russians—for it was clear that he admired the position of power they had made for themselves in world affairs— we judged to be the product of a sense of personal shortcoming which he made some effort to repair. Apart from these two individual accents the content of his views grew almost wholly from his needs for object appraisal and for social adjustment.

CHAPTER 10

OPINIONS AND

PERSONALITIES

THE impression generally left by a series of intensive case studies is one of almost boundless individual variation. If the studies are faithful to their subject matter they show us living people who are as distinctive as the ones we meet in everyday life. Such descriptive abundance is requisite in order to show the lawfulness within each personality. It is thus an essential step on the way to more general propositions about fundamental processes. The very wealth of individuality, however, looms as an obstacle to generalization. The comparative study of cases—the comparison of individual lives that differ in so many particulars—can be successfully carried out only when variables have been selected which draw attention to significant generalities beneath the crowding multitude of surface features. Generalities of this kind we have sought in our descriptive and functional analysis of opinions. In this chapter we shall undertake to gather and appraise our findings. What have we learned from our attempt to describe the opinions held by our ten men? What have we learned by examining the expressive nature of their opinions? What have we learned by considering their opinions with respect to object appraisal, social adjustment, and externalization? What have they taught us about the commerce between men's opinions and their informational environment?

In order to summarize the information in such a way that it can be taken in at a glance, we shall set out our findings in six tables. These tables consist simply of condensed statements of relevant findings for each subject; they will serve as points of departure for our discussion of what we believe we have learned.

Describing an Opinion

In selecting men to serve in our study, it was our aim to include a wide variety of opinion about Russia. At the outset, the idea of representing the positions of our respondents on some spectrum of favorableness or unfavorableness was appealing. Variety we achieved, as the summary of opinions in Table 1 attests, but our notion of a simple spectrum soon faded. At best, such a spectrum is constructed by pool-

TABLE 1

SUMMARY DESCRIPTION OF OPINIONS ABOUT RUSSIA

Chatwell   Object characteristics: moderate salience; high differentiation; long-range optimistic time perspective, vaguer in short range; major aspects: *police state* (−), advocate of world Communism (−), developing nation (+)

Orientation: approach-hostility (counteraction and interdependence)

Policy stand: strengthen UN; reassure Russia from U.S. position of strength

Lanlin   Object characteristics: low moderate salience; rather low differentiation; time perspective, easy optimism; major aspects: *evil leaders seeking world domination* (−), backward country of great resources and ignorant people (−)

Orientation: *avoidance*, hostility, approach (make friends but keep powder dry)

Policy stand: vigorous U.S. stand if Russia refuses to be reasonable

Sullivan   Object characteristics: very high salience; high cognitive (but low affective) differentiation; optimistic historical time perspective, vague short-run perspective; major aspects: *experiment in social welfare* (+), alternative to moribund capitalism (+), ideological opponent of U.S. (+), temporary police state (±)

Orientation: *approach*

Policy stand: opposed to actual U.S. policy and any conceivable one; has no positive stand

Daniel   Object characteristics: moderate salience; considerable differentiation; broad time perspective; major aspects: *social welfare state* (+), limitations on freedom and democracy (−), religion and morality (−)

Orientation: *approach*-avoidance

Policy stand: favors U.S. stand from position of strength; opposes cooperation that might jeopardize security

TABLE 1 (*Continued*)

SUMMARY DESCRIPTION OF OPINIONS ABOUT RUSSIA

Hodder Object characteristics: very low salience; very little differentiation; time perspective restricted to present; major aspects: *Communists as destructive, grasping, atheistic force of evil* (−), impairment of freedom (−), international menace (−)
Orientation: *avoidance*-hostility
Policy stand: favors U.S. stand from position of strength, opposing Russia wherever she creates disturbance

Clark Object characteristics: very low salience; very little differentiation; narrow time perspective; major aspects: *international greed* (−), atheistic immorality (−)
Orientation: *avoidance*
Policy stand: confused; call Russia's bluff, with preventive war if necessary—but also trade, cooperation on live-and-let-live basis; probably *no* real policy stand

Kleinfeld Object characteristics: considerable salience; considerable differentiation; rather narrow, pessimistic time perspective; major aspects: *world domination* (−), social welfare state (+), limitations on freedom and democracy (−), treatment of Jews and minorities (±)
Orientation: *avoidance*-approach
Policy stand: cooperation to avoid provocation; avoidance of war at all costs

Rock Object characteristics: rather low salience; little differentiation; time perspective, long-run pessimism—expects Communistic Europe; major aspects: *religion and morality* (−), threat of war (−), restriction of personal freedom (−)
Orientation: *avoidance*-hostility
Policy stand: diplomacy from U.S. position of strength

Upjohn Object characteristics: low salience, little differentiation; narrow time perspective; major aspects: *greedy expansion and threat of war* (−), religion and morality (−), restriction of freedom (−), material progress and contribution to World War II (+)
Orientation: *avoidance*-hostility
Policy stand: diplomacy from position of strength, risking war if necessary

Osgood Object characteristics: low salience; moderate differentiation; time perspective, long-run optimism; major aspects: *disruption in international relations and U.S. domestic conflict* (−), restriction in individual freedom (−), part in World War II (+), internal development (+)
Orientation: *avoidance*
Policy stand: maintain peace by strong stand against Russian expansion, aid to democracies

ing or ordering an arbitrary set of expressed opinions in the interest of giving an individual an overall "score." Whether one uses a Guttman scale for performing the operation, i.e., determining what the scale shall be and then placing the subject along it, or uses some other method, the result in the present case would be stunting and artificial. For demographic purposes, perhaps, it might be worth knowing that Hodder, Lanlin, Upjohn all had about the same position on a "Communism Scale." Our interest lay elsewhere. The question we posed was "How may a man's opinion on an issue be fruitfully described?"

Object characteristics. The Russias to which our ten men were reacting were different objects, differently composed. That these objects of opinion shared common features reflecting world events and constancies in the information environment is evident. But the first and most striking impression we got in talking with our respondents was that the Russia to which each referred was a conception selectively fashioned, a reflection of individuality. It was soon apparent to us that we could not begin describing an attitude until the qualitative pattern of its object had been set forth.

First as to content.

To the majority of our subjects Russia was conceived as a disruptive force in the international scene and as a threat to the United States. But only to Chatwell and Sullivan did the challenge of Russia assume a markedly ideological character. Greedy aims of world domination, concrete and personified, were seen by others. The aims, the evil, the immorality of Russia sensed by most of our subjects were properties of specific men or of cliques, not of a system or of a set of ideas called Marxism. Restriction in individual freedom figured importantly in the image most of the men had of Russia. It had no place, however, in the impoverished conception held by Clark, whose own feeling of freedom was so poorly defined. Lanlin took cognizance of the authoritarian features of the Russian system, but his version of the business ethic was concerned with the uses to which dictatorial power is put rather than with its bare existence; this feature of Russia did not stand out for him. The ideological Sullivan, exposed as he was to unquestionable facts about the Russian police state, took embarrassed notice of them, assigning them a subsidiary and well-rationalized place in his image of the land of hope.

A few of our men found a place in their conceptions for the social welfare aspirations of Russia. This feature stood out, for example, in Sullivan's image, less so in Daniel's. For most, it was an aspect of Russia that had little centrality.

Not only were the objects of our men's attitudes constructed of different content, but they were differently organized. The men varied greatly in the extent to which Russia presented a *differentiated* image in their thinking. At one extreme was Chatwell with his many-faceted view of Russia. Clark and Hodder provide the contrast in the barren poverty of their conceptions. But there were interesting variations that defy alignment on a single dimension. Sullivan, for example, vied with Chatwell in the detail with which his picture of Russia was sketched; cognitively speaking, Russia was well differentiated for him. But so imperative was his need to see the Soviet Union as the promised land that he assimilated every feature, even the least tractable, to an affectively dominated totality of incarnate good.

To speak of differentiation is, however, insufficient. For in each man's conception, *hierarchically organized* as it was, some features dominated the picture at the expense of others. For Chatwell, several themes jostled for the central positions, while in the less differentiated opinions of Clark and Hodder the single theme of evil malice occupied an otherwise empty stage. The single aspect that we judged to be most dominant in each case is italicized in Table 1.

These aspects were not conceived in neutral tones. Each of the aspects of Russia to which our men attended presented itself laden with what we have termed *object value*, an immediate and self-evident goodness or badness, desirability or fearsomeness. The signs ($+$, $-$) in the lists of major aspects in Table 1 represent our rough categorization of the value that each of these object features had for the men. It is interesting to observe that whenever "world domination" occurs as a differentiated aspect, it receives negative valuation; similarly with "religion and morality" and with "impairment of freedom," Sullivan being the sole exception in regard to the latter.

What of the overall value set on Russia? It is difficult to describe with any precision save to say that the picture each had of Russia as a totality grew out of those few dominant features that stood at the top of his hierarchy of attention. It was as if, in each case, certain features were the principal determinants of the image as a whole. Abridgment of freedom, persecution of religion, threat to peace—from these the larger view grew. Some of our men could tolerate aspects of Russia that were discordant with their overall view; others could see nothing discrepant. Chatwell could see good things, but they did not dilute his overall negative valuation based on what he conceived as the major issues. If he could do this by virtue of the highly articulate image he had constructed, Osgood could do the same by virtue of the loose-knittedness of his image. To Sullivan, on the other hand, every seeming Russian cloud was a threat to his favorable views until he found its silver lining.

Two other object characteristics that we distinguished were *salience* and *time perspective*. With the exception of Sullivan and to a lesser degree Kleinfeld, Russia was not particularly salient in the lives of our men; there were many other matters that preoccupied them more. There was for most of them, therefore, little occasion to elaborate a highly developed time perspective on Russian affairs. Two of our subjects, Chatwell and Sullivan, showed a longer perspective, the former in terms of explicit events, the latter in terms of a rather un-articulated conception of historical necessities. For the rest, time perspective was little more than generalized optimism or pessimism.

Orientation. The orientations of our men toward Russia, how they were set to react, may be described in terms of *approach, avoidance,* and *hostility.* This classification recommended itself to us on grounds of logical comprehensiveness and as preferable to the stock "pro-con" distinction, but we take little satisfaction in it. Only Sullivan among our subjects was set squarely in the direction of approach. Two of the men seemed straightforwardly avoidant: Clark and Osgood. Each of them viewed Russia with repugnance, but in neither were there appreciable tendencies to punish or destroy her. More common was some balance of avoidant and hostile orientations, with the accent on the former. Predominant in the feelings of Hodder, Rock, and Upjohn was the desire to be freed from the threat they saw Russia posing. If necessary they would support, though reluctantly, hostile action toward Russia. Daniel and Kleinfeld shared an ambivalence between avoidance and approach, with different emphases. Each was drawn toward some features of Russia, repelled by others, but there was little hostility in the orientation of either. No subject is harder to place in terms of this scheme than Chatwell, whose ideal was an inter-dependent world in which Russia would have a major place, a state of affairs unfortunately prevented by Russian policies. If anything, his orientation harmoniously combined approach and hostility: military preparedness in the context of firm internationalism.

In spite of the negative value with which Russia appeared in the attitudes of most of our men, none of them could be classified as primarily destructive in his orientation. We suspect that unalloyed hostile orientations were and are a rarity in peacetime American attitudes.

Policy stand. Here we consider the "final common path" taken by a person's attitudes into publicly formulated issues. Put crudely, the issue of the day was: Should the United States attempt to "cooperate" with Russia, in the hope that cooperation in the spirit of give-and-take would evoke a reasonable response, or should the United States "get tough" with Russia, negotiating only from a position of strength? Under Secretaries Byrnes and Marshall, the country was becoming increasingly committed to the latter alternative, after unfortunate experience with the former.

All but a few of our subjects stood firmly behind this emergent American policy, though with individual qualifications such as, for instance, Chatwell's prior emphasis on support of the United Nations. Only Sullivan as an acknowledged deviant was entirely out of step—so much so that his policy stand could only be a negative one.

It is when one observes the compression of rich individual opinions into the "yeas" and "nays" of policy stand that one senses the relatively narrow range of alternatives by which individual opinion can express itself on public matters. It is no surprise to find a plenitude of different motives bringing men together in a common stand on policy. What strikes one forcibly, however, is the complexity of attempting to link deeper-lying motives with position on such specific matters as the Truman Doctrine. In many ways, the policies upon which these men must take a stand have little directly to do with the substance of their opinions: the question always is whether a given policy proposal will serve as an adequate channel through which the more amorphous underlying opinions may be expressed.

We regard the rubrics under which we have described the opinions of our ten men as a minimum list. There are many and varied categories which might be applied to such a task. Our objective has been to choose descriptive terms that keep contact with those commonly found in the opinion literature and that can also be related to descriptions of more general psychological functioning.

In most general terms, our description has been threefold. First, to characterize the phenomenology of an opinion in terms of the object toward which it was directed. About *what* was the opinion? The "what" in this case refers to the object as experienced: not Russia as a political entity but as a psychic entity, one man's Russia. Eventually, the transmutation of the external events that constitute Russia into an individual impression of Russia will be rendered more comprehensible by psychological research on the higher mental processes. Even prior to such elucidation, we feel that a description of opinion is empty unless it includes a description of the object of the opinion.

The second aspect of opinion to be described is what we have called orientation: the readiness of the individual to approach, avoid, or attack the object of his opinion. The specific forms of carrying out these orientations are many where Russia is concerned. The general rubrics we have used may serve to remind the analyst of opinion that one must go beyond describing orientation in the language of "pro" and "con."

Finally, there is the question of how the rich complexity of an attitude is fitted to the final common path of a stand on some particular policy. We have sought to underline the subtlety of this process in our description of policy stand.

Commerce with the Informational Environment

The range and diversity of information available to a man limit, of course, the kinds of attitudes he is likely to form. There is a crude correspondence between our men's attitudes taken in the gross and the content of the mass media analyzed in Chapter 5. But people may and do exercise control over the kind of information that will in fact be available to them. The sources of information on which our men relied, as itemized in Table 2, indicate that they did indeed pick and choose, and it was equally apparent that their selectivity was systematic in reflecting preference for one kind of information over another— whether the medium was the Jesuit *America*, the *New York Times*, or, in Hodder's case, a near vacuum of political information.

In some of our cases, a distinction can be made between *line* and *filler sources:* Lanlin, for example, took his line on Russia from Catholic publications, but drew detail in a rather inattentive way from the popular media. Several others, among them notably Chatwell and Sullivan, had their individual line so well internalized that all they sought from their purposeful reading and talk was filler detail—or challenge. Still others seemed to wander aimlessly among congenial sources without retaining very much.

More interesting psychologically than the selection of a congenial informational environment was the manner in which the subjects displayed functional selectivity in the information to which they reacted. Perhaps the first generalization one can make is that information impinging on a person appears to become relevant to his attitudes only when it "engages" or "fits" his preconceptions about the attitude object. Various lines of experimental evidence as well as observations on our intensively studied cases point to some such generalization. Yet as it stands the statement is too sweeping to be justified. Some degree of general curiosity remained in nearly all our subjects. Lanlin, for all his efforts to write off information about Russia that did not fit his conceptions, could be reached with discordant information

TABLE 2

SUMMARY OF FINDINGS RELEVANT TO COMMERCE WITH THE INFORMATIONAL
ENVIRONMENT

Chatwell Information score 51 out of possible 53 (Rank 1)

Reads widely and critically for "filler" information but provides
own "line" ; values being informed

Tests own ideas in argument; frequent discussion of world affairs

IAT: skeptical of challenging items, readily supplies context

Information well organized and accessible; flexible to convincing
burden of fact

Lanlin Information score 34 (Rank 8)

Line sources: Catholic publications, priests; Boston papers, popular magazines, radio followed inattentively for filler

Rarely discusses Russia, but has argued with Communists in his
union

IAT: thinks aloud, progressively shifting item toward own point
of view

Information not organized; unlikely to be shifted by information
per se

Sullivan Information score 50 (Rank 2.5)

Systematic reading of quality papers provides filler for own Marxist line; disregards radical and liberal press; values being informed

Discussion of Russia and Communism a favorite pastime

IAT: highly sensitive to information conflicting with own views;
assimilates it drastically

Not open to change via new information

Daniel Information score 38 (Rank 7)

Scans local and liberal papers for lead stories and labor news; follows opposition columnists; no line source on Russia

Sensitized to issue of Communism in union; knows few Communists

IAT: accepts each item with little distortion, no forced contexts

Attitudes toward Russia open to impact from new information

Hodder Information score 28 (Rank 10)

Virtually no reading; rare and inattentive radio listening

Depends on talk for information, but talk is mostly kidding and
rarely extends from ward to world politics

IAT: comprehension insufficient for items to be really challenging;
insufficient context

Inattentive to new information about Russia

Clark Information score 30 (Rank 9)

Line sources Catholic; reads local papers from front to back but
registers little

Never talks politics

TABLE 2 (*Continued*)

SUMMARY OF FINDINGS RELEVANT TO COMMERCE WITH THE INFORMATIONAL
ENVIRONMENT

Clark (*continued*)	IAT: holds new items at antiseptic distance; evasive, untouched by them Attitudes inaccessible to information; information registered not retained in usable form
Kleinfeld	Information score 50 (Rank 2.5) Casual and sporadic reading of newspapers, "Fascist" and Communist; mass media do not provide line; nevertheless values information *per se* Discusses Russia with wife and her family, regarded as more pro-Russian than he IAT: responsive to both positive and negative information Interested and open to change via information, but skeptical toward sources
Rock	Information score 41 (Rank 6) Follows Boston papers, popular magazines; indications of Catholic sources; no claim to be informed Little political discussion IAT: challenging information fits rapidly into context without strain Main views fairly rigid; details accessible to new information
Upjohn	Information score 43 (Rank 4.5) No special line; follows local papers, popular magazines, news magazine inattentively; need to be informed a reaction to desire for Clinic approval Rarely discusses foreign affairs; leaves to wife IAT: momentarily shaken by information not fitting readily into context, but this is social embarrassment, not change of views Attitudes not very responsive to information
Osgood	Information score 43 (Rank 4.5) No special line; casual reading of Boston papers, news magazine Little discussion of Russia and no argument IAT: assimilates positive and negative information without difficulty; attitudes unchallenged by acceptance of positive items without distortion Open to new information; core of attitude unlikely to be touched by it

and enticed to play with it in an exploratory way. He was, as we know, rather intrigued with the notion that people in his position in Russia got more money than he earned. Sullivan, too, was not completely closed to information that ran counter to his favorable thinking about the Soviet Union in spite of his very strong commitments.

Nonetheless, it was clear that our subjects had characteristic ways of coping with the informational environment so as to minimize the disruptive effects of knowledge incongruent with beliefs. One of the most fruitful investigatory tools that we had at our disposal was the *Information Apperception Test* (*IAT*) in which the subject was given a "fact" about Russia, negative, positive, or neutral in tone, and asked to "explain" it and indicate what it might mean. While the strategies for dealing with challenging items of information were varied, they can be summarized briefly in the following terms:

1. *Denial:* categorization of the item as false or unproven.

2. *Skepticism about source:* the veracity of the source is doubted, and the item held at a distance.

3. *Ascription of motive:* the *ad hominem* argument that avoids direct evaluation of the alleged fact by questioning the motives for its having been advanced.

4. *Isolation:* neutralization of an item that is accepted, by keeping it apart from the significant context of one's attitude.

5. *Minimization:* placing an accepted fact in context so that it appears unimportant or atypical.

6. *Interpretation:* placing an accepted fact in context so that it takes on a meaning other than the unwelcome one that it immediately presents.

7. *Misunderstanding:* distorted perception of the presenting fact; a special case is motivated failure to perceive any meaning in the item.

8. *Thinking away:* moving from a correct original perception of the item to quite other conclusions, via a loose chain of thought.

It was usual for several of these devices to be employed together in digesting unpalatable items. In reading the protocols, we were often reminded of the legendary farmer who countered the charge that he had broken a borrowed tool with the rejoinder that he had returned it intact, it was broken when he got it, and he had never borrowed it in the first place. Typical performance on this test would, in fact, be rather disillusioning if one did not recognize that the very procedure we have chosen to use stacks the cards against human rationality. After all, human action would be a sorry chaos if people were to revamp their basic attitudes for each incompatible fact that came into their ken. As Krech and Crutchfield [1] emphasize, adjustive behavior requires the stabilizing keel that strong cognitive structures such as attitudes provide. The balance between flexibility and stabil-

[1] David Krech and R. Crutchfield, *Theory and problems of social psychology,* New York, McGraw-Hill Book Co., 1948.

ity that is essential for effectiveness would seem to require revision of attitudes in the light of some preponderance of evidence, rather than ready influence by the isolated fact. No such preponderance of evidence could, of course, be incorporated in our test. The responses nevertheless bring to light striking individual differences in characteristic modes of coping with the informational environment.

Among our men, Sullivan came closest to the proverbial farmer in the defensive antics by which he maneuvered each item into pro-Russian position. For Chatwell, each item fell into the well-articulated context that he provided. His critical skepticism came through on the test, but the items presented no real challenge to his intellectual nimbleness. Rock, too, had little difficulty in supplying interpretative context. But in his case items were assimilated to a less differentiated, more rigid core of solid disapproval. Three of our subjects (in addition to Chatwell) displayed remarkable openness to opposite-toned items in the *IAT*. For Daniel and Kleinfeld this was hardly surprising: Russia for them was compounded of attractive and repellent features, and their ambivalent conceptions found ready place for both favorable and unfavorable items. What we have called "thinking away" is illustrated by Lanlin's favorite strategy. He would start with a correct rehearsal of the presented item, and, thinking aloud, talk himself to a quite different position in little contact with the original stimulus. Clark evasively held most items at an antiseptic distance; from his behavior on the test it is not surprising that he registered little from his page-by-page progression through the evening paper. And as for Hodder, he simply lacked sufficient context for many of the items to be meaningful.

Some of the men, it therefore seems, were relatively open to new information. But this openness could be a step toward attitude change only for persons, like Chatwell, with well-organized opinions, in which a change at one point in the structure was likely to have wide ramifications. For Osgood, with his loosely gathered views, openness had no such implication. Others, like Lanlin and Sullivan, had effective ways of fending off the consequences of discordant information while they still registered it in a form likely to be convertible for other uses. Especially where there was "idle curiosity" or interest in information for its own sake, data seemed to be stored away in a form compatible with the person's strongly held opinions, yet capable of being recovered and reorganized should it acquire new relevance to changing attitudes or situations. There remained some, notably Clark, whose defense against the information environment was so drastic as to defeat the possibility of recovery. Impoverishment is the inevitable result of such a strategy.

The matter of "recoverability" or "convertibility" of past information acquires importance from its possible significance for attitude change. Where an individual's stock of information is convertible to a new set of needs, values, or expectations, attitude change is perhaps less difficult cognitively. One can, under such conditions, undertake "object reappraisal." Where information is so rigidly structured as to be nonconvertible, or where it has been dealt with by exclusion, opinion change becomes increasingly difficult.

The Expressive Nature of Opinions

In several respects the opinions of our ten men exhibited congruence with their general styles of thought and action. Their views were influenced by those relatively stable traits or characteristics which confer a certain personal consistency on many different kinds of behavior. Some of these qualities are probably innately determined, others have become habituated through long adjustive use.

Our chief findings concerning the expressive nature of opinions have been assembled in Table 3. The entries after each subject's name begin with his I.Q. as estimated from the *Wechsler-Bellevue Adult Intelligence Test*, together with his rank order in the group of ten. This is followed directly by the score and rank order on the *Wells Alpha Examination*. Other entries summarize our observations concerning the qualitative aspects of our subjects' thinking; still others indicate general traits of mood and feeling. Our studies convinced us that both intellectual and temperamental qualities can be reflected in opinions.

Intellectual qualities. Through an unintentional bias in selection we found ourselves studying an intellectually superior group of men. According to the figures offered by Wechsler,[2] nine of our subjects belonged in the top ten per cent of the general population, seven in the top five per cent. Even Hodder, who stood lowest in our group, struck us as decidedly competent in dealing with practical affairs and their more immediate implications. Our findings therefore contribute little to the understanding of the opinions of people with genuinely limited intellectual ability. They do display, however, great individual differences in the qualitative use of mind, differences which often prove to be closely connected with other features of personality.

[2] David Wechsler, *The measurement of adult intelligence,* 3rd ed., Baltimore, Williams and Wilkins, 1944.

TABLE 3

SUMMARY OF FINDINGS RELEVANT TO THE EXPRESSIVE NATURE OF OPINIONS

Chatwell   Wechsler-Bellevue I.Q. 142 (rank 1); Alpha score 205.5 (rank 1)
Quick, versatile, flexible, retentive mind
Facile thinking at abstract level
Generalized predominance of intellectual control over feeling
Optimistic mood

Lanlin   Wechsler-Bellevue I.Q. 120 (rank 9); Alpha score 120 (rank 7)
Resistant to abstraction and ideological issues
Indifferent to distant impersonal problems
Controlled, ordered, modulated, disliking excess and violence

Sullivan   Wechsler-Bellevue I.Q. 128 (rank 3.5); Alpha score 119 (rank 8)
Careless generalization
Marked emotionality and impulsivity
Underlying depressive tone

Daniel   Wechsler-Bellevue I.Q. 128 (rank 3.5); Alpha score 140.5 (rank 4)
Deliberate and fair, counteracting impulsiveness
Limited insight into other viewpoints
Steady holding to thought trains, undistracted

Hodder   Wechsler-Bellevue I.Q. 113 (rank 10); Alpha score 61.5 (rank 10)
Limited education
Lack of practice and motive in using mind
Vivid concreteness, poor abstraction

Clark   Wechsler-Bellevue I.Q. 126 (rank 6.5); Alpha score 158 (rank 2)
Constriction of interest
Insecurity, ambivalence, indecisiveness
Conventional and stereotyped
Drab tone, tendency toward bitter pettiness

Kleinfeld   Wechsler-Bellevue I.Q. 123 (rank 8); Alpha score 150 (rank 3)
Gluttonous appetite for facts and information
Deliberate, cultured detachment
Passivity and mildly toned pessimism

Rock   Wechsler-Bellevue I.Q. 126 (rank 6.5); Alpha score 106 (rank 9)
Intellectual procedure conjunctive with feeling rather than with
    logic ("feeling type")
Deep and bitter resignation to evil in world

Upjohn   Wechsler-Bellevue I.Q. 127 (rank 5); Alpha score 121 (rank 6)
Disjunctiveness in thinking
Indifferent to theory and abstraction
Preference for action and specific policies; amenities rather than
    principles
Uncertainty about novel policies
Bustling energy

Osgood   Wechsler-Bellevue I.Q. 129 (rank 2); Alpha score 130 (rank 5)
Indifferent to theory and abstraction
Ideas not sharply defined
Fair-minded detachment, delayed expression of own convictions

We were aware that our occupational bias would dispose us to set unduly high standards of abstractness and precision of thinking. Lest it seem, in what follows, that we criticize from a lofty academic standpoint the thought processes displayed by our subjects, we should make at this point an explicit statement of the conditions under which their thinking was done. In the first place, most of the men did not feel a sense of immediate concern about Russia; their thoughts on the subject did not enlist their maximum interest. Only in the case of Sullivan was Russia a topic of deep preoccupation. Secondly, the opinions were elicited in interviews and discussions for which the men were more or less unprepared; they were asked to start, in effect, with "off-the-cuff" judgments, even though they were given plenty of time and encouragement to elaborate their views. Several of the men found this situation agreeably challenging, but perhaps only Chatwell, with his legal training and delight in argument, was prepared to use it for a maximum display of intellectual power. In the third place, our subjects were at the mercy of their sources of information. We could not expect them, in the main, to have more complex ideas about Russia than those which appeared in the papers, news broadcasts, magazines, and other commonly available sources. Sullivan, Chatwell, Daniel and Kleinfeld had made some effort to increase their information, but the other men were more or less dependent upon what happened to come their way.

It is safe to assume, therefore, that our subjects' opinions about Russia did not represent their top level of intellectual performance. Yet most opinions on public questions are formed under circumstances just as casual as those described here. Ideal conditions of full information, enlisted interest, and leisure are anything but common. Most people's political opinions depend upon easily available information, do not enlist major motives, and develop in such "off-the-cuff" conversations as happen to arise. It is important to examine the expressive elements in opinions under these common circumstances.

The majority of our subjects showed little interest in *abstraction*. They exhibited a strong preference for fairly concrete ways of thinking. Only Chatwell seemed able to operate with pleasurable ease in the realms of abstract thought. Ideological convictions have played a prominent part in the Russian Communist movement, but most of our subjects seemed inclined to overlook this important fact. They failed to perceive Russia as an ideological force; she loomed in their minds purely as a political one.

Avoidance of abstract issues did not prevent shrewd judgments concerning concrete problems. If our men often neglected Russian

ideology, they were by no means disposed to overlook Soviet political
realism. For the most part they perceived the leaders of the Russian
state as a small group of smart but unscrupulous politicians seeking
territory, wealth, power, and a strategic place in world affairs. The
Russian people were perceived as much like the American people except that they had let themselves be robbed of liberties and information and therefore could exert no control over the ambitions of their
leaders.

The preference shown by most of our subjects for the concrete,
practical, and personal, as contrasted with abstractions and ideologies,
can justly be considered an expressive feature of their opinions. It
was not shown exclusively in their views about Russia. There was
a congruent preference for concreteness in the *Vigotsky* and *Rorschach
Tests,* in the *Wechsler-Bellevue Test,* in the systems of personal values,
indeed in the whole orientation to the world. Conversely, Chatwell
displayed an interest in abstraction and a capacity for theorizing in
almost every test or interview, and Sullivan's liking for large ideas
was manifested in every topic he discussed. Whatever their origin,
these preferences seemed to be both deep and wide, affecting with
marked consistency many different kinds of behavior.

When we attempted to work out the differentiated aspects under
which Russia appeared to our subjects we encountered further variations in their processes of thought. In several of the men there was
a lack of sharp *differentiation among ideas.* Sometimes this led to
contradictory statements, but not so much because the thinking was
illogical as because the ideas were not sharply enough defined to
create a sense of collision. Albert Rock, for example, found no discomfort in the juxtaposition of Catholic spirituality, Protestant indi-
vidualism, and workaday materialism that constituted his value system, and he opposed with a single mass of undifferentiated feeling
the Russian attacks on religion, the family, and the business entrepre-
neur. All in all, our study of the transcribed interviews showed that
most of our men were working with ideas which did not have the
stable meaning and sharp boundaries most conducive to effective
thinking.

This tendency in our subjects can be somewhat better understood
by utilizing the concept of *intellectual control over feeling.* Our men
certainly did not lack the intellectual capacity to arrive at differentiated
ideas. When they failed to do so, it was usually because of a failure
to prevent antipathies, fears, and strongly felt preferences from dominating their intellectual procedure. Even in our small sample it

proved possible to discern three patterns of relationship between feeling and its control in matters of opinion.

1. In some cases *thinking was predominant over feeling*. Intellectual appraisal governed the arousal of feeling and steered the engagement of values. This pattern was best exemplified in Chatwell, whose
thoughts generally moved faster than his feelings, producing a quick
and accurate analysis of the existing situation which then served to
guide the enlistment of feeling. This capacity enabled him to engage
quite a variety of different feelings in his total attitude toward Russia:
anger at the police state, admiration for internal economic development, sympathy on account of past injustices at the hands of capitalist
nations, resistance to imperialistic expansion.

2. In other cases *feeling was predominant over thinking*. Appraisal
of the facts was subordinated to expressing the attitudes or affects
aroused by the topic. Albert Rock provided the clearest example of
this pattern. Rock was more interested in expressing his strong feelings and settled convictions than he was in building an independent
framework of ideas. His religious outlook, his kindly charity, his sympathy for the underdog, his fear of bigger business competitors, his
respect for hard work and good craftsmanship: these and similar
preferences gave the push to his opinions, and he was not apt to weigh
against each other the intellectual by-products of his different feelings.
In Sullivan also it was possible to discern the constant pressure of
affect-laden convictions, even when factual information was fairly
abundant.

3. In still other cases *both thinking and feeling were constricted*.
Feelings were governed not by intellectual control but by generalized
inhibition and withdrawal of affect. Our most extreme case was Clarence Clark, who showed scarcely any interest in debatable topics or
in matters remote from the round of his daily life. Clark neither
thought nor felt about Russia except in the vague sense of an unwelcome threat to his settled values. A milder form of this procedure
could be observed in Lanlin, whose opinions were expressed, and
apparently also held, in a modulated, conciliatory fashion well-designed
to keep feeling at a manageable level. In both men the pattern of
constriction was highly generalized, showing itself repeatedly throughout the whole range of their behavior.

Temperamental qualities. In several cases the opinions of our
subjects were unmistakably influenced by *prevailing mood tone*.
Qualities such as optimism or pessimism, confidence or helplessness,
buoyancy or resignation must be regarded on the whole as fairly stable
and enduring features of personality, even though they are sometimes

subject to great change. Three of our men were largely resigned to a personal fate that seemed full of heaviness. Hilary Sullivan expected little for his own life, though much for that better world order that would follow the historical demise of capitalism. Albert Rock was trying to make the best of an unhappy marriage and a burden of anxieties, confident of grace before his God. Clarence Clark had adapted himself to a narrow round of activities and interests, hoping a little apprehensively that his son would do better in life. Resignation did not, of course, produce uniform opinions about Russia, but we could scarcely claim to understand the opinions of these three men without taking into account the emotional coloring that appeared in all their behavior. Mildly toned pessimism was apparent in Kleinfeld's outlook, and a certain growing desperation could be detected in Upjohn's vehement opinions. Osgood's contented feeling that everything would come out all right, Hodder's almost unfailing trust in human friendliness, Lanlin's confidence that reasonableness would prevail, Daniel's firm determination to keep inching along toward a better industrial system, Chatwell's rosy hopes for ultimate international law and order —all these could be listed on the brighter side of the mood picture. Our study showed that mood tone was to some extent a generalized product of life experience; being generalized, it colored our men's opinions about Russia without necessarily serving an adjustive function with respect to that particular topic.

The importance of differences in *action level* can best be indicated by taking two extreme cases: the bustling Grafton Upjohn and the quiet Benjamin Kleinfeld. Upjohn was a man who habitually used action both to forward his own interests and to blow off the steam generated by his resentfulness and conflicts. He tended to externalize his problems, blame the environment, and feel at his best when taking vigorous action of some kind. This quality had a definite effect on his opinions about Russia: he was much clearer about specific policies and lines of possible action than he was about the general issues raised by long-range Russian intentions. His preference for action was also responsible for his frequent self-contradictions. Thinking of each item about Russia with reference to its action possibilities, he often did not stop to consider the purely logical relationships among his various ideas. Kleinfeld, in contrast, showed in his opinions a clear intrusion of the passivity and sense of helplessness that characterized his general attitude toward people and problems of relationship. Although he disapproved of Russian expansion, he believed that the only hope of peace lay in giving no offense to the Russians.

Differences in action level, like those in mood tone, are certainly not unrelated to life experience, and they may possibly be altered by further life experience. They are nevertheless fairly stable and fairly general, deserving a place in any account of the expressive nature of opinions.

To sum up the implications of our findings in regard to the expressive nature of opinions: a man's opinions inevitably bear his personal stamp. His capacities for abstract or practical thinking, for intense feeling, for forthright action set limits on his response to public issues and, indeed, on what he makes of any significant event that impinges on him. His intellectual and temperamental qualities, general features of his behavior stabilized in the complex interaction of constitution and personal history, give distinctive form to his opinions about Russia no less than they do to his copings with a psychologist's ink blots. Even when his opinions serve the most minimal function in his life strategies—as when they are produced more or less *ad hoc* to satisfy the importunacies of an interviewer—they carry his signature. If the trivial ink blot evokes a valid sample of his personal style, so does a question about Russia. The tasks are more similar than might appear at first glance.

In the expressive nature of opinions lies the element of validity in the earlier approach to the determinants of opinion that sought correlations between traits and attitudes, a tactic the general sterility of which we noted in Chap. 2. Surely there is correspondence between attitudes and personality traits if we but know where to look. But the complexities of this relationship as our ten men bring it before us leave little doubt as to where the earlier search for simple correlations went astray. Armed with attitude tests and scales that compressed the rich dimensionality of a person's opinions into a single score—of radicalism or of favorableness to X—the investigators of the 1920's hoped to establish correlations with analogous measures of personality, measures that were often scarcely more satisfactory. Our data support no illusory hope that favorableness to Russia can be traced to any single trait or complex of traits. They do strongly support the assumption, firmly rooted in personality research, that there is congruence among the various instances of a person's thinking, feeling, and deciding about features of his world.

Object Appraisal

One of the uses of opinions is to assist in the never-ending process of object appraisal. Each person is constantly trying to size up the world around him and to place it in relation to his major interests,

TABLE 4

Summary of Findings Relevant to Object Appraisal

Chatwell   Beneficiary of current socioeconomic order
                Desires world that permits free exercise of talent, initiative, choice,
                    change, opportunity for distinction
                High value on social control through legal system

Lanlin   Satisfaction with work and prospects in business corporation
                Attaches special value to economic security achieved by owner-
                    ship of property
                Sees Russia as run by clique showing bluff but really dependent
                    on us

Sullivan   Has renounced hope of personal security and success
                Barring early war, Russia not related to personal fortunes
                Sees Russia as sole hope of progress toward a just and secure
                    future world order

Daniel   Sees personal career as injured and children's careers as endan-
                    gered by lack of educational opportunities and employment se-
                    curity
                Goals of union work similar to Russian welfare state
                Satisfied by role in union work
                High value on religion and standards of personal morality

Hodder   Desires world that will be open, friendly, fair-minded
                Sees Communist leaders as small group of demanding, unapproach-
                    able, unfriendly men

Clark   Central interest to maintain precarious economic security and
                    middle-class status
                Excludes problems and threats not immediately pressing

Kleinfeld   Strong interest in fair treatment for ethnic minorities
                Adherent of Zionist movement
                Believes in democratic ideals, a "principled liberal"
                Wants protection but also freedom for small business man

Rock   Predominantly religious and moral conception of universe
                High value on family and sanctity of marriage
                Favors free enterprise but with some protection in business
                Admires individual craftsmanship
                Satisfied by role of helper of the poor

Upjohn   Cherishes goal of comfortable, gentlemanly living
                Wants to be one of the socially elect
                Possibility of accumulating wealth essential to both these desires
                High value on warm, stable family circle

Osgood   Beneficiary of current socioeconomic order, no interest in change
                Sees no good in Russia except where system resembles ours
                Satisfied by role of volunteer in civic betterment

ongoing concerns, and cherished aspirations (Table 4). An opinion on any given topic represents a person's way of defining a relationship between the demands of the outside object and the requirements of his own interests. Defining the relationship serves to reduce ambiguity in the interest of channelizing feeling and action.

In essence, object appraisal may be thought of as the process of testing reality in order to assess its relevance to one's ongoing enterprises. It comprises those activities whereby the events and issues in the person's world are appraised for their relationship to his motives, goals, values, and interests. And these activities are various indeed. One man feels impelled to scan events and issues·in order that he may assure a proper balance in his views. Another, who handles the topic of Russia and Communism as something to be avoided, operates with a dense filter rather than a scanner when it comes to appraising events. This initial hospitality or selective inhospitality to events is one feature of object appraisal, and the difference among our various subjects was striking. Chatwell and Clark represent extremes in sheer openness, but each of our other subjects differs qualitatively in his initial receptivity to the happenings around him.

A person's initial orientation to events is not to be thought of as serving purely autistic needs. However much Clark would like to shut out the unpleasant and threatening array of events in the information environment, he can proceed only so far without encountering another hazard. For there are two requirements that must be met in one's dealings with the world. The first can be summed up as a demand to maximize gratification: to keep the world congruent with one's needs, aspirations, and enterprises. But there is a second requirement in adjustment: a need to minimize surprise. If Clark is going to pursue his enterprises in a world of events and people, he must at least know the outline of the world around him. If he does not, he will inevitably trip on the unpleasant rocks he does not want to see or consider. And at the other extreme Chatwell can scarcely devote all his energies to seeing the pattern whole and seeing it clear. For he in turn has needs to be gratified and values to be sustained, lest he become another version of the man who knows all about art but doesn't know what he likes.

The degree to which and the manner in which one exposes oneself to events is closely linked to how one *relates* these events to ongoing enterprises and values. In each man we find an effort to make the world congruent with or supportive of his way of life—within the limits imposed by the requirements of minimizing surprise, for contact with reality must remain the *pied à terre*. To understand how events are related to a person's interests it is necessary first to devise some coherent schema for describing these interests.

In reviewing the life patterns of our ten men, we have developed a tentative approach to this objective. We find it necessary to consider: (1) the pattern of his personal goals, (2) the locus of his important frustrations, (3) the directions of his success, (4) the vested interests he may have acquired in particularly satisfying modes of activity, (5) the extended interests he may have in other people and groups, and (6) the moral values and ethical principles for which he stands. All of these are important in the process of adjusting the events of the world to one's ongoing interests.

One great benefit we derived from our intensive study of ten men was a much sharper and more concrete understanding of these components. To a certain extent our subjects' interests could be deduced from economic position, religious affiliation, and similar gross social facts, but these relationships threw little light on the actual processes whereby events were "taken in," related to internal requirements, and formed into opinions. Each man appraised Russia in his own particular fashion. He viewed the topic selectively, and his choice of items reflected an attempt to fit it into a pattern of interests strongly colored by personal experience.

As regards *goals* it was clear that economic success, for example, meant different things to different people. Upjohn craved a higher income in order to achieve the goal of comfortable, gentlemanly living as one of the socially elect. Rock, whose current income was greater, viewed such goals with contempt and preferred to use his profits to strengthen his business, secure his children's future, and increase his support of the church. Chatwell, whose economic prospects were even better, thought of wealth mainly as a support for energetic activity, as a means, perhaps, whereby he might become free to run for political office. Kleinfeld, in contrast, hoped the day might come when he would have leisure to pursue his intellectual and artistic interests. All of these men perceived the possible threat of Communist doctrine with respect to private wealth, but the threat was directed at very different conceptions as to what would constitute a better life.

In several cases the opinions about Russia showed the influence of personal experiences of *frustration*. Ernest Daniel, the ardent union worker, attributed his difficulties partly to the fact that he had not been encouraged to pursue his education to the point where he would qualify for a secure job. In his views on Russia he singled out for special emphasis the system of free higher education and the policy of encouraging able men to secure specialized training. Kleinfeld's bitter experiences with antisemitism caused him to place strong emphasis on Russian policy with respect to ethnic minorities and with respect to the Zionist movement. In a similar way other subjects exhibited very personal conceptions of what was wrong with the world, and their ideas about Russia were correspondingly selective.

The selective process was equally guided by personal experiences of *success*. As examples we might mention Chatwell's emphasis on freedom and initiative, privileges which he had used to great advantage, and Lanlin's admiration for the American business system within which he had achieved a sense of importance and security. Each used these successful patterns as yardsticks against which to measure the image of Russia. Indeed, the only way in which we were able to make Lanlin give pause to the subject of Russia was to present an item to him for comment about the comparably greater earning power of the managerial class in Russia.

As we have noted, a man's interests come to include certain highly specific modes of activity which yield him personal satisfaction. Rock, for example, found great satisfaction in the activity of visiting the poor; if this function were taken from him by state intervention, his own life would be emotionally impoverished. Similarly, Osgood's participation in private civic activities and Chatwell's delight in argumentative court procedures represented sources of emotional income with which it would be difficult to dispense. Perhaps the most interesting example is that of Daniel, who strongly favored a number of the Communist economic goals but who with equal vehemence preferred the means of attaining them (collective bargaining between unions and management) that had brought him personal success. Several of our men thus exhibited a *vested interest in a particular mode of activity* which, for reasons not always even remotely economic, had come to play a vital part in their lives.

Our understanding of opinions was helped by analyzing these highly personal patterns of interest, but we could not fully explain our men's views on a basis so purely individualistic. It was necessary to consider, for one thing, those other people in our subjects' lives whose interests had become to some extent their interests, those *extensions of the self* which Allport[3] evaluates as one of the earmarks of maturity. When Daniel, for example, talked about educational opportunities he was thinking of his children as well as himself. When he spoke of employment security he had in mind not only his personal fortunes but also the fortunes of the fellow union members with whose interests

[3] Gordon W. Allport, *Personality: a psychological interpretation*, New York, Henry Holt & Co., 1937.

he was identified. Many of our men were strongly identified with other individuals and with groups. Rock, Lanlin, and Upjohn were especially concerned about their children, Osgood with his friends and business associates, Kleinfeld with the fortunes of the Jews. No analysis of interests can be complete without including these extensions of the individual self.

Nor can the understanding of interests be complete without reference to *moral values and ethical ideals*. Daniel was again a case in point. His sympathy for Communist goals suggested that he would favor a tolerant and fairly trustful attitude toward Russia, but in point of fact he believed that we should increase our armaments and do everything in our power to maintain our advantage in atomic weapons. This paradox proved explicable only when we took into account the high value placed by Daniel on religion and the religious sanction in personal morality. He appeared to feel that the Russians could not be trusted because they lacked this indispensable control over rapacity and aggression. Ideals were important to most of our subjects. Sullivan and Chatwell were uncompromising exponents of intellectual honesty. Kleinfeld was a principled liberal. Hodder stood for friendliness and the doctrine of "live and let live." In short, our men stood for values as well as personal considerations of gain and happiness.

And so we see the concrete effects of interest in the selection of events and issues and in their transformation into the texture of a man's opinions. Goals, successes, frustrations, preferred modes of activity, one's extended interests in others, and one's deeper values—all of them are operative in determining the pattern of object appraisal. It is evident that the emergence of an opinion, a crystallized definition of relationship between the demands of some outside object and the requirements of the person's ongoing interests, represents an economical solution to the inherently complex problem of serving one's own gratification while remaining in contact with reality.

We did not observe our subjects in the act of newly forming their opinions about Russia, and we therefore learned little about the mechanisms that might be employed. It was evident, of course, that most of the subjects had used short-cuts to opinion formation rather than trying to work out full opinions of their own. Some had adopted the overall attitude of their church, or of some other membership or reference group, without much independent attempt at object appraisal. Some had rather easily assimilated Russia to pre-existing categories, such as "ungodly" or "subversive," and thus brought the topic into the sphere of an attitude already prepared. These short-cuts were made easier by the remoteness of the topic, the lack of information about it, and the feeling that the individual citizen could exert little influence upon policy. Our men differed somewhat in their feeling of distance from the topic of Russia. Some of them, particularly Hodder and Clark, seemed to have little sense that the activities of Russia could ever disturb the course of their daily lives. They recognized that war might occur, but they did not think of this as directly threatening the round of life to which they were accustomed. Others viewed the topic with greater concern and a more vivid awareness of possible consequences. None of them, however, felt an urgent sense of crisis with respect to the topic.

Analysis of object appraisal, as the term is used here, has been the prerogative of students of the cognitive processes; it has rarely become a focal concern of recent students of opinion or of personality. Yet an opinion cannot be fully understood without taking into account its status as a hypothesis about the nature of the "real" in the person's social environment. Having an opinion about Russia is more than being "for" or "against" Russia: it is a way of "perceiving" or "knowing" Russia by inference from available information, and with reference to personal values, interests, and ongoing concerns. The selectivity of perception, inference, and memory, the reconciling of bias and evidence—all of these are considerations in understanding the status of an opinion in the functioning of a man's personality.

Let it be clear, however, that emphasis upon the object-appraising function of an opinion is not a bid for the reinstatement of that admirable fiction, the "rational man." We are not proposing that the process is a kind of calculus of interest, wherein the person accurately appraises the relation of the world to his goals and decides his best line accordingly. Our insistence upon object appraisal as a cognitive activity stems from broader considerations. It is apparent, when one looks closely at a life, that the formation of an opinion does reflect a drive toward rational decision in terms of one's interests. We are rational according to our lights, but the lights may be dim indeed. The case material we have examined gives ample evidence of the highly selective ways in which Russia may be viewed and of the distorted manner in which inferences about her may be made. But at the same time there is also evidence of nicety, finesse, and reason. What is critical to emphasize is that opinions must also serve functions other than object appraisal. For, as we have repeatedly noted, opinions are also vehicles by which we orient ourselves to the social groups in our environment and a means whereby internal problems are externalized and acted out in the everyday world. Each of these functions limits and restricts the other.

We have devoted so much attention to object appraisal out of a sense that the time has come, given the assimilation of Freud's great insights, to look again at the manner in which and the degree to which man deals rationally with the world around him in the light of his interests. Perhaps the anti-intellectualism of the past half-century has abated sufficiently so that the problem of rationality can be approached again without embarrassment or bias.

Social Adjustment

In addition to their service in the cause of object appraisal, opinions play a part in maintaining relationships with other people. They provide a possible topic for social interaction, and they can thus serve as a vehicle for facilitating, maintaining, or disrupting one's contact with the individuals and groups that make up one's social environment. Our subjects showed us several different ways in which opinions become involved in the process of social adjustment. The most relevant findings in each case are summarized in Table 5.

It is important to distinguish between "membership groups" and "reference groups," which present somewhat different problems of adjustment. By "membership groups" we mean, of course, the people with whom an individual is in direct contact and fairly frequent interaction. By "reference groups," in contrast, we signify those groups with which the individual identifies himself, accepting their standards for self-evaluation. (We neglect for simplicity "negative reference groups" from which the person would distinguish himself.) In some cases there is no difference between the two groups; membership and reference groups are one and the same. In other cases there is considerable divergence, and the reference groups may be of fairly remote and idealized character. The distinction between "expressed" opinions and "held" opinions is particularly relevant in this connection. Interaction with membership groups is obviously conducted only with expressed opinions, whereas opinions silently held can be of distinct service in mediating a person's relation to his reference groups.

Interaction with membership groups creates and maintains a more or less common information environment. To some extent the individual derives his information from the group, and if he acquires information from some other source he is likely to transmit it in conversation and thus make it a part of the group's knowledge. This consideration is particularly important for people who, like Sam Hodder, derive practically the whole of their information from talk with their friends.

TABLE 5

Summary of Findings Relevant to Social Adjustment

Chatwell   Debate used to establish competitive dominance among peers
Identification with ideal of free rational man
Conformity to Western liberal culture as exemplified in early environment

Lanlin   Conformity to human environment, on which he depends for guidance
Identification with management and men of property

Sullivan   Desire for approval, restricted to small circle of friends
Desire to shock, anger, and expose; to be noticed for individuality
Identification with remote group of radical intellectual world reformers

Daniel   Identification with laboring class and union organization
No anxiety connected with disagreement with others
High value on religion and standards of personal morality

Hodder   Information environment derived from personal contacts
Conformity to Catholic values
Opinions create no disharmony, possibly affirm membership in immediate groups but not important in this respect

Clark   Conformity to restrictive middle-class values, modified by certain resentments
Indecisive evasiveness as means of avoiding aggression and counter-aggression

Kleinfeld   Identification with Jews in general
Membership in small group, mostly of relatives
Identification with ideal of the cultured liberal

Rock   Conformity to views of parents and of Catholic church
Can disagree with people but prefers to avoid debatable issues
Conformity to Catholic middle-class environment

Upjohn   Identification with conservative upper-class group
Need to have and expound opinions that affirm identity with this group

Osgood   Values friends, strong need not to disagree
Opinions needed as material for social interaction
Fully identified with principal membership groups

In our group of ten men we noticed a variety of ways in which opinions became implicated in social adjustment. Sometimes they were used in the interests of conformity or identification, serving to facilitate and maintain relationships with a group in which the person valued his membership. In other cases they were used to differentiate oneself from a group, even to disrupt a group, or to establish a relationship of competitive dominance or of superiority to a given group.

The outstanding example in which conformity was not a motive was Hilary Sullivan, who liked to express radical opinions where they were most apt to shock and annoy his hearers. He could take pleasure in baiting conservative business men with statements about Communist excellences and the coming demise of the capitalist system. And by analyzing typical capitalist pronouncements and unveiling the prejudice of the daily press, he was able to establish his position as a man of superior wisdom and insight. In most of his membership groups Sullivan seemed concerned to emphasize his individuality, to differentiate himself from the rest of the group. There was only one membership group, a small circle of like-minded friends, with which he felt any sense of kinship. His real identification was with a remote and idealized reference group, one with which he had scarcely any contact except through reading: the group of radical intellectuals who could penetrate the veils of *status quo* ideology and foresee the inevitable movement of historical processes.

The case of Chatwell provides another illustration. Opinions served him well as means of establishing competitive dominance over his peers. He found pleasurable challenge in debate. Like Sullivan he was not strongly identified with his membership groups, which in any event were quite transient during his college and Army years. His identification was with a stable reference group, the aristocracy of free, independent, rational men that has long figured as an ideal in Western liberal culture. As already noted, when he entered the congenial law office and found in it a certain embodiment of his ideal reference group he began to show increasing signs of cautious conformity.

Sullivan and Chatwell were our outstanding nonconformists in relation to their membership groups. It is significant that their nonconformist attitudes were "carried," so to speak, by strong identification with remote and idealized reference groups conceived to be greatly superior. They were not made anxious by disagreement with those around them, but it is likely that they would be disturbed if they persistently lapsed from the standards of their reference groups.

Turning now to men in whom conformity was a stronger motive, we find illuminating examples in the otherwise divergent personalities of Upjohn and Kleinfeld. These two men had the common problem that their membership groups did not satisfy their aspirations; they were eager to find and affirm membership in circles that represented their ideal reference groups. Upjohn was obliged to move in middle-class circles, but he aspired to regain the upper-class status once occupied by his family and he sought every opportunity to demonstrate his membership in upper-class groups. Kleinfeld was gravely dissatisfied with his business associates and not altogether mollified by the immediate circle made up mostly of his relatives. He hoped to achieve actual membership among the cultured, talented liberals who constituted his chief reference group. Upjohn seized upon the social prestige of Harvard, Kleinfeld upon its intellectual prestige, to perceive us as embodiments of reference groups, and each exerted himself to affirm temporary membership. This proved to entail having an informed and elaborate series of opinions about Russia, and both men did their best to produce or improvise the material they believed would satisfy our expectations. Their behavior contrasted sharply with that of Ernest Daniel, whose secure identification with the laboring man made him indifferent to our approval of his views. He was pleased that we heard him with such patience, but he uttered his opinions with self-respecting finality and showed no sign of modulating them to please listeners who were not of the laboring class.

For Daniel and the other five men there was no fundamental difference between membership and reference groups. Lanlin, to be sure, felt identified with management and ownership, but this created a disharmony of outlook neither with his fellow salesmen nor with his neighbors. Rock, Clark, and Hodder were identified with the Catholic middle-class groups which formed their immediate social environment, as was Osgood with his upper-middle-class business friends in a prosperous suburb. Our four Catholic men made but little use of political opinions as a means of expressing conformity in membership groups. It seemed likely that their membership in a clearly defined religious body reduced the need to use opinions as a means of affirming solidarity. Osgood, however, clearly felt the need to have opinions as material for the social interaction he so greatly valued. The exchange of opinions was one of his chief means of enjoying friendships.

It was of interest to observe individual differences in the tactics of conformity as shown not only in our interviews but in the subjects' whole account of their views. Two examples must suffice here. Osgood presented, at the outset of any conversation, the very picture of tolerant fair-mindedness. He saw virtue in every point of view. As time advanced, however, he evinced quite positive opinions on certain points and expressed himself with warm partisanship, often rejecting the very arguments in which he had at first perceived merit. It appeared that his initial hospitality to all possible opinions was a kind of unwitting technique for feeling out the other party, finding out what the climate would be before committing himself to a decided stand. Osgood had little use for argument; he wanted to express his opinions only when the consequence would be substantial agreement and an increase of harmonious interaction.

Somewhat more difficult was the task of Clarence Clark, whose desire for conformity was constantly undercut by feelings of resentful aggression. He, too, wanted to avoid an argument, which might release unmanageable quantities of aggression and counter-aggression, but he was also blocked in expressing sentiments of full conformity. He met this situation by a practiced technique of evasiveness. He took no stand on the merits of a question, but rather than suggesting, as did Osgood, that each viewpoint had its merits he was apt to imply that each argument was a little at fault. Yet the undertone of criticism was never sufficient to become a basis for contention. Clark was expert in shrugging his shoulders and pointing out that you could not be sure of anything anyway.

For each man, opinions had significance as a means of affirming to himself or others what he "was" socially. Opinions provided routes to identifying with or rejecting groups. To recognize this is a far cry, however, from the view that a person's opinions are but a mirroring of his group memberships, another of the simplistic half-truths that our cases tend to refute. The function of social adjustment is only part of the story, and even this part concerns a more complicated range of phenomena than conformity alone.

"Social influence" on opinions is neither a matter simply of conformity needs, rebelliousness, "prestige suggestion" or any of the other simple and sovereign doctrines. It is, rather, the resultant of a deeply complex process of attempting to find and proclaim one's social identity. Our opinions are as much a badge of social membership as anything else: a badge worn for informing others who we are and for confirming identity to ourselves. And finally, however important is the social adjustive function of an opinion, there are other needs to be served as well: object appraisal, discussed in the preceding section, and externalization to which we turn next.

The emphasis on diversity that our natural history approach has entailed implies no counsel of despair in regard to studying on a larger scale the social influences on opinion. It should be possible to arrive at indices of different major varieties of social orientation—

a task on which David Reisman [4] has made a promising start in his fertile if speculative distinction between "inner-directed" and "other-directed" personalities. Only as order is brought into our understanding of social motivation can the psychologist's concern with underlying processes be brought in contact with the sociologist's description of group uniformities.

Externalization

We speak of externalization when the evidence shows that a person has responded to an external event in a way that is colored by unresolved inner problems. Outside events are treated as if they were analogous to inner ones, and the attitude taken toward them corresponds in some way to the attitude that is taken toward the inner struggle. In attempting to appraise the object the person unwittingly carries on some of the work that is necessary in dealing with inner problems, and he may even be able to achieve a significant reduction of anxiety by taking a stand with respect to the external version of his conflict.

The chief manifestations of this process in the present group of subjects are summarized in Table 6. What we have learned from our case studies can be indicated in four main propositions: (1) covert strivings influence selectivity in the perception of objects; (2) the subject's attitude toward the object is influenced by the one he takes toward the covert striving; (3) the subject's attitude is further influenced by his preferred adjustive strategies; and (4) the amount and importance of externalization differ greatly in different cases. These propositions will be discussed in turn.

1. *Covert strivings influence selectivity in the perception of objects.* The presence of a covert striving, whether repressed or merely suppressed, creates a predisposition to perceive this striving in the object. For evidence of this process we need only run through our list of subjects noting the differences in their images of Russia. Sullivan's defeated hopes caused him to emphasize the optimism and youthful vigor of the Russian Communists. Daniel's passivity and dependence put an accent on security and the Russian policy of pushing the training of talented men. Kleinfeld's problem with aggression and inferiority disposed him to perceive the Russians as unfortunate underdogs who might nevertheless become dangerously savage. Chatwell's covert desires for greater independence and greater productivity led him to stress Russian progress in these directions. Clark saw the Rus-

---

[4] David Riesman, *The lonely crowd,* New Haven, Yale University Press, 1950.

TABLE 6

SUMMARY OF FINDINGS RELEVANT TO EXTERNALIZATION

Chatwell   Rational mastery: faith in system of law
              Independent self-sufficiency: economic decentralization
              Productivity: Russian economic upbuilding

Lanlin   Dependence: human environment seen as guiding, management
              as providing
              Demandingness: condemnation of unruly demandingness of Rus-
              sians

Sullivan   Personal aggressiveness: movement of protest
              Insecurity: identification with world movement
              Despondency: frustration seen as part of historic necessity on way
              to better future

Daniel   Passivity: Russian state pushing talented people forward
              Dependence: security in Russia
              Fear of aggression and retaliation, need for control: condemnation
              of Russian attitude toward morality and religion, belief in mili-
              tary preparedness

Hodder   Guilt feelings over past delinquencies: attribution of more serious
              evil intentions to Russians

Clark   Economic greed: Russians seen as greedy, employers as extor-
              tionate
              Suspiciousness: Russians seen as suspicious
              Inferiority feelings: fantasy of being big man in Russia

Kleinfeld   Repressed aggression, helplessness: policy of appeasement
              Identification with underdog: United States as top dog
              Rebellion against parental restrictions: doctrine of personal free-
              dom

Rock   Repression and reaction-formation against family-directed aggres-
              sion: censuring of Russian attack on family life
              Indignation because virtues unrecognized: Russians seen as un-
              grateful
              Rebelliousness: occasional sympathy for Russia as youthful rebel

Upjohn   Appropriative tendencies (status and wealth): Russians rejected
              as rude, grabbing peasants
              Inferiority feelings: admiration for strong stands against Russia

Osgood   Aggression: criticism of brutality
              Inferiority feelings: admiration for strength and assertiveness

sians as greedy and suspicious, Lanlin found them full of unruly demandingness, Osgood was particularly impressed by their brutality. Hodder pictured the Communist leaders as men of delinquent intention, while Rock noted their ingratitude and their assault on the sanctity of the home. Finally, Upjohn pictured the Russians as covetously grabbing wealth and status, indeed as veritable pigs at the trough. Our men tended to use different imagery in describing Russia, and their preferred images were often clearly related to covert strivings as revealed by projective and other indirect procedures. We were not in a good position to note significant gaps in their perception of Russia, but these also might be expected to show a relationship to covert strivings and apprehensions.

2. *Attitudes toward objects are influenced by attitudes toward covert strivings.* For the most part our men were disposed to condemn the behavior of the Russians that corresponded to their own covert strivings. They externalized the conflict, both the unruly striving and the necessity for its control. Upjohn, for example, proposed firm measures to contain the gobbling pigs, and Rock was uncompromising in his opposition to Russian laxity with respect to the institution of marriage. In such cases the person used the external replica of his problem as a means of strengthening his control over disruptive inner forces. Wish was not fulfilled in the projected medium; it was treated rather with a firm dose of control.

In some cases, however, the subject tended to sympathize with a perceived tendency in Russia that was denied satisfaction in himself. This was true of Chatwell, for example, who frankly admired Russian industrial productivity while lamenting the lack of productivity in his own highly verbal occupation. It was also true in one respect of Osgood, who envied the Russians their confident assertiveness, and of Rock, who on occasion felt paternally tolerant toward the youthful rebelliousness of Communist policy. Probably it was best exemplified in the case of Sullivan, who had long since abandoned the hope of personal success but who held in the highest esteem a nation that could give full expression to its urge for a better place in a better world. We came to feel that externalized wishes might be fulfilled under two circumstances: when the corresponding wish in the person was obstructed, as in the case of Chatwell, more by outer circumstances than by anxiety; and when, as in the cases of Sullivan and Rock, the externalized wish could be placed at a distance and seen as a somewhat remote historical tendency. In any other circumstances the wish seemed to prove a threat even when externalized, and it was given a properly energetic belaboring.

3. *Attitudes toward objects are further influenced by preferred adjustive strategies.* Sometimes our subjects' opinions, and especially their suggestions as regards policy, seemed to be influenced by satisfaction with an adjustive strategy that had worked well in their personal lives. Lanlin, for example, who had found happiness in salesmanship, proposed to ease the international situation by letting the Russian people know what we had to offer, whereas Upjohn, who had gradually achieved a good capacity for firm decisiveness, especially during his military service, advocated a strong policy line toward Russia even if it should result in war. The only one of our subjects who placed much faith in the United Nations organization and in international law was Chatwell, whose personal success turned on both the rational mastery of inner impulse and the searching legalistic process of competitive debate. Daniel's advocacy of distrustful preparedness corresponded to the attitude he had learned to take in his successful union contests with management. It was pointed out in our discussion of object appraisal that a person's interests often include the preserving of specific lines of action which have brought personal gratification. We can now add that our men sometimes externalized their experience of successful adjustive strategy and applied it to the international scene.

In other cases an adjustive strategy was externalized which represented the most that a person dared to do in his personal life. Kleinfeld offered a case in point when he declared that the Russians must be appeased lest they break out in open aggression, thus advocating a strategy he had found necessary in order to exist as a small shopkeeper and as a Jew. Similarly, Clark found it as difficult to conceive of definite policies toward Russia as he found it to take definite stands in any kind of contention. These men externalized strategies which had been found personally gratifying only in the sense that they had prevented the development of serious anxiety. The threat of anxiety prevented them from using the international scene as a realm in which stronger tactics might be risked.

4. *The amount and importance of externalization differs greatly in different cases.* In some instances we felt that covert conflicts exerted scarcely any effect beyond coloring or accenting certain features in the perception of the object. The opinion orientation held by the subject was not significantly altered by the externalization. Osgood, for example, selectively criticized Russian brutality and selectively admired Russian assertiveness, but his opinion orientation was not thereby deflected from the shape it took as a consequence of object appraisal and of his particularly strong concern with social adjustment. The

most extreme contrasting case was that of Sullivan, whose externalization of personal problems on the worldwide screen of history was an essential element in maintaining a bare minimum of self-respect and courage. Perhaps these two can be taken as limiting cases between which we would expect to find the large bulk of the population. At all events we became convinced that externalization was but one of three ways in which the total economy of adjustment effected the formation of opinions. It must always be considered in relation to object appraisal and social adjustment.

That these observations on externalization emerged from a study of attitudes toward Russia has a special importance. Remote and affect-laden as Russia was to most Americans, the topic doubtless afforded more opportunities for externalization than others that might have been selected. Yet there was ample occasion for object appraisal in more realistic vein. In this respect our topic contrasts sharply with that of antisemitism, the focus of the California studies of the "authoritarian personality." [5] In the nature of the case, the more extreme forms of prejudice are overwhelmingly irrational, that is to say projective, externalized in content. The dynamic account given by the California authors of the correspondence they found between *extreme* prejudice and a particular configuration of personality is an excellent instance of what we mean by externalization. Our topic, however, is probably more representative of the variety of ways in which personality is involved in political thinking.

The Function of an Opinion

In the preceding discussion, we have been impelled to treat the function of an opinion as a resultant or compromise between reality demands, social demands, and inner psychological demands. The three are inseparable. Emphasis upon the first alone leads one to the rationalism of the 19th century writers on opinion who, like A. Lawrence Lowell [6] in later years, would admit for study only those opinions based on "adequate knowledge." Emphasis on social factors alone leads to a passive conception of the individual, a mirror of culture or society. Emphasis on externalization alone is the route to the kind of irrationalism that marked the earliest impact of the psychoanalytic movement. Only by emphasis on the three together can one arrive

[5] T. W. Adorno, D. J. Levinson, Else Frenkel-Brunswik, and R. N. Sanford, *The authoritarian personality*, New York, Harper and Brothers, 1950.

[6] A. Lawrence Lowell, *Public opinion and popular government*, New York, Longmans, Green and Co., 1926.

at an adequate picture of the complex adjustments that go into the formation of a man's opinions.

Perhaps the greatest service that can be rendered by the present theory of attitude function comes in the consideration of attitude change. Why do attitudes change? Why, for example, did the Bennington students investigated by Newcomb [7] move in the direction of New Deal liberalism in their years at college? Why did the voting population of the United States solidify in Democratic and Republican preference along social class lines in 1932, after three years of disastrous depression? Why do adolescents so frequently shift in the direction of less antipathy toward authority upon reaching the early twenties? In none of these instances can an answer be essayed simply in terms of a shift in the relation of the reality situation to personal interests and values, a change in social factors, or an alteration in the inner economy of personality. Each may be a precipitating factor, indeed the sole precipitating factor in attitude change. But the process of change involves a shift in the balance of all factors. Psychological comprehensiveness requires that all be taken into account. In the case of the Bennington students described by Newcomb, the need to conform to the prevailing liberal atmosphere of the college, or to resist it, was indeed a factor. At the same time, the informational environment to which the girls had to adapt changed markedly: they were exposed to new knowledge, new kinds of sentiments, new media of communication, and new events in the world. Nor should one overlook the unique problem of the adolescent in our culture on the verge of becoming an adult. The passage is a difficult one and, as anyone knows who has counseled college students, the personality problems are exigent. There is often a need to find oneself, to stake out one's autonomy and achieve independence from one's family background. Surely all these factors are required for a full explanation of change.

Hypothetically, we can go farther than this in proposing a relationship between our three-fold analysis and the conditions of change in opinions. People's attitudes on topics of public concern involve an admixture of the three sorts of determinants. But people presumably differ, as our subjects did in regard to Russia, in the extent to which one or another predominates in the basis for their opinions about a given topic. The thinking of people at large on various public issues may involve different weightings of the broadly realistic, social, and

[7] Theodore M. Newcomb, *Personality and social change,* New York, The Dryden Press, 1943.

projective components, and these may differ on the same issue from one time to another. One might guess, for example, that Senator McCarthy injected a stronger tinge of projective externalizing into thinking about Russia and Communism than existed before him; he certainly reflected and perhaps brought about a heightening in the pressures toward conformity. These differences in the functional determination of opinions may be expected to have important consequences for the circumstances of their probable change.[8]

To the extent that object appraisal predominates, the person tends to react rationally, according to his lights and according to the information at his disposal. In terms of this function, his interests and values stand to be advanced by flexibility on his part in assimilating the implication of new facts. Conventional educational campaigns rest heavily on the assumption that the attitudes to be affected are rooted primarily in object appraisal. The failure of some programs, for instance some attempts to reduce race prejudice by supplying information, can perhaps be attributed to mistakenness in this assumption.

To the extent that a person's attitudes are primarily rooted in his social adjustments, he is less oriented toward the facts than toward what others think. Probably the effective strategy for changing opinions serving this function is that of the propagandist who relies on "prestige suggestion"—creating the "impression of universality," drawing on testimonials, and discrediting the group support of opposing views. This strategy is often effective, but not always. It has been remarked that such techniques in the hands of the advertising man, while they may give competitive advantage to one product over equivalent ones, do not always transfer effectively to the "selling" of ideas. For opinions are imbedded in larger systems of value or belief that give them support, and one does not "change" a single opinion by invoking a reference group or a figure of prestige without also providing the person with material for revised object appraisal.

To the extent that a person's attitudes serve to externalize inner problems, and are therefore embedded in his defenses against obscure and unresolved tensions, we may expect them to be rigid and not particularly amenable either to reason and fact or to simple social manipu-

[8] A framework for the study of attitude change bearing striking resemblance to ours has recently been presented by I. Sarnoff and D. Katz, The motivational bases of attitude change, *Journal of Abnormal and Social Psychology*, 1954, **49**, 115–124. The hypotheses they propose are concerned with the conditions affecting attitude change when attitudes serve different functions for the individual. The experimental research within this framework, in progress at the University of Michigan, may be expected to throw further light on the relation between the function of an opinion and its susceptibility to change.

lation. Anything that increases his anxiety and sense of threat may be expected to heighten their rigidity. Reassurance and permissiveness are the conditions under which such attitudes are most accessible to change, while firm authority may suppress one "symptom" in favor of another. The history of Sullivan's shift from Catholicism to Communism, like the reverse shift that seems more common among contemporary public figures, illustrates a signal feature of attitude change when externalization is primary: it is saltatory, moving from one equilibrium to a dynamic near-equivalent that may differ radically in manifest content. Rigidity is not the same as stability, which more truly characterizes the slower but more predictable adjustments in opinion that result from object appraisal in the face of changing reality.

If this analysis of the conditions of attitude change is correct—and it is supported not only by impressions from our cases, but also by the burden of much contemporary work in clinical and social psychology—it becomes important to devise rigorous and objective means of assessing the contribution of the different functional supports to people's opinions on given issues. Ways of doing so seem entirely within the range of feasible attainment.

In considering the nature of opinions, their functions in an ongoing personality, and the conditions under which they may change, we have been impressed again and again by three things—and it is appropriate that we reiterate them in this closing paragraph. The first is that there is no rigid or one-to-one relationship between the opinions a person develops and the underlying needs or dynamics of his personality. Two men, both characterized by strong and unacceptable aggressive urges, may develop opinions that are at polar extremes: the one displacing his aggression by channeling it into feelings of bitter enmity toward Russia, the other avoiding the issue by urging the course of isolation from the world. The opinions that develop in a man are multiple in their determinants. They reflect his needs, his characteristic ways of coping with these needs, his expressive style, his strivings for social adjustment, and the manner in which through contact with the environment his values have been engaged by events about him. One cannot look closely at a man's opinions without being impressed by the pluralism of determinants that bring them into being. This is not to say that opinions are indeterminate in their origin, but only that their origin is complex. A second and closely related conclusion is that opinions serve several functions for their holder: they aid him in appraising the value-relevance of the events he encounters; they serve his adjustments to the groups in which he participates and give him a badge of identity with his significant reference groups;

and they provide an occasion for coping externally with analogues of still unresolved inner problems. In any given instance, an opinion or a fabric of opinions may serve one function more than another, but it is our impression that virtually always they serve all of them in some degree. Finally, it is only when we recognize the embeddedness of opinions in the functioning of personality that we can begin to understand the significance of an opinion and the conditions of its change.

APPROACHES

TO OPINIONS

AND PERSONALITY

IMPLICATIONS FOR THE STUDY OF PERSONALITY

Our exploration of ten adult men—men very much in the midst of life—has led us perforce to look at the field of personality research in a somewhat new perspective. Pathology was not a matter of concern: these were stable men, at least to the extent that they were functioning without seeking or receiving professional psychological help. Nor were we diverted by the exigent need to gather data to aid in therapy. Moreover, our interest led us to consider not only the classical inner dynamics of these lives, but also their world views.

What have we learned of interest to the student of personality from the many hours we spent with these men?

The first conclusion is that one gains rich insight into the functioning of personality by considering not only the deep dynamics but also the level that is closely in contact with events in the world. Various theorists have spoken of manifestations of personality as "wheat" and "chaff," the former leading to deep knowledge of underlying trends, the latter leading only to trivial knowledge about transitory states. Granting that the distinction is not without some virtue, it is nonetheless true that one may learn much and go deep into the consistency of a personality without searching for basic hostility or underlying latent homosexuality. The pattern of a man's expressed opinions and values tells one much, often more when it comes to prediction than his responses to projective techniques that appear to indicate, say, underlying masochism and self-destructiveness.

There are here two important and related points. One of them is substantive: about the organization of personality. The other is methodological: about the devices and procedures one may fruitfully use in the study of personality. The two are best separated for discussion.

The manner in which a person copes with his problems is the most revealing thing about him. The solutions to his problems are conserved in the form of values: ways of looking at and evaluating himself, the people about him, and the world around him. Those values represent a resultant of the contacts and struggles between a motivated individual and the surrounding world. From them one can infer much about the kinds of underlying problems with which the person has had to deal.

One's attitudes, examined for their consistencies and patterning, provide an excellent basis for inferring such values. In this sense, the student of personality cannot overlook the study of sentiments and opinions as an approach to his subject matter. To know the manner in which ego functioning proceeds, one literally must examine the attitude-value patterns of his subjects.

This brings us to the methodological problem. In the past decades it has often been assumed that the only "valid" approach to personality lay in indirect, projective, or "keyhole" methods. There is a possibly apocryphal story about the selection of officers for duty in the tropics and the arctic in which the whole gamut of projective psychological tests and physiological measures was employed, along with a brief questionnaire that included an item on the candidate's preference for one or the other climate. According to the story, the only item that correlated with later performance was the preference item. One can infer much about a person by letting him tell what he likes, what moves him to action, what he is like.

Among the most revealing procedures used in our investigation was a two-hour interview on "Personal Values and Religious Sentiments" which began with a question on "What things really matter to you most in life?" and moved widely over the topic of philosophy of life. To be sure, there were evasions and prettifications in the record, but withal one obtained a picture of the person that was consistent with and in some ways more revealing than later information obtained by more conventional projective techniques.

In what way more revealing? The "blind analyses" of our subjects' *Rorschach* and *TAT* records were, in the opinion of the Diagnostic Council, rather consistent in under-rating the capacities, the strengths, and the stability of our subjects. Skillful though they were, these analyses contained too often the kind of statement so familiar to the user of these tools. This subject had depressive trends, that one was somewhat crippled in responding to inner promptings, another had conflicts about his masculinity. While these diagnoses were "revealing" they were often misleading in the sense that they failed to discover the effective, in some cases creative, ways in which the subject had learned to cope with and overcome his difficulties. The planful, value-guided aspects of personality functioning simply did not come through on these tests. Often, the liabilities of a person's adjustment were amplified while his assets were damped by the nature of the instruments employed.

Interview material, in contrast, may tend to exaggerate the assets, but we came to the conclusion that recorded interviews formed a much-needed bridge between overt and covert levels of personality. When it is possible to study at leisure a transcript of all that was said in an interview, the material yields unsuspected riches. Slips of the tongue, hesitations, self-contradictions, preferred figures of speech, and the transitions from one topic to another all lend themselves to analysis as manifestations of covert process. These manifestations do not yield the rich picture of underlying motives and unwitting assumptions that can often be derived from an analysis of fantasy. But they enjoy one great advantage over the findings of projective tests: they show the actual effect of covert processes on conscious thought and behavior. The most difficult problem in interpreting fantasy material is to decide upon its importance in the actual functioning of the personality. Do the fantasies reveal tensely suppressed strivings that are ever ready to disrupt behavior, do they disclose wishes that demand at least symbolic satisfaction in life, or do they show tendencies that exert no real influence over the contemporary personality? Recorded interviews can sometimes play the crucial part in answering such questions. They show us the actual transactions between overt and covert processes, thus allowing us to observe what would otherwise be precariously inferred.

The contemporary trend toward a closer scrutiny of ego-functioning is, we feel, a step toward better balance in personality diagnosis. We would go a step further and suggest that progress could be further aided by the utilization of rather simple interviews on major values and sentiments.

Closely related to the points just made is the conclusion we have reached concerning the inadequacy of current conceptions of ego-defense that have grown largely out of psychoanalytic theory. The traditional defenses about which Anna Freud and others have written so ably—repression, undoing, denial, reaction formation, and the rest—while they are adequate as far as they go, leave out of account a wide variety of tactics employed by normal individuals. That is to say, the traditional defense mechanisms appear to us to represent techniques of defense used *in extremis*. In many spheres of their lives, our subjects never got into dilemmas of such severity as to be forced into reaction formation or projection or even repression. Insofar as one can single out a particular flaw in current views of ego defense it is that writers on the subject have failed to mention the tremendous importance of constructive strategies as a means of avoiding the vicissitudes that make crippling defenses necessary.

The matter can be approached obliquely by an example outside the field of opinion. The child psychiatrist D. M. Levy has commented that in cases of enuresis—even cases of traceable psychogenic origin—one of the therapist's major allies is an alarm clock. If one has the child set the alarm clock to awaken him before his bladder becomes distended, it is frequently possible to reduce materially the incidence of bed-wetting. By so doing, one relieves the guilt and shame felt by the subject and makes it easier for him to cope with his underlying psychological difficulties. Where there are no apparent underlying difficulties, the alarm clock has the effect of preventing guilt reactions from developing and becoming a new source of difficulty.

Our subjects, too, were capable of avoiding difficulties by constructive action. They could often prevent things from occurring that might disrupt them or, more positively, they could plan events in such a way that they could operate effectively and thus grow increasingly competent in dealing with still other situations. Dana Osgood chose those areas of activity in which he could gain acceptance in the community and at the same time discharge his own nurturant needs. Lanlin prevented the occurrence of disruptive surprises by the simple device of list-making-for-the-morrow. Sullivan knew the situations in which to argue and the ones in which to wear his "cap and bells." Chatwell knew that a small law firm would land him in fewer autonomy conflicts than a large law office. We cannot emphasize too strongly that these are not instances of mere avoidance. They were the constructive ways by which our subjects learned to make the most they could of their capacities and limitations.

Indeed, opinions and values may themselves serve as constructive means of avoiding the critical vicissitudes that require extreme defenses. Here we are speaking of the entire pattern of a man's opinions of the world about him—his philosophy of life, if you will. A striking example is provided by Albert Rock. Impressive as was the picture of strength that Rock presented, his was not an untroubled soul. Beneath the surface, we knew him as a man of strong anger, guilt, and anxiety—as well as of responsibility and compassion. To be sure, symptoms of these latent passions came through here and there; that is how we learned of them. Psychopathology would appropriately dwell on these. We are more impressed, however, by the way in which his version of the Catholic faith fulfilled his life and obviated the need for more drastic defense. Through his good works of visitation, through the sense of rightness and appropriateness emanating from his Catholic world view, his life took on meaning and order that gave him deep gratification while it held unruly impulse in check. Similar processes could be traced in others among our men.

It is also the case, to be sure, that opinions, rather than obviating the need for drastic defense, may reflect the inadequacy of such defenses already in being. This is typical of the externalizing function of an opinion. Upjohn's projection of his own capacity and hostility on to others was, as we saw, a standard feature of his attitude structure.

Whether one's philosophy of life turns out to be a guarantor of serenity that saves one from crippling defensive tactics, or whether it turns out to be a by-product of crippling defenses: how this issue is determined, we do not know. It is our conviction that the matter is central in understanding personality. It cannot be approached unless and until as much time is spent on understanding a man's values and philosophy as is spent on his underlying, basic strivings.

IMPLICATIONS FOR THE STUDY OF OPINION

Our major object in the present research has been to explore the relationship between opinion and personality. The principal conclusions of this aspect of the inquiry have been embodied in the final chapter. There remain to be noted, however, some additional methodological and substantive implications.

The first has to do with the dogma of objectivity and permissiveness in the conduct of opinion interviewing—whether that interviewing be of a polling type or of the more open-ended variety. The open-ended interview, with its neutral exploration of the person's general view of a topic, does to be sure provide valuable material that allows the analyst to infer the characteristics of opinion structure in a "resting state." And indeed the balanced, carefully pretested poll question does maximize the possibility of determining how the person will take his policy stand on an issue when he is free of biasing pressures. But this is only part of the story.[1] Some of our most valuable procedures—valuable because they brought to light critical features of a man's opinions—departed radically from the permissive, objective spirit. There is nothing sacred, we held, about neutrality and permissiveness in the opinion interview.

We have already summarized what we learned from the *Information Apperception Test*. This device used affectively loaded stimulus items to evoke responses in which we could observe the individual's opinions in use, coping with novel and challenging bits of environmental information. We could never have gained the insights furnished by this test had we maintained strict neutrality in the tasks we put to our subjects. Departing even farther from neutrality and permissiveness was the *Stress Interview,* in which we attempted to apply strong pressures to the victim's opinions, pressures cut to their measure. Again the returns were rich. Not only did a man's responses in the *Stress Interview* tell us much about his habitual reaction to social pressure and contradiction, but we were also able to arrive at a clearer picture of the organization of his opinions and sentiments than would otherwise have been possible. The *Stress Interview* provided an opportunity to see on which points a man would give, on which stand fast.

We would certainly not advocate discarding the non-directive approach. It supplies an indispensable point of reference in the description of opinions. We argue rather that the information it provides needs to be supplemented by more dynamic methods that show how a person's opinions are deflected by situational pressure and become involved in his coping with new experience. One of the drawbacks of the permissive interview has been the difficulty of predicting from a person's responses in this highly special situation his actions and expressions of opinion in diverse situations of everyday life. It is possible to use the items on a questionnaire to provide challenge to a subject's opinions, the better to assess the degree to which they will be maintained in the face of challenge. Indeed, and this is a more

---

[1] For a further exploration of this issue, see J. Dollard, Under what conditions do opinions predict behavior? *Public Opinion Quarterly,* 1948, **12,** 623–632; and M. B. Smith, Comment on the "Implications of separating opinions from attitudes," *Public Opinion Quarterly,* 1954, **18,** 254–270.

radical departure from convention, we believe that the interviewer himself can be used and should be used in the same way to provide challenge. To be sure, there are problems involved in gaining rapport and in maintaining it under such a regimen. But they are hardly insuperable. Not until there is more effort expended in testing such possibilities will we know how the interviewer's role can be altered in such a way as to be used for probing a respondent's opinions. It is our conviction that the present adherence to the "interviewer as neutral recorder" is more a matter of cultural lag than anything else.

A second point has to do with "depth" devices used in opinion surveying. Psychologists versed in the ways of personality diagnosis have urged that projective questions and other projective methods might be adapted to use in door-to-door interviewing to increase the depth of information obtained. Our own experience with projective methods as a means of getting richer data on opinions was anything but successful. The *Cartoon Stereotype Test,* the *Argument Completion Test,* and other procedures that were partially dependent on projective methods were not conspicuously useful in digging up new or surprising aspects of opinion. Rather, it was our experience that the best method of getting richer material about a man's opinion was by the rather naive and direct device of asking him to talk about those things that mattered most to him as far as the world was concerned and then to direct him from general values to the specific topic under discussion. It was by getting some sense of the person's major interests and enterprises that we were able to put his opinions into a context. One does not have to use highly unreliable "keyhole" methods to get at this broader context of values and general interests. To hark back to the previous point about the role relationship between interviewer and respondent, it is quite apparent that this part of an interview would have to be conducted in a permissive vein and would have to precede the point at which the interviewer put informational or conformity pressures on the respondent.

A third general conclusion concerns the complexity of opinions and the implications of this complexity for attitude measurement. Recent rapid advances in the theory and technique of attitude measurement— Guttman's scale analysis and Lazarsfeld's latent structure analysis are the most familiar examples [2]—have yet to take this complexity into account. Characteristically, they have conceived of attitudes as a matter of pro-ness and con-ness, with perhaps intensity also included.

[2] Cf. S. A. Stouffer et al., *Measurement and prediction,* Princeton, Princeton University Press, 1950; P. F. Lazarsfeld (ed.), *Mathematical thinking in the social sciences,* Glencoe, Ill., Free Press, 1954.

Provocative as are the mathematical models on which these methods are based, we would question whether it is reasonable to expect them to generate the dimensions required for an adequate description of opinion. A sense of the units or dimensions adequate for describing the nature of an opinion comes rather from intensive explorations such as the present inquiry. We suspect that the cart has somehow got before the horse. Refinements of measurement are essential, but they must be built around close acquaintance with the phenomenon to be measured.

There is one additional feature of contemporary methods of attitude scaling that requires comment. It is a necessity of scale construction that a formal attitude dimension or latent structure must order or account for common variance in a *group* of subjects. For example, in order to conclude that an attitude dimension like "morale" exists, it must be shown that a group of subjects can be ordered in terms of this dimension by some such device as a Guttman scalogram. This, in essence, is the objective of attitude scaling: to order an array of individuals rather than to examine the pattern of opinion within a given individual.[3] Again, it is our conviction that the task of arraying individuals along common attitude dimensions, i.e., arraying them in terms of basic likeness of attitudes will be more readily accomplished after we have developed a surer sense of the setting of an opinion within the individual and its functional significance for him.

[3] There are, to be sure, techniques that have as their purpose the discernment of intra-individual patterns. Examples are provided by Stephenson's Q-technique, recently described in W. Stephenson, *The study of behavior: Q-technique and its methodology*, Chicago, University of Chicago Press, 1953. The present discussion is not addressed to such methods which are not, of course, concerned with attitudes scaling in the traditional sense.

INDEX